OEL ⌁ DEUTERONOMY ⌁ KINGS
ANIAH ⌁ HEBREW
CHRONICLES ⌁ ECC ASTES
ATIANS ⌁ EXODUS ⌁ PHILEMON
LEVITICUS ⌁ HAGGAI ⌁ PSALMS
MIAH ⌁ EZEKIEL ⌁ ESTHER ⌁ JOB
PHILIPPIANS ⌁ JAMES ⌁ NAHUM
ADIAH ⌁ TIMOTHY ⌁ EPHESIANS
GALATIANS ⌁ ACTS ⌁ JEREMIAH
I ⌁ SONG OF SOLOMON ⌁ JUDE
ROMANS ⌁ REVELATION ⌁ LUKE
LACHI ⌁ HEBREWS ⌁ MATTHEW
DEUTERONOMY ⌁ KINGS ⌁ JOEL
EWS ⌁ MALACHI ⌁ ZEPHANIAH
NS ⌁ NUMBERS ⌁ REVELATION
MATTHEW ⌁ TITUS ⌁ PROVERBS
ANS ⌁ JONAH ⌁ RUTH ⌁ EXODUS
ESSALONIANS ⌁ PSALMS ⌁ JOB
SAMUEL ⌁ COLOSSIANS ⌁ JOHN
MOTHY ⌁ EPHESIANS ⌁ NAHUM
CHARIAH ⌁ JUDGES ⌁ OBADIAH
UDE ⌁ THESSALONIANS ⌁ EZRA
NICLES ⌁ SONG OF SOLOMON
ON ⌁ AMOS ⌁ MATTHEW ⌁ LUKE
NTHIANS ⌁ JONAH ⌁ HEBREWS

THE READER'S DIGEST BIBLE

LARGE-TYPE EDITION

THE READER'S DIGEST BIBLE

CONDENSED FROM
THE REVISED STANDARD VERSION
OLD AND NEW TESTAMENTS

LARGE-TYPE EDITION
VOLUME III

General Editor
BRUCE M. METZGER
Ph.D., D.D., L.H.D., D.Theol.
Princeton Theological Seminary

Published by
Reader's Digest Fund for the Blind, Inc.
with permission of
THE READER'S DIGEST ASSOCIATION
PLEASANTVILLE, NEW YORK
LONDON, MONTREAL, SYDNEY, CAPE TOWN, HONG KONG

Note:
The full-length text of
the Revised Standard Version
is available from the following:

Holman Bible Publishers
Thomas Nelson Publishers
Oxford University Press Inc.
World Bible Publishers Inc.
The Zondervan Corporation

Third Printing 1988

The Reader's Digest Bible, Large-Type Edition,
was first published in 1986.

CONTENTS

CONTENTS

THE
NEW TESTAMENT

INTRODUCTION
TO THE
NEW TESTAMENT

The New Testament is the distinctively Christian portion of the Bible. It consists of twenty-seven documents, varying greatly in length, each of which is traditionally known as a "book."

The first four books, the Gospels, record the fundamental facts about Jesus Christ, his birth, ministry, teaching, death, and resurrection. Three of the Gospels—Matthew, Mark, and Luke—are known collectively as the Synoptics, because they follow much the same plan and tell much the same story (in the present version some of this repetition from Gospel to Gospel has been eliminated). John's Gospel is rather different. It contains no parables in the Synoptic sense, and it provides a number of incidents, and sayings of Jesus, not given by the other three evangelists. Also, John frequently weaves Jesus' words so closely with his own deeply meditated interpretations of them that it is often hard to find the break between the two.

Composition of the Gospels is assigned by most scholars to a thirty-year period, about A.D. 65 to A.D. 95. It is thought that Mark wrote first, and John last. The books of Matthew and Luke, both of which made use of Mark's work as well as other sources, appeared in between.

The fifth book of the New Testament, the Acts of the Apostles, records the growth and spread of Christianity during the generation after Christ's resurrection. Written by Luke as a continuation of his Gospel, the narrative of Acts focuses first on the work of the chief apostle, Peter, and then on the far-flung missionary labors of Paul.

The next twenty-one books are all letters, or epistles, by which early church authorities sought to provide guidance in the Christian way of life. Thirteen of these letters are attributed to the apostle Paul, and were written mostly to local churches he had personally founded. Paul's letters, containing some of the best-known passages in world literature, were in circulation even before the written Gospels, starting about A.D. 51 with his first letter to the Thessalonians. This was only some twenty years after Christ's death and resurrection.

The final book of the New Testament, Revelation, belongs to a class of literature called apocalyptic. By means of an elaborate symbolism it announces the disclosure, or revelation, of God's will for the future, the consummation of the divine purpose.

All the books of the New Testament were originally written in koine, the everyday Greek of the time, which was spoken by most peoples of the Roman Empire. The various books show different levels of competence in koine, the most highly literary being the Letter to the Hebrews and 1 Peter. Least polished are the Gospel of

Mark and Revelation. As scholars have shown, certain turns of expression in the Greek of the Gospels reflect traces of an underlying Aramaic idiom, which was the mother tongue of Jesus and his disciples.

The original manuscripts of the books of the New Testament have not survived. Almost all of the thousands of copies made during the first three or four centuries, painstakingly handwritten by scribes, have also disappeared. The reasons for the unfortunate loss are obvious: the writing material then commonly used, papyrus, soon wore out, and during persecutions the Christian Scriptures were often hunted out and destroyed.

The oldest existing portion of the New Testament is a tiny scrap of papyrus, dating from about A.D. 125, which contains a few verses from the Gospel of John. The oldest considerable manuscripts of the New Testament, containing most of John's Gospel and some of the letters of Paul, are two papyrus books dating from about A.D. 200. The earliest existing copy of the entire

New Testament is the famous volume known as Codex Sinaiticus, dating from about A.D. 350, now preserved in the British Library, London. Aside from these treasured volumes, more than five thousand other Greek manuscripts of the New Testament, whole or in part, are known to exist today.

At first the books of the New Testament were probably written on scrolls, making it impracticable to include many of them in a single scroll. When Christians, in the second century, began using the codex, or page form of manuscript, it became possible to collect in one volume all the New Testament books. With this physical assembling, questions about what to include in the volume became urgent, and churchmen had to decide on a canon for the New Testament.

Derived from Greek, the word canon denotes a measuring rod, thus indicating a rule or norm. Applied to the Scriptures, the word came to mean a list of those books that were considered authoritative, marking them off in a special way from the rest of early Christian literature. The test for canonicity most frequently applied seems to have been twofold: apostolic authorship, or at least apostolic content, as well as agreement with what was called the rule of faith, that is, a general harmony with the rest of Scripture.

Exactly when it was in the first centuries that the present books were admitted into the New Testament canon, and in what manner, is hard to say, since explicit information has been lost to history. Apparently the process went rapidly in some parts of the early church, more slowly in others. During the second century most churches came to accept a canon that included the four Gospels, Acts, and most of the epistles. At length, official pronouncements were made, first by bishops of provincial churches, then by synods and church councils. Prior to these statements, however, there existed the intuitive insight of individual Christians regarding the inherent significance of these books. Saint Athanasius, in A.D. 367, was the first of whom there is record to name the present twenty-seven books as exclusively canonical.

THE GOSPEL ACCORDING TO

MATTHEW

In his account of the ministry of Jesus Christ, Matthew repeatedly shows how the words and deeds of Jesus fulfil Old Testament predictions, and frequently he touches on the relation of Jesus' teachings to Jewish law. These and other features indicate that the writer's main purpose is to proclaim Jesus' mission as part of a divine plan, and to demonstrate to Jewish readers that Jesus is the royal Messiah. Also characteristic of this Gospel is the fullness with which it records Jesus' message.

While Matthew's account is based largely on that of Mark, it also provides much additional information, for instance, on the birth of Jesus, on certain sayings of Jesus about the church, and on Jesus' final commission to teach and baptize all nations. Though the framework of the narrative is biographical, Matthew tends to group his materials by subject, rather than presenting them in strict chronological order. The method can best be appreciated in the five distinctive and lengthy discourses given by Jesus, each of which is actually a collection of Jesus' teachings on a specific theme. Among the five is the well-known Sermon on the Mount.

———

Now THE BIRTH of Jesus Christ took place in this way. When his mother Mary had been betrothed to Joseph, before they came together she was found to be with child of the Holy Spirit; and her husband Joseph, being a just man and unwilling to put her to shame, resolved to divorce her quietly. But an angel of the Lord appeared to him in a dream, saying, "Do not fear to take Mary your wife, for that which is conceived in her is of the Holy Spirit; she will bear a son, and you shall call him Jesus, for he will save his people from their sins."

All this took place to fulfil what the

Lord had spoken by the prophet, "Behold, a virgin shall conceive and bear a son, and his name shall be called Emmanuel" (which means, God with us). When Joseph woke, he did as the angel commanded; he took his wife, but knew her not until she had borne a son; and he called him Jesus.

Now when Jesus was born in Bethlehem of Judea in the days of Herod the king, wise men from the East came to Jerusalem, saying, "Where is he who has been born king of the Jews? For we have seen his star in the East, and have come to worship him." At this, Herod was troubled, and assembling the chief priests and scribes, he inquired where the Christ was to be born. They told him, "In Bethlehem of Judea; for so it is written by the prophet: 'And you, O Bethlehem, in the land of Judah, are by no means least among the rulers of Judah; for from you shall come a ruler who will govern my people Israel.' "

Secretly Herod summoned the wise men and ascertained from them what time the star appeared. "Go, and when you have found the child," he said, "bring me word, that I too may come and worship him."

They went their way, and lo, the star which they had seen in the East went before them, till it came to rest over the place where the child was. Going into the house, they saw the child with Mary his mother, and they fell down and worshiped him, and they offered him gifts, gold and frankincense and myrrh. Then, being warned in a dream not to return to Herod, they departed to their own country by another way.

Now an angel appeared to Joseph in a dream and said, "Rise, take the child and his mother, and flee to Egypt, and remain there till I tell you; for Herod is about to search for the child, to destroy him." And he took them by night and departed. This was to fulfil what the Lord had spoken by the prophet, "Out of Egypt have I called my son."

When Herod saw that he had been tricked, he was in a furious rage, and he sent and killed all the male children in Bethlehem and in all that region who were two years old or under, according to the time which he had ascertained. Then was fulfilled what was spoken by the prophet

Jeremiah, "A voice was heard in Ramah, wailing and loud lamentation, Rachel weeping for her children; she refused to be consoled, because they were no more."

After Herod died, an angel appeared in a dream to Joseph in Egypt, saying, "Rise, take the child and his mother, and go to the land of Israel, for those who sought the child's life are dead." And they went to the land of Israel, but when Joseph heard that Archelaus reigned over Judea in place of his father Herod, he was afraid, and being warned in a dream he withdrew to the district of Galilee. And they dwelt in a city called Nazareth, that what was spoken by the prophets might be fulfilled, "He shall be called a Nazarene."

IN THOSE DAYS came John the Baptist, preaching in the wilderness of Judea, "Repent, for the kingdom of heaven is at hand." For this is he who was spoken of by the prophet Isaiah when he said, "The voice of one crying in the wilderness: Prepare the way of the Lord, make his paths straight." Now John wore a garment of camel's hair, and a leather girdle, and his food was locusts and wild honey. The people of Jerusalem and all Judea and the region about the Jordan went out to him, and they were baptized by him in the river Jordan, confessing their sins.

But when he saw many of the Pharisees and Sadducees coming for baptism, he said, "You brood of vipers! Who warned you to flee from the wrath to come? Bear fruit that befits repentance, and do not presume to say to yourselves, 'We have Abraham as our father'; for I tell you, God is able from these stones to raise up children to Abraham. Even now the axe is laid to the root of the trees; every tree therefore that does not bear good fruit is cut down and thrown into the fire.

"I baptize you with water for repentance, but he who is coming after me is mightier than I, whose sandals I am not worthy to carry; he will baptize you with the Holy Spirit and with fire. His winnowing fork is in his hand, and he will clear his threshing floor and gather his wheat into the granary, but the chaff he will burn with unquenchable fire."

Then Jesus came from Galilee to John,

to be baptized by him. John would have prevented him, saying, "I need to be baptized by you, and do you come to me?"

"Let it be so now," Jesus answered, "for thus it is fitting for us to fulfil all righteousness." When Jesus was baptized, the heavens were opened and he saw the Spirit of God descending like a dove, and alighting on him; and a voice from heaven said, "This is my beloved Son, with whom I am well pleased."

Then Jesus was led by the Spirit into the wilderness to be tempted by the devil. He fasted forty days and forty nights, and the tempter came and said, "If you are the Son of God, command these stones to become loaves of bread." But he answered, "It is written, 'Man shall not live by bread alone, but by every word that proceeds from the mouth of God.' "

The devil took him to the holy city, and set him on the pinnacle of the temple, and said, "If you are the Son of God, throw yourself down; for it is written, 'He will give his angels charge of you,' and 'On their hands they will bear you up, lest you strike your foot against a stone.' " Jesus said, "Again it is written, 'You shall not tempt the Lord your God.'"

Then the devil took him to a very high mountain, and showed him all the kingdoms of the world, and he said, "All these I will give you, if you will fall down and worship me." Then Jesus said, "Begone, Satan! for it is written, 'You shall worship the Lord your God and him only shall you serve.'" The devil left him, and behold, angels came and ministered to him.

Now when Jesus heard that John had been arrested, he withdrew into Galilee and dwelt in Capernaum by the sea. From that time he began to preach, saying, "Repent, for the kingdom of heaven is at hand."

As he walked by the Sea of Galilee, he saw two brothers who were fishermen casting a net; Simon who is called Peter, and Andrew. "Follow me," he said, "and I will make you fishers of men." Immediately they followed him. Then he saw two other brothers, James and John, in the boat with Zebedee their father, mending their nets, and he called them. Immediately they left the boat and followed him.

JESUS WENT ABOUT all Galilee, teaching in synagogues, preaching the gospel of the kingdom, and healing every disease and infirmity among the people. As his fame spread throughout all Syria, they brought him all the sick and the demoniacs, and he healed them.

Seeing the great crowds that followed him, he went up on the mountain and sat down. When his disciples came, he taught them, saying:

"Blessed are the poor in spirit, for theirs is the kingdom of heaven.

"Blessed are those who mourn, for they shall be comforted.

"Blessed are the meek, for they shall inherit the earth.

"Blessed are those who hunger and thirst for righteousness, for they shall be satisfied.

"Blessed are the merciful, for they shall obtain mercy.

"Blessed are the pure in heart, for they shall see God.

"Blessed are the peacemakers, for they shall be called sons of God.

"Blessed are those who are persecuted

for righteousness' sake, for theirs is the kingdom of heaven.

"Blessed are you when men revile you and persecute you and utter all kinds of evil against you falsely on my account. Rejoice and be glad, for your reward is great in heaven, for so men persecuted the prophets who were before you.

"You are the salt of the earth; but if salt has lost its taste, how shall its saltness be restored? It is no longer good for anything except to be thrown out and trodden under foot by men.

"You are the light of the world. A city set on a hill cannot be hid. Nor do men light a lamp and put it under a bushel, but on a stand, and it gives light to all in the house. Let your light so shine before men, that they may see your good works and give glory to your Father who is in heaven.

"Think not that I have come to abolish the law and the prophets; I have come not to abolish them but to fulfil them. For truly, I say to you, till heaven and earth pass away, not an iota, not a dot, will pass from the law until all is accomplished.

Whoever then relaxes one of the least of these commandments and teaches men so, shall be called least in the kingdom of heaven; but he who does them and teaches them shall be called great in the kingdom of heaven. For I tell you, unless your righteousness exceeds that of the scribes and Pharisees, you will never enter the kingdom of heaven.

"You have heard that it was said to the men of old, 'You shall not kill; and whoever kills shall be liable to judgment.' But I say to you that every one who is angry with his brother shall be liable to judgment; whoever insults his brother shall be liable to the council, and whoever says, 'You fool!' shall be liable to the hell of fire. So if you are offering your gift at the altar, and remember that your brother has something against you, leave your gift and go; first be reconciled to your brother, and then come and offer your gift. Make friends quickly with your accuser, while you are going with him to court, lest your accuser hand you over to the judge, and the judge to the guard, and you be put in prison; truly, I say to you, you will never get out till you have paid the last penny.

"You have heard that it was said, 'You shall not commit adultery.' But I say to you that every one who looks at a woman lustfully has already committed adultery with her in his heart. If your right eye causes you to sin, pluck it out; and if your right hand causes you to sin, cut it off; it is better that you lose one of your members than that your whole body be thrown into hell.

"It was also said, 'Whoever divorces his wife, let him give her a certificate of divorce.' But I say to you that every one who divorces his wife, except on the ground of unchastity, makes her an adulteress; and whoever marries a divorced woman commits adultery.

"Again you have heard that it was said to the men of old, 'You shall not swear falsely, but shall perform to the Lord what you have sworn.' But I say to you, Do not swear at all, either by heaven, for it is the throne of God, or by the earth, for it is his footstool, or by Jerusalem, for it is the city of the great King. And do not swear by your head, for you cannot make one hair white or black. Let what you say be simply 'Yes' or 'No'; anything more than this comes from evil.

"You have heard that it was said, 'An eye for an eye and a tooth for a tooth.' But I say to you, Do not resist one who is evil. But if any one strikes you on the right cheek, turn to him the other also; and if any one would sue you and take your coat, let him have your cloak as well; and if any one forces you to go one mile, go with him two miles. Give to him who begs from you, and do not refuse him who would borrow from you.

"You have heard that it was said, 'You shall love your neighbor and hate your enemy.' But I say to you, Love your enemies and pray for those who persecute you, so that you may be sons of your Father who is in heaven; for he makes his sun rise on the evil and on the good, and sends rain on the just and on the unjust. For if you love those who love you, what reward have you? Do not even the tax collectors do the same? And if you salute only your brethren, what more are you doing than others? Do not even the Gentiles do the same? You, therefore, must be perfect, as your heavenly Father is perfect.

"Beware of practicing your piety before men in order to be seen by them; for then you will have no reward from your Father who is in heaven.

"Thus, when you give alms, sound no trumpet before you, as the hypocrites do in the synagogues and in the streets, that they may be praised. Truly, I say to you, they have received their reward. But when you give alms, do not let your left hand know what your right hand is doing, so that your alms may be in secret; and your Father who sees in secret will reward you.

"And when you pray, you must not be like the hypocrites; for they love to stand and pray in the synagogues and at the street corners, that they may be seen by men. Truly, I say to you, they have received their reward. But when you pray, go into your room and shut the door and pray to your Father who is in secret; and your Father who sees in secret will reward you.

"And in praying do not heap up empty phrases as the Gentiles do; for they think that they will be heard for their many words. Do not be like them, for your Father knows what you need before you ask him. Pray then like this:

"Our Father who art in heaven, hallowed be thy name. Thy kingdom come, thy will be done, on earth as it is in heaven. Give us this day our daily bread; and forgive us our debts, as we also have forgiven our debtors; and lead us not into temptation, but deliver us from evil.

"For if you forgive men their trespasses, your heavenly Father also will forgive you; but if you do not forgive men their trespasses, neither will your Father forgive your trespasses.

"And when you fast, do not look dismal, like the hypocrites, for they disfigure their faces that their fasting may be seen by men. Truly, I say to you, they have received their reward. But when you fast, anoint your head and wash your face, that your fasting may not be seen by men but by your Father who is in secret; and your Father who sees in secret will reward you.

"Do not lay up for yourselves treasures on earth, where moth and rust consume and where thieves break in and steal, but lay up for yourselves treasures in heaven, where neither moth nor rust consumes and where thieves do not break in and steal. For where your treasure is, there will your heart be also.

"The eye is the lamp of the body. So, if your eye is sound, your whole body will be full of light; but if your eye is not sound, your whole body will be full of darkness. If then the light in you is darkness, how great is the darkness!

"No one can serve two masters; for either he will hate the one and love the other, or he will be devoted to the one and despise the other. You cannot serve God and mammon.

"Therefore I tell you, do not be anxious about your life, what you shall eat or what you shall drink, nor about your body, what you shall put on. Is not life more than food, and the body more than clothing? Look at the birds of the air: they neither sow nor reap nor gather into barns, and yet your heavenly Father feeds them. Are you not of more value than they? And which of you by being anxious can add one cubit to his span of life? And why are you anxious about clothing? Consider the lilies of the field, how they grow; they neither toil nor spin; yet I tell you, even Solomon in all his glory was not arrayed like one of these. But if God so clothes the grass of the field, which today is alive and tomorrow is thrown into the oven, will he not much more clothe you, O men of little faith? Therefore do not be anxious, saying, 'What shall we eat?' or 'What shall we drink?' or 'What shall we wear?' For the Gentiles seek all these things; and your heavenly Father knows that you need them all. But seek first his kingdom and his righteousness, and all these things shall be yours as well.

"Therefore do not be anxious about tomorrow, for tomorrow will be anxious for itself. Let the day's own trouble be sufficient for the day.

"Judge not, that you be not judged. For with the judgment you pronounce you will be judged, and the measure you give will be the measure you get. Why do you see the speck that is in your brother's eye, but do not notice the log that is in your own eye? Or how can you say to your brother,

'Let me take the speck out of your eye,' when there is the log in your own eye? You hypocrite, first take the log out of your own eye, and then you will see clearly to take the speck out of your brother's eye.

"Do not give dogs what is holy; and do not throw your pearls before swine, lest they trample them under foot and turn to attack you.

"Ask, and it will be given you; seek, and you will find; knock, and it will be opened to you. For every one who asks receives, and he who seeks finds, and to him who knocks it will be opened. Or what man of you, if his son asks him for bread, will give him a stone? Or if he asks for a fish, will give him a serpent? If you then, who are evil, know how to give good gifts to your children, how much more will your Father who is in heaven give good things to those who ask him! So whatever you wish that men would do to you, do so to them; for this is the law and the prophets.

"Enter by the narrow gate; for the gate is wide and the way is easy, that leads to destruction, and those who enter by it are many. For the gate is narrow and the way is hard, that leads to life, and those who find it are few.

"Beware of false prophets, who come to you in sheep's clothing but inwardly are ravenous wolves. You will know them by their fruits. Are grapes gathered from thorns, or figs from thistles? So, every sound tree bears good fruit, but the bad tree bears evil fruit. A sound tree cannot bear evil fruit, nor can a bad tree bear good fruit. Every tree that does not bear good fruit is cut down and thrown into the fire. Thus you will know them by their fruits.

"Not every one who says to me, 'Lord, Lord,' shall enter the kingdom of heaven, but he who does the will of my Father who is in heaven. On that day many will say to me, 'Lord, Lord, did we not prophesy in your name, and cast out demons in your name, and do many mighty works in your name?' And then will I declare to them, 'I never knew you; depart from me, you evildoers.'

"Every one then who hears these words of mine and does them will be like a wise man who built his house upon the rock;

and the rain fell, and the floods came, and the winds blew and beat upon that house, but it did not fall, because it had been founded on the rock. And every one who hears these words of mine and does not do them will be like a foolish man who built his house upon the sand; and the rain fell, and the floods came, and the winds blew and beat against that house, and it fell; and great was the fall of it."

When Jesus finished, the crowds were astonished at his teaching, for he taught them as one who had authority, and not as their scribes.

Afterward, when he came down from the mountain, great crowds followed him, and as he entered Capernaum, a centurion came forward, beseeching, "Lord, my servant is lying paralyzed at home, in terrible distress." Jesus said, "I will come and heal him." But the centurion answered, "Lord, I am not worthy to have you come under my roof; but only say the word, and my servant will be healed. For I am a man under authority, with soldiers under me; and I say to one, 'Go,' and he goes, and to another, 'Come,' and he comes, and to my slave, 'Do this,' and he does it."

At this, Jesus marveled, and he said to those who followed, "Truly, I say to you, not even in Israel have I found such faith. I tell you, many will come from east and west and sit at table with Abraham, Isaac, and Jacob in the kingdom of heaven, while the sons of the kingdom will be thrown into the outer darkness; there men will weep and gnash their teeth." Then to the centurion he said, "Go; be it done for you as you have believed." And the servant was healed at that very moment.

Now when Jesus saw great crowds around him, he gave orders to go over to the other side of the Sea of Galilee, and he got into the boat with his disciples. And behold, there arose a great storm, so that the boat was being swamped by the waves; but he was asleep. They woke him, saying, "Save, Lord; we are perishing." And he said, "Why are you afraid, O men of little faith?" Then he rose and rebuked the winds and the sea; and there was a great calm. "What sort of man is this," they marveled, "that even winds and sea obey him?"

When they came to the other side, to the country of the Gadarenes, two fierce demoniacs came out of the tombs, and they cried, "What have you to do with us, O Son of God? Have you come here to torment us before the time?" Now a herd of swine was feeding there, and the demons begged, "If you cast us out, send us into the swine." He said to them, "Go," and they went into the swine; and the whole herd rushed down the steep bank and perished in the waters. The herdsmen fled to the city and told what had happened, and all the city came out, and when they saw Jesus, they begged him to leave their neighborhood.

Getting into a boat, he crossed over again, and as he passed on from there, he saw a man called Matthew sitting at the tax office; and he said, "Follow me." And he rose and followed him. And as Jesus sat at table in Matthew's house, many tax collectors and sinners came and sat down. Then the Pharisees said to his disciples, "Why does your teacher eat with tax collectors and sinners?" When Jesus heard it, he said, "Those who are well have no need of a physician, but those who are sick. Go and learn what this means, 'I desire mercy, and not sacrifice.' For I came not to call the righteous, but sinners."

Then the disciples of John came and asked, "Why do we and the Pharisees fast, but your disciples do not fast?"

"Can the wedding guests mourn," Jesus said, "as long as the bridegroom is with them? The days will come when the bridegroom is taken away from them, and then they will fast."

Afterward, a dumb demoniac was brought to Jesus. And when the demon had been cast out, the dumb man spoke; and the crowds marveled, saying, "Never was anything like this seen in Israel." But the Pharisees said, "He casts out demons by the prince of demons."

WHEN JESUS SAW the crowds that followed him, he had compassion for them, because they were harassed and helpless, like sheep without a shepherd. "The harvest is plentiful," he said to his disciples, "but the laborers are few; pray therefore the Lord of the harvest to send out laborers into his harvest." Then he gave his twelve disciples authority to cast out unclean spirits, and to heal every disease and infirmity. The names of the twelve are these: first, Simon called Peter, and Andrew his brother; James and John the sons of Zebedee; Philip and Bartholomew; Thomas and Matthew the tax collector; James the son of Alphaeus, and Thaddaeus; Simon the Cananaean, and Judas Iscariot, who betrayed him.

These twelve Jesus sent out, charging them, "Go nowhere among the Gentiles, and enter no town of the Samaritans, but go rather to the lost sheep of the house of Israel. And preach as you go, saying, 'The kingdom of heaven is at hand.' Heal the sick, raise the dead, cleanse lepers, cast out demons. You received without paying, give without pay. Take no gold, nor silver, nor copper in your belts, no bag for your journey, nor two tunics, nor sandals, nor a staff; for the laborer deserves his food. And whatever town or village you enter, find out who is worthy in it, and stay with him until you depart. As you enter the house, salute it. And if the house is worthy, let your peace come upon it; but if it is not worthy, let your peace return to you. And if any one will not receive you or listen to your words, shake off the dust from your feet as you leave. Truly, I say to you, it shall be more tolerable on the day of judgment for the land of Sodom and Gomorrah than for that town.

"Behold, I send you out as sheep in the midst of wolves; so be wise as serpents and innocent as doves. Beware of men; for they will deliver you up to councils, and flog you in their synagogues, and you will be dragged before governors and kings for my sake, to bear testimony before them and the Gentiles. When they deliver you up, do not be anxious how you are to speak or what you are to say; for what you are to say will be given to you in that hour; for it is not you who speak, but the Spirit of your Father speaking through you. Brother will deliver up brother to death, and the father his child, and children will rise against parents and have them put to death; and you will be hated by all for my name's sake. But he who endures to the end will be saved. When they persecute you in one town, flee to the next; for truly, I say to you, you will not have gone through all the towns of Israel, before the Son of man comes.

"A disciple is not above his teacher, nor a servant above his master; it is enough for the disciple to be like his teacher, and the servant like his master. If they have called the master of the house Beelzebul, how much more will they malign those of his household.

"So have no fear of them; for nothing is covered that will not be revealed, or hidden that will not be known. What I tell you in the dark, utter in the light; and what you hear whispered, proclaim upon the housetops. And do not fear those who kill the body but cannot kill the soul; rather fear him who can destroy both soul and body in hell. Are not two sparrows sold for a penny? And not one of them will fall to the ground without your Father's will. But even the hairs of your head are all numbered. Fear not, therefore; you are of more value than many sparrows. So every one who acknowledges me before men, I also will acknowledge before my Father who is in heaven; but whoever denies me before men, I also will deny before my Father who is in heaven.

"Do not think that I have come to bring peace on earth; I have not come to bring peace, but a sword. For I have come to set a man against his father, and a daughter against her mother, and a daughter-in-law against her mother-in-law; and a man's foes will be those of his own household. He who loves father or mother more than me is not worthy of me; and he who loves son or daughter more than me is not worthy of me; and he who does not take his cross and follow me is not worthy of me. He who finds his life will lose it, and he who loses his life for my sake will find it.

"He who receives you receives me, and he who receives me receives him who sent me. He who receives a prophet because he is a prophet shall receive a prophet's reward, and he who receives a righteous man because he is a righteous man shall receive a righteous man's reward. And whoever gives to one of these little ones even a cup of cold water because he is a disciple, truly, I say to you, he shall not lose his reward."

WHEN JOHN THE Baptist heard in prison about the deeds of the Christ, he sent his disciples to ask, "Are you he who is to come, or shall we look for another?" Jesus answered, "Go and tell John what you hear and see: the blind receive their sight and the lame walk, lepers are cleansed and the deaf hear, the dead are raised up, and the poor have good news preached to them. And blessed is he who takes no offense at me."

Then he spoke to the crowds concerning John: "What did you go out into the wilderness to behold? A reed shaken by the wind? Why then did you go out? To see a man clothed in soft raiment? Behold, those who wear soft raiment are in kings' houses. Why then did you go out? To see a prophet? Yes, I tell you, and more than a prophet. This is he of whom it is written, 'Behold, I send my messenger before thy face, who shall prepare thy way before thee.' Truly, I say to you, among those born of women there has risen no one greater than John the Baptist; yet he who is least in the kingdom of heaven is greater than he. From the days of John the Baptist until now the kingdom of heaven has suffered violence, and men of violence take it by force. For all the prophets and the law prophesied until John; and if you are willing to accept it, he is Elijah who is to come. He who has ears to hear, let him hear. But to what shall I compare this generation? It is like children sitting in the market places and calling to their playmates, 'We piped to you, and you did not dance; we wailed, and you did not mourn.' For John came neither eating nor drinking, and they say, 'He has a demon'; the Son of man came eating and drinking, and they say, 'Behold, a glutton and a drunkard, a friend of tax collectors and sinners!' Yet wisdom is justified by her deeds."

Then he began to upbraid the cities where most of his mighty works had been done, because they did not repent. "Woe to you, Chorazin! woe to you, Bethsaida! for if the mighty works done in you had been done in Tyre and Sidon, they would have repented long ago in sackcloth and ashes. But I tell you, it shall be more tolerable on the day of judgment for Tyre and Sidon than for you. And you, Capernaum, will you be exalted to heaven? You shall be brought down to Hades. For if the mighty works done in you had been done in Sodom, it would have remained until this day. But I tell you that it shall be more tolerable on the day of judgment for the land of Sodom than for you."

At that time Jesus declared, "I thank thee, Father, Lord of heaven and earth, that thou hast hidden these things from the wise and understanding, and revealed them to babes; yea, Father, for such was thy gracious will. All things have been delivered to me by my Father; and no one knows the Son except the Father, and no one knows the Father except the Son and any one to whom the Son chooses to reveal him. Come to me, all who labor and are heavy laden, and I will give you rest. Take my yoke upon you, and learn from me; for I am gentle and lowly in heart, and you will find rest for your souls. For my yoke is easy, and my burden is light."

From there he went on, and he entered a

synagogue, and behold, there was a man with a withered hand. The Pharisees asked him, "Is it lawful to heal on the sabbath?" so that they might accuse him.

"What man of you," he said, "if he has one sheep and it falls into a pit on the sabbath, will not lay hold of it and lift it out? Of how much more value is a man than a sheep! So it is lawful to do good on the sabbath." Then he said to the man, "Stretch out your hand." The man stretched it out, and it was restored, whole like the other. But the Pharisees went out and took counsel against him, how to destroy him. Jesus, aware of this, withdrew from there. And many followed him, and he healed them all, and ordered them not to make him known.

Then a blind and dumb demoniac was brought to him, and he healed him, so that he spoke and saw. All the people were amazed, and said, "Can this be the Son of David?" But when the Pharisees heard it they said, "It is only by Beelzebul, the prince of demons, that this man casts out demons."

Knowing their thoughts, Jesus said to

them, "Every kingdom divided against itself is laid waste, and no city or house divided against itself will stand; and if Satan casts out Satan, he is divided against himself; how then will his kingdom stand? And if I cast out demons by Beelzebul, by whom do your sons cast them out? Therefore they shall be your judges. But if it is by the Spirit of God that I cast out demons, then the kingdom of God has come upon you. Or how can one enter a strong man's house and plunder his goods, unless he first binds the strong man? Then indeed he may plunder his house. He who is not with me is against me, and he who does not gather with me scatters. Therefore I tell you, every sin and blasphemy will be forgiven men, but the blasphemy against the Spirit will not be forgiven. And whoever says a word against the Son of man will be forgiven; but whoever speaks against the Holy Spirit will not be forgiven, either in this age or in the age to come.

"Either make the tree good, and its fruit good; or make the tree bad, and its fruit bad; for the tree is known by its fruit. You brood of vipers! how can you speak good, when you are evil? For out of the abundance of the heart the mouth speaks. I tell you, on the day of judgment men will render account for every careless word they utter; for by your words you will be justified, and by your words you will be condemned."

Some of the scribes and Pharisees said, "Teacher, we wish to see a sign from you." But he answered, "An evil and adulterous generation seeks for a sign; but no sign shall be given to it except the sign of the prophet Jonah. For as Jonah was three days and three nights in the belly of the whale, so will the Son of man be three days and three nights in the heart of the earth. The men of Nineveh will arise at the judgment with this generation and condemn it; for they repented at the preaching of Jonah, and behold, something greater than Jonah is here. The queen of the South will arise at the judgment with this generation and condemn it; for she came from the ends of the earth to hear the wisdom of Solomon, and behold, something greater than Solomon is here."

While he was still speaking, his mother

and his brothers stood outside, asking to speak to him. But he replied to the man who told him, "Who is my mother, and who are my brothers?" Stretching out his hand toward his disciples, he said, "Here are my mother and my brothers! For whoever does the will of my Father in heaven is my brother, and sister, and mother."

That same day Jesus went out and sat beside the sea, and great crowds gathered, so that he sat in a boat while the crowd stood on the beach. And he told them many things in parables, saying, "The kingdom of heaven may be compared to a man who sowed good seed in his field; but while men were sleeping, his enemy came and sowed weeds among the wheat, and went away. So when the plants came up and bore grain, then the weeds appeared also. And the servants of the householder came and said to him, 'Sir, did you not sow good seed in your field? How then has it weeds?' He said to them, 'An enemy has done this.' The servants said to him, 'Then do you want us to go and gather them?' But he said, 'No; lest in gathering the weeds you root up the wheat along with them. Let both grow together until the harvest; and at harvest time I will tell the reapers, Gather the weeds first and bind them in bundles to be burned, but gather the wheat into my barn.' "

Another parable he put before them, saying, "The kingdom of heaven is like a grain of mustard seed which a man took and sowed in his field; it is the smallest of all seeds, but when it has grown it is the greatest of shrubs and becomes a tree, so that the birds of the air come and make nests in its branches." And he told them another parable. "The kingdom of heaven is like leaven which a woman took and hid in three measures of flour, till it was all leavened." All this Jesus said to the crowds in parables; indeed he said nothing to them without a parable. This was to fulfil what was spoken by the prophet, "I will open my mouth in parables, I will utter what has been hidden since the foundation of the world."

When he left the crowds and went into the house, his disciples came to him, saying, "Explain to us the parable of the weeds of the field." He answered, "He who sows the good seed is the Son of man; the field is the world, and the good seed means the sons of the kingdom; the weeds are the sons of the evil one, and the enemy who sowed them is the devil; the harvest is the close of the age, and the reapers are angels. Just as the weeds are gathered and burned with fire, so will it be at the close of the age. The Son of man will send his angels, and they will gather out of his kingdom all causes of sin and all evildoers, and throw them into the furnace of fire; there men will weep and gnash their teeth. Then the righteous will shine like the sun in the kingdom of their Father. He who has ears, let him hear."

When Jesus had finished these parables, he went away. And coming to his own country he taught in the synagogue, so that they were astonished, and said, "Where did this man get this wisdom and these mighty works? Is not this the carpenter's son? Is not his mother called Mary? And are not his brothers James and Joseph and Simon and Judas? And are not all his sisters with us? Where then did this man get all this?" And they took offense at him.

But Jesus said, "A prophet is not without honor except in his own country and in his own house." And he did not do many mighty works there, because of their unbelief.

At that time Herod the tetrarch heard about the fame of Jesus; and he said to his servants, "This is John the Baptist, he has been raised from the dead; that is why these powers are at work in him." For Herod had seized John and put him in prison for the sake of Herodias, his brother Philip's wife; because John said to him, "It is not lawful for you to have her." Herod wanted to put him to death, but he feared the people, because they held John to be a prophet.

When Herod's birthday came, the daughter of Herodias danced before the company, and pleased Herod, so that he promised with an oath to give her whatever she might ask. Prompted by her mother, she said, "Give me the head of John the Baptist on a platter." The king was sorry, but because of his oaths and his guests he commanded it to be done. John was beheaded in the prison, and his head was brought on a platter and given to the girl, and she brought it to her mother. Then John's disciples took the body and buried it; and they went and told Jesus.

Now when Jesus heard this, he withdrew from there in a boat to a lonely place. The crowds followed by land, and as he went ashore he saw a great throng, and he had compassion on them, and healed their sick. When it was evening, the disciples said, "The day is now over; send the crowds into the villages to buy food for themselves."

"They need not go away," Jesus said. "You give them something to eat." They said, "We have only five loaves and two fish."

Then Jesus ordered the crowds to sit down on the grass; and taking the five loaves and the two fish he looked up to heaven, and blessed, and broke and gave the loaves to the disciples, and the disciples gave them to the crowds. They all ate and were satisfied, and they took up twelve baskets full of the broken pieces left over. Those who ate were about five thousand men, besides women and children.

Then he made the disciples get into the boat and go before him to the other side, while he dismissed the crowds. After that he went up on the mountain by himself to pray. The boat by this time was many furlongs distant from the land, beaten by the waves; for the wind was against them. And in the fourth watch of the night he came to them, walking on the sea. But when the disciples saw him walking on the sea, they were terrified, saying, "It is a ghost!" And they cried out for fear. But immediately he spoke to them, saying, "Take heart, it is I; have no fear."

"Lord," said Peter, "if it is you, bid me come to you on the water." He said, "Come." So Peter got out of the boat and walked on the water and came to Jesus. But when he saw the wind, he was afraid, and beginning to sink he cried out, "Lord, save me." Jesus immediately reached out his hand and caught him, saying, "O man of little faith, why did you doubt?" When they got into the boat, the wind ceased, and those in the boat worshiped him, saying, "Truly you are the Son of God." And when they had crossed over, they came to land at Gennesaret. Then Pharisees and scribes came to Jesus from Jerusalem and said, "Why do your disciples transgress the tradition of the elders? For they do not wash their hands when they eat."

"And why," he answered, "do you transgress the commandment of God for the sake of your tradition? For God commanded, 'Honor your father and your mother,' and, 'He who speaks evil of father or mother, let him surely die.' But you say, 'If any one tells his father or his mother, What you would have gained from me is given to God, he need not honor his father.' So, for the sake of your tradition, you have made void the word of God. You hypocrites! Well did Isaiah prophesy of you when he said, 'This people honors me with their lips, but their heart is far from me; in vain do they worship me, teaching as doctrines the precepts of men.' "

Then he called the people to him and said, "Hear and understand: not what goes into the mouth defiles a man, but what comes out of the mouth, this defiles a man." And the disciples said, "Do you know that the Pharisees were offended when they heard this saying?"

"Every plant," he answered, "which my heavenly Father has not planted will be rooted up. Let them alone; they are blind guides. And if a blind man leads a blind man, both will fall into a pit." But Peter said, "Explain the parable to us."

"Are you also still without understanding?" he said. "Do you not see that whatever goes into the mouth passes into the stomach, and so passes on? But what comes out of the mouth proceeds from the heart, and this defiles a man. For out of the heart come evil thoughts, murder, adultery, fornication, theft, false witness, slander. These are what defile a man; but to eat with unwashed hands does not defile a man."

Now Jesus withdrew to the district of Tyre and Sidon, and there a Canaanite woman came to him and cried, "Have mercy on me, O Lord, Son of David; my daughter is severely possessed by a demon." But he did not answer her a word. And his disciples begged him, "Send her away, for she is crying after us." He answered, "I was sent only to the lost sheep of the house of Israel." But the woman knelt before him, saying, "Lord, help me."

"It is not fair," he answered, "to take the children's bread and throw it to the dogs." Then she said, "Yes, Lord, yet even the dogs eat the crumbs that fall from their masters' table."

"O woman," Jesus answered, "great is your faith! Be it done for you as you desire." And her daughter was healed instantly.

Passing along the Sea of Galilee, Jesus went up on the mountain, and great crowds came to him, bringing the sick, and he healed them. And the throng wondered, when they saw the dumb speaking, the maimed whole, the lame walking, and the blind seeing; and they glorified the God of Israel.

Then he called his disciples and said, "I have compassion on the crowd, because they have been with me now three days, and have nothing to eat; and I am unwilling to send them away hungry, lest they faint on the way." The disciples said, "Where are we to get bread enough in the desert to feed so great a crowd?" Jesus said, "How many loaves have you?" They said, "Seven, and a few small fish." Commanding the crowd to sit on the ground, he took the seven loaves and the fish, and having given thanks he broke them and gave them to the disciples, and the disciples gave them to the crowds. And they all ate and were satisfied; and they took up seven baskets full of the broken pieces left over. Those who ate were four thousand men, besides women and children. After sending away the crowds, he got into the boat and went to the region of Magadan.

Now the Pharisees and Sadducees came, and to test him they asked for a sign from heaven. He answered, "When it is evening, you say, 'It will be fair weather; for the sky is red.' And in the morning, 'It will be stormy today, for the sky is red and threatening.' You know how to interpret the appearance of the sky, but you cannot interpret the signs of the times. An evil and adulterous generation seeks for a sign, but no sign shall be given to it except the sign of Jonah." So he left them and departed.

When the disciples reached the other side, they had forgotten to bring any bread. Jesus said, "Take heed and beware of the leaven of the Pharisees and Sadducees." And they discussed it among themselves, saying, "We brought no bread." But Jesus, aware of this, said, "O men of little faith, why do you discuss among yourselves the fact that you have no bread? Do you not yet perceive? Do you not remember the five loaves of the five thousand, and how many baskets you gathered? Or the seven loaves of the four thousand, and how many baskets you gathered? How is it that you fail to perceive that I did not speak about bread? Beware of the leaven of the Pharisees and Sadducees." Then they understood.

When Jesus came into the district of Caesarea Philippi, he asked his disciples, "Who do men say that the Son of man is?" They said, "Some say John the Baptist, others say Elijah, and others Jeremiah or one of the prophets." He said to them, "But who do you say that I am?" Simon Peter replied, "You are the Christ, the Son of the living God."

"Blessed are you, Simon Bar-Jona!" Jesus answered, "for flesh and blood has not revealed this to you, but my Father who is in heaven. And I tell you, you are Peter, and on this rock I will build my church, and the powers of death shall not prevail against it. I will give you the keys of the kingdom of heaven, and whatever you bind on earth shall be bound in heaven, and whatever you loose on earth shall be loosed in heaven." Then he strictly charged the disciples to tell no one that he was the Christ.

From that time Jesus began to show his disciples that he must go to Jerusalem and suffer many things from the elders and chief priests and scribes, and be killed, and on the third day be raised. And Peter began to rebuke him, saying, "God forbid, Lord! This shall never happen to you." But he turned and said to Peter, "Get behind me, Satan! You are a hindrance to me; for you are not on the side of God, but of men." Then he told his disciples, "If any man would come after me, let him deny himself and take up his cross and follow me. For whoever would save his life will lose it, and whoever loses his life for my sake will find it. For what will it profit a man, if he gains the whole world and forfeits his life? Or what shall a man give in return for his life? For the Son of man is to come with his angels in the glory of his Father, and then he will repay every man for what he has done. Truly, I say to you, there are some standing here who will not taste death before they see the Son of man coming in his kingdom."

After six days Jesus took Peter and James and John and led them up a high mountain apart. And he was transfigured before them, and his face shone like the sun, and his garments became white as light. And behold, there appeared to them Moses and Elijah, talking with him. And Peter said to Jesus, "Lord, it is well that we are here; if you wish, I will make three booths here, one for you and one for Moses and one for Elijah." He was still speaking, when lo, a bright cloud overshadowed them, and a voice from the cloud said, "This is my beloved Son, with whom I am well pleased; listen to him." When the disciples heard this, they fell on their faces, and were filled with awe. But Jesus came and touched them, saying, "Rise, and have no fear." When they lifted up their eyes, they saw no one but Jesus only.

As they were coming down the mountain, Jesus commanded them, "Tell no one the vision, until the Son of man is raised from the dead." And they asked, "Then why do the scribes say that first Elijah must come?" He replied, "Elijah does come, and he is to restore all things; but I tell you that Elijah has already come, and they did not know him, but did to him whatever they pleased. So also the Son of man will suffer at their hands." Then the disciples understood that he was speaking of John the Baptist.

When they came to the crowd, a man knelt before him and said, "Lord, have mercy on my son, for he is an epileptic and he suffers terribly; for often he falls into the fire, and often into the water. And I brought him to your disciples, and they could not heal him."

"O faithless and perverse generation," Jesus answered, "how long am I to be with you? How long am I to bear with you? Bring him here to me." And Jesus rebuked the demon and it came out, and the boy was cured instantly. Then the disciples asked Jesus privately, "Why could we not cast it out?" And he said, "Because of your little faith. For truly, I say to you, if you have faith as a grain of mustard seed, you will say to this mountain, 'Move from here to there,' and it will move; and nothing will be impossible to you."

As they were gathering in Galilee, Jesus said to the disciples, "The Son of man is to be delivered into the hands of men, and they will kill him, and he will be raised on the third day." And they were greatly distressed. When they came to Capernaum, the collectors of the half-shekel tax said to Peter, "Does not your teacher pay the tax?" He said, "Yes." And when he came home, Jesus spoke to him first, saying, "What do you think, Simon? From whom do kings of the earth take toll or tribute? From their sons or from others?" When Peter said, "From others," Jesus said, "Then the sons are free. However, not to give offense to them, go to the sea and cast a hook, and take the first fish that comes up, and when you open its mouth you will find a shekel; take that and give it to them for me and for yourself."

AT THAT TIME the disciples came to Jesus, saying, "Who is the greatest in the kingdom of heaven?" Calling a child, he put him in the midst of them, and said, "Truly, I say to you, unless you turn and become like children, you will never enter the kingdom of heaven. Whoever humbles himself like this child, he is the greatest in the kingdom of heaven. Whoever receives one such child in my name receives me; but whoever causes one of these little ones who believe in me to sin, it would be better for him to have a great millstone fastened round his neck and to be drowned in the depth of the sea. Woe to the world for temptations to sin! For it is necessary that temptations come, but woe to the man by whom the temptation comes!

"See that you do not despise one of these little ones; for I tell you that in heaven their angels always behold the face of my Father who is in heaven. What do you think? If a man has a hundred sheep, and one of them has gone astray, does he not leave the ninety-nine on the mountains and go in search of the one that went astray? And if he finds it, truly, I say to you, he rejoices over it more than over the ninety-nine that never went astray. So it is not the will of my Father that one of these little ones should perish.

"If your brother sins against you, go and tell him his fault, between you and him alone. If he listens to you, you have gained your brother. But if he does not listen, take one or two others along with you, that every word may be confirmed by the evidence of two or three witnesses. If he refuses to listen to them, tell it to the church; and if he refuses to listen even to the church, let him be to you as a Gentile and a tax collector. Truly, I say to you, whatever you bind on earth shall be bound in heaven, and whatever you loose on earth shall be loosed in heaven. Again I say to you, if two of you agree on earth about anything they ask, it will be done for them by my Father in heaven. For where two or three are gathered in my name, there am I in the midst of them."

Then Peter said, "Lord, how often shall

my brother sin against me, and I forgive
him? As many as seven times?"

"I do not say to you seven times," Jesus
answered, "but seventy times seven.
Therefore the kingdom of heaven may be
compared to a king who wished to settle
accounts with his servants. One was
brought who owed him ten thousand talents; and as he could not pay, his lord
ordered him to be sold for payment, with
his wife and children and all that he had.
The servant fell on his knees, imploring,
'Lord, have patience with me, and I will
pay you everything.' Out of pity the king
released him and forgave him the debt.
That same servant, as he went out, came
upon one of his fellow servants who owed
him a hundred denarii; and seizing him by
the throat he said, 'Pay what you owe.'
The man fell down and besought him,
'Have patience with me, and I will pay
you.' But he refused and put him in prison
till he should pay the debt. When his fellow servants saw this, they were greatly
distressed, and they went and reported to
their lord all that had taken place. Then
the king summoned him and said, 'You

wicked servant! I forgave you all that debt because you besought me; and should not you have had mercy on your fellow servant, as I had mercy on you?' And in anger the king delivered him to the jailers, till he should pay all his debt. So also my heavenly Father will do to every one of you, if you do not forgive your brother from your heart."

When Jesus had finished these sayings, he left Galilee for Judea. And Pharisees came to test him by asking, "Is it lawful to divorce one's wife for any cause?" He answered, "Have you not read, that he who made them from the beginning made them male and female, and said, 'For this reason a man shall leave his father and mother and be joined to his wife, and the two shall become one flesh'? So they are no longer two but one flesh. What therefore God has joined together, let not man put asunder."

"Why then," they said, "did Moses command one to give a certificate of divorce, and to put her away?"

"For your hardness of heart," he answered, "Moses allowed you to divorce your wives, but from the beginning it was not so. And I say to you: whoever divorces his wife, except for unchastity, and marries another, commits adultery."

The disciples said, "If such is the case of a man with his wife, it is not expedient to marry."

"Not all men," Jesus said, "can receive this saying, but only those to whom it is given. For there are eunuchs who have been so from birth, and there are eunuchs who have been made eunuchs by men, and there are eunuchs who have made themselves eunuchs for the sake of the kingdom of heaven. He who is able to receive this, let him receive it."

Then children were brought to him that he might lay his hands on them and pray. When the disciples rebuked the people, Jesus said, "Let the children come to me, and do not hinder them; for to such belongs the kingdom of heaven." And he laid his hands on them and went away.

And behold, one came up to him, saying, "Teacher, what good deed must I do, to have eternal life?" And he said to him, "Why do you ask me about what is good? One there is who is good. If you would enter life, keep the commandments." He said, "Which?" And Jesus said, "You shall not kill, You shall not commit adultery, You shall not steal, You shall not bear false witness, Honor your father and mother, and, You shall love your neighbor as yourself." The young man said, "All these I have observed; what do I still lack?" Jesus said, "If you would be perfect, go, sell what you possess and give to the poor, and you will have treasure in heaven; and come, follow me." When the young man heard this he went away sorrowful; for he had great possessions.

And to his disciples Jesus said, "Truly, I say to you, it will be hard for a rich man to enter the kingdom of heaven. Again I tell you, it is easier for a camel to go through the eye of a needle than for a rich man to enter the kingdom of God." The disciples were greatly astonished, and said, "Who then can be saved?" But Jesus looked at them and said, "With men this is impossible, but with God all things are possible." Then Peter said, "Lo, we have left everything and followed you. What then shall we have?" Jesus said, "Truly, I say to you, in the new world, when the Son of man shall sit on his glorious throne, you who have followed me will also sit on twelve thrones, judging the twelve tribes of Israel. And every one who has left houses or brothers or sisters or father or mother or children or lands, for my name's sake, will receive a hundredfold, and inherit eternal life. But many that are first will be last, and the last first.

"For the kingdom of heaven is like a householder who went out early in the morning to hire laborers for his vineyard. After agreeing with the laborers for a denarius a day, he sent them into his vineyard. And going out about the third hour he saw others standing idle in the market place, and he said, 'You go into the vineyard too, and whatever is right I will give you.' So they went. About the sixth hour and the ninth hour he did the same. And about the eleventh hour he went out and found others standing, and he said, 'Why do you stand here idle all day?' They said, 'Because no one has hired us.' He said, 'You go into the vineyard too.'

"Now when evening came, the owner of

the vineyard said to his steward, 'Call the laborers and pay them their wages, beginning with the last, up to the first.' When those hired about the eleventh hour came, each of them received a denarius. When the first came, they thought they would receive more; but each of them also received a denarius. And they grumbled at the householder, saying, 'These last worked only one hour, and you have made them equal to us who have borne the burden of the day and the scorching heat.' But he replied, 'I am doing you no wrong; did you not agree with me for a denarius? Take what belongs to you, and go; I choose to give to this last as I give to you. Am I not allowed to do what I choose with what belongs to me? Or do you begrudge my generosity?' So the last will be first, and the first last."

As THEY WERE going up to Jerusalem, Jesus took the twelve disciples aside and said, "Behold, we are going up to Jerusalem; and the Son of man will be delivered to the chief priests and scribes, and they will condemn him to death, and deliver him to the Gentiles to be mocked and scourged and crucified, and he will be raised on the third day."

And when they drew near to Jerusalem and came to the Mount of Olives, Jesus sent two disciples, saying, "Go into the village opposite you, and immediately you will find an ass tied, and a colt with her; untie them and bring them to me. If any one says anything to you, you shall say, 'The Lord has need of them,' and he will send them immediately." This took place to fulfil what was spoken by the prophet, "Behold, your king is coming to you, humble, and mounted on an ass, and on a colt, the foal of an ass."

The disciples brought the ass and the colt, and put their garments on them, and Jesus sat thereon. The crowd spread garments on the road, and cut branches from trees and spread them also, and they shouted, "Hosanna to the Son of David! Blessed is he who comes in the name of the Lord! Hosanna in the highest!" And all Jerusalem was stirred.

Entering the temple, Jesus drove out all who sold and bought there, and he overturned the tables of the money-changers and the seats of those who sold pigeons. He said, "It is written, 'My house shall be called a house of prayer'; but you make it a den of robbers."

And the blind and the lame came to him in the temple, and he healed them. But when the chief priests and the scribes saw the wonderful things that he did, and the children crying out, "Hosanna to the Son of David!" they were indignant. "Do you hear what these are saying?" they asked. Jesus said, "Yes; have you never read, 'Out of the mouth of babes and sucklings thou hast brought perfect praise'?" And leaving them, he went out of the city and lodged at Bethany.

The next day in the city the chief priests and the elders came to him as he was teaching in the temple, and said, "By what authority are you doing these things, and who gave you this authority?"

"I also will ask you a question," Jesus said, "and if you tell me the answer, then I also will tell you by what authority I do these things. The baptism of John, whence was it? From heaven or from men?"

They argued with one another, "If we say, 'From heaven,' he will say to us, 'Why then did you not believe him?' But if we say, 'From men,' we are afraid of the multitude; for all hold that John was a prophet." So they answered Jesus, "We do not know."

"Neither will I tell you," he said, "by what authority I do these things. Now what do you think? A man had two sons; and he went to the first and said, 'Son, go and work in the vineyard today.' And he answered, 'I will not'; but afterward he repented and went. And the man went to the second and said the same; and he answered, 'I go, sir,' but did not go. Which of the two did the will of his father?" They said, "The first."

"Truly," said Jesus, "the tax collectors and the harlots go into the kingdom of God before you. For John came to you in the way of righteousness, and you did not believe him, but the tax collectors and the harlots believed him; and even when you saw it, you did not afterward repent and believe him."

Again Jesus spoke in parables, saying,

"The kingdom of heaven may be compared to a king who gave a marriage feast for his son, and he sent his servants to call those who were invited to the marriage feast; but they would not come. Again he sent other servants, saying, 'Tell those who are invited, Behold, I have made ready my dinner, my oxen and my fat calves are killed, and everything is ready; come to the marriage feast.' But they made light of it and went off, one to his farm, another to his business, while the rest seized his servants, treated them shamefully, and killed them. The king was angry, and he sent his troops and destroyed those murderers and burned their city. Then he said to his servants, 'The wedding is ready, but those invited were not worthy. Go therefore to the thoroughfares, and invite to the marriage feast as many as you find.' And those servants went out into the streets and gathered all whom they found, both bad and good; so the wedding hall was filled with guests. But when the king came in to look at the guests, he saw there a man who had no wedding garment; and he said, 'Friend, how did you get in here without a wedding garment?" And he was speechless. Then the king said to the attendants, 'Bind him hand and foot, and cast him into the outer darkness; there men will weep and gnash their teeth.' For many are called, but few are chosen."

Now the Pharisees took counsel how to entangle Jesus in his talk, and they sent their disciples to him, along with the Herodians. "Teacher, we know that you are true," they said, "and teach the way of God truthfully, and care for no man; for you do not regard the position of men. Tell us, then, what you think. Is it lawful to pay taxes to Caesar, or not?"

"Why put me to the test, you hypocrites?" he said. "Show me the money for the tax." They brought him a coin, and he asked, "Whose likeness and inscription is this?" They said, "Caesar's." Then he said, "Render therefore to Caesar the things that are Caesar's, and to God the things that are God's." Marveling, they left him and went away.

The same day Sadducees, who say that there is no resurrection, came to him, saying, "Teacher, Moses said, 'If a man dies, having no children, his brother must marry the widow, and raise up children for his brother.' Now there were seven brothers among us; the first married, and died, and having no children, left his wife to his brother. So too the second and third, down to the seventh. After them all, the woman died. In the resurrection, therefore, to which of the seven will she be wife? For they all had her."

"You are wrong," Jesus answered, "because you know neither the scriptures nor the power of God. For in the resurrection they neither marry nor are given in marriage, but are like angels in heaven. And as for the resurrection of the dead, have you not read what was said to you by God, 'I am the God of Abraham, and the God of Isaac, and the God of Jacob'? He is not God of the dead, but of the living." And the crowd was astonished at his teaching.

When the Pharisees heard that he had silenced the Sadducees, they came together, and one of them asked him a question, to test him. "Teacher, which is the great commandment in the law?" He said, "You shall love the Lord your God with all your heart, and with all your soul, and with all your mind. This is the great and first commandment. And a second is like it, You shall love your neighbor as yourself. On these two commandments depend all the law and the prophets."

Then Jesus asked the Pharisees a question. "What do you think of the Christ? Whose son is he?" They said, "The son of David." He said, "How is it then that David, inspired by the Spirit, calls him Lord, saying, 'The Lord said to my Lord, Sit at my right hand, till I put thy enemies under thy feet'? If David thus calls him Lord, how is he his son?" No one was able to answer, nor from that day did any one dare to ask him any more questions.

Then said Jesus to the crowds and to his disciples, "The scribes and the Pharisees sit on Moses' seat; so practice and observe whatever they tell you, but not what they do; for they preach, but do not practice. They bind heavy burdens, hard to bear, and lay them on men's shoulders; but they themselves will not move them with their finger. They do all their deeds to be seen by men; for they make their phylacteries broad and their fringes long, and they love the place of honor at feasts and the best seats in the synagogues, and salutations in the market places, and being called rabbi by men. But you are not to be called rabbi, for you have one teacher, and you are all brethren. And call no man your father on earth, for you have one Father, who is in heaven. Neither be called masters, for you have one master, the Christ. He who is greatest among you shall be your servant; whoever exalts himself will be humbled, and whoever humbles himself will be exalted.

"But woe to you, scribes and Pharisees, hypocrites! because you shut the kingdom of heaven against men; for you neither enter yourselves, nor allow those who would enter to go in. Woe to you, scribes and Pharisees, hypocrites! for you traverse sea and land to make a single proselyte, and when he becomes a proselyte, you make him twice as much a child of hell as yourselves.

"Woe to you, blind guides, who say, 'If any one swears by the temple, it is nothing; but if any one swears by the gold of the temple, he is bound by his oath.' You blind fools! For which is greater, the gold or the temple that has made the gold sacred? And you say, 'If any one swears by the altar, it is nothing; but if any one swears by the gift that is on the altar, he is bound by his oath.' You blind men! For which is greater, the gift or the altar that makes the gift sacred? So he who swears by the altar, swears by it and by everything on it; and he who swears by the temple, swears by it and by him who dwells in it; and he who swears by heaven, swears by the throne of God and by him who sits upon it.

"Woe to you, scribes and Pharisees, hypocrites! for you tithe mint and dill and cummin, and have neglected the weightier matters of the law, justice and mercy and faith; these you ought to have done, without neglecting the others. You blind guides, straining out a gnat and swallowing a camel!

"Woe to you, scribes and Pharisees, hypocrites! for you cleanse the outside of the cup and of the plate, but inside they are full of extortion and rapacity. You blind Pharisee! first cleanse the inside of the cup and of the plate, that the outside also may be clean.

"Woe to you, scribes and Pharisees, hypocrites! for you are like whitewashed tombs, which outwardly appear beautiful, but within they are full of dead men's bones and all uncleanness. So you also outwardly appear righteous to men, but within you are full of hypocrisy and iniquity.

"Woe to you, scribes and Pharisees, hypocrites! for you build the tombs of the prophets and adorn the monuments of the righteous, saying, 'If we had lived in the days of our fathers, we would not have taken part with them in shedding the blood of the prophets.' Thus you witness against yourselves, that you are sons of those who murdered the prophets. Fill up, then, the measure of your fathers. You serpents, you brood of vipers, how are you to escape being sentenced to hell? Therefore I send you prophets and wise men and scribes, some of whom you will kill and crucify, and some you will scourge in your synagogues and persecute from town to town, that upon you may come all the righteous blood shed on earth, from the blood of innocent Abel to the blood of Zechariah the son of Barachiah, whom you murdered between the sanctuary and the altar. Truly, I say to you, all this will come upon this generation.

"O Jerusalem, Jerusalem, killing the prophets and stoning those who are sent to you! How often would I have gathered your children together as a hen gathers her brood under her wings, and you would not! Behold, your house is forsaken and desolate. For I tell you, you will not see me again, until you say, 'Blessed is he who comes in the name of the Lord.' "

As JESUS WAS leaving the temple, his disciples pointed out to him the buildings of the temple. But he answered, "You see all these, do you not? Truly, I say to you, there will not be left here one stone upon another, that will not be thrown down." And as he sat on the Mount of Olives, the disciples came to him privately, saying, "Tell us, when will this be, and what will be the sign of your coming and of the close of the age?"

"Take heed," Jesus answered, "that no one leads you astray. For many will come in my name, saying, 'I am the Christ,' and they will lead many astray. And you will hear of wars and rumors of wars; see that you are not alarmed; for this must take place, but the end is not yet. For nation will rise against nation, and kingdom against kingdom, and there will be famines and earthquakes in various places: all this is but the beginning of the birth-pangs. Then they will deliver you up to tribulation, and put you to death; and you will be hated by all nations for my name's sake. And then many will fall away, and betray one another, and hate one another. And many false prophets will arise and lead many astray. And because wickedness is multiplied, most men's love will grow cold. But he who endures to the end will be saved. And this gospel of the kingdom will be preached throughout the whole world, as a testimony to all nations; and then the end will come.

"So when you see the desolating sacrilege spoken of by the prophet Daniel, standing in the holy place (let the reader understand), then let those who are in Judea flee to the mountains; let him who is on the housetop not go down to take what is in his house; and let him who is in the field not turn back to take his mantle. And alas for those who are with child and for those who give suck in those days! Pray that your flight may not be in winter or on a sabbath. For then there will be great tribulation, such as has not been from the beginning of the world until now, no, and never will be. And if those days had not been shortened, no human being would be saved; but for the sake of the elect those days will be shortened. Then if any one says to you, 'Lo, here is the Christ!' or 'There he is!' do not believe it. For false Christs and false prophets will arise and show great signs and wonders, so as to lead astray, if possible, even the elect. Lo, I have told you beforehand. So, if they say to you, 'Lo, he is in the wilderness,' do not go out; if they say, 'Lo, he is in the inner rooms,' do not believe it. For as the lightning comes from the east and shines as far as the west, so will be the coming of the

Son of man. Wherever the body is, there the eagles will be gathered together.

"Immediately after the tribulation of those days the sun will be darkened, and the moon will not give its light, and the stars will fall from heaven, and the powers of the heavens will be shaken; then will appear the sign of the Son of man in heaven, and then all the tribes of the earth will mourn, and they will see the Son of man coming on the clouds of heaven with power and great glory; and he will send out his angels with a loud trumpet call, and they will gather his elect from the four winds, from one end of heaven to the other.

"From the fig tree learn its lesson: as soon as its branch becomes tender and puts forth its leaves, you know that summer is near. So also, when you see all these things, you know that he is near, at the very gates. Truly, I say to you, this generation will not pass away till all these things take place. Heaven and earth will pass away, but my words will not pass away.

"But of that day and hour no one knows, not even the angels of heaven, nor the Son, but the Father only. As were the days of Noah, so will be the coming of the Son of man. For as in those days before the flood they were eating and drinking, marrying and giving in marriage, until the day when Noah entered the ark, and they did not know until the flood came and swept them all away, so will be the coming of the Son of man. Then two men will be in the field; one is taken and one is left. Two women will be grinding at the mill; one is taken and one is left. Watch therefore, for you do not know on what day your Lord is coming. But know this, that if the householder had known in what part of the night the thief was coming, he would have watched and would not have let his house be broken into. Therefore you also must be ready; for the Son of man is coming at an hour you do not expect.

"Who then is the faithful and wise servant, whom his master has set over his household, to give them their food at the proper time? Blessed is that servant whom his master when he comes will find so doing. Truly, I say to you, he will set him over all his possessions. But if that wicked servant says to himself, 'My master is delayed,' and begins to beat his fellow servants, and eats and drinks with the drunken, the master of that servant will come on a day when he does not expect him and at an hour he does not know, and will punish him, and put him with the hypocrites; there men will weep and gnash their teeth.

"Then the kingdom of heaven shall be compared to ten maidens who took their lamps and went to meet the bridegroom. Five of them were foolish, and five were wise. For when the foolish took their lamps, they took no oil with them; but the wise took flasks of oil with their lamps. As the bridegroom was delayed, they all slumbered and slept. But at midnight there was a cry, 'Behold, the bridegroom! Come out to meet him.' Then all those maidens rose and trimmed their lamps. And the foolish said to the wise, 'Give us some of your oil, for our lamps are going out.' But the wise replied, 'Perhaps there will not be enough for us and for you; go rather to the dealers and buy for yourselves.' And while they went to buy, the bridegroom came, and those who were ready went in with him to the marriage feast; and the door was shut.

Afterward the other maidens came also, saying, 'Lord, lord, open to us.' But he replied, 'Truly, I say to you, I do not know you.' Watch therefore, for you know neither the day nor the hour.

"For it will be as when a man going on a journey called his servants and entrusted to them his property; to one he gave five talents, to another two, to another one, to each according to his ability. Then he went away. He who had received the five talents went at once and traded with them; and he made five talents more. So also, he who had the two talents made two talents more. But he who had received the one talent went and dug in the ground and hid his master's money. Now after a long time the master of those servants came and settled accounts with them. And he who had received the five talents came forward, bringing five talents more, saying, 'Master, you delivered to me five talents; here I have made five talents more.' His master said, 'Well done, good and faithful servant; you have been faithful over a little, I will set you over much; enter into the joy of your master.' And he also who had the two talents came forward, saying, 'Master, you delivered to me two talents; here I have made two talents more.' His master said, 'Well done, good and faithful servant; you have been faithful over a little, I will set you over much; enter into the joy of your master.'

"Then he who had received the one talent came forward. 'Master, I knew you to be a hard man,' he said, 'reaping where you did not sow, and gathering where you did not winnow; so I was afraid, and I went and hid your talent in the ground. Here you have what is yours.' But his master answered him, 'You wicked and slothful servant! You knew that I reap where I have not sowed, and gather where I have not winnowed? Then you ought to have invested my money with the bankers, and at my coming I should have received what was my own with interest. So take the talent from him, and give it to him who has the ten talents. For to every one who has will more be given, and he will have abundance; but from him who has not, even what he has will be taken away. And cast the worthless servant into the outer darkness; there men will weep and gnash their teeth.'

"When the Son of man comes in his glory, and all the angels with him, then he will sit on his glorious throne. Before him will be gathered all the nations, and he will separate them one from another as a shepherd separates the sheep from the goats, and he will place the sheep at his right hand, but the goats at the left. Then the King will say to those at his right hand, 'Come, O blessed of my Father, inherit the kingdom prepared for you from the foundation of the world; for I was hungry and you gave me food, I was thirsty and you gave me drink, I was a stranger and you welcomed me, I was naked and you clothed me, I was sick and you visited me, I was in prison and you came to me.'

"Then the righteous will answer, 'Lord, when did we see thee hungry and feed thee, or thirsty and give thee drink? And when did we see thee a stranger and welcome thee, or naked and clothe thee? And when did we see thee sick or in prison and visit thee?' And the King will answer, 'Truly, I say to you, as you did it to one of the least of these my brethren, you did it to me.'

"Then he will say to those at his left hand, 'Depart from me, you cursed, into the eternal fire prepared for the devil and his angels; for I was hungry and you gave me no food, I was thirsty and you gave me no drink, I was a stranger and you did not welcome me, naked and you did not clothe me, sick and in prison and you did not visit me.'

"Then they also will answer, 'Lord, when did we see thee hungry or thirsty or a stranger or naked or sick or in prison, and did not minister to thee?' Then he will answer them, 'Truly, I say to you, as you did it not to one of the least of these, you did it not to me.' And they will go away into eternal punishment, but the righteous into eternal life."

WHEN JESUS HAD finished all these sayings, he said to his disciples, "You know that after two days the Passover is coming, and the Son of man will be delivered up to be crucified."

Then the chief priests and the elders

gathered in the palace of the high priest Caiaphas, and took counsel together in order to arrest Jesus by stealth and kill him. But they said, "Not during the feast, lest there be a tumult among the people."

Now when Jesus was at Bethany in the house of Simon the leper, a woman came up to him with an alabaster flask of very expensive ointment, and she poured it on his head as he sat at table. But the disciples were indignant at this, saying, "Why this waste? The ointment might have been sold for a large sum, and given to the poor." Jesus said, "Why do you trouble the woman? She has done a beautiful thing to me. For you always have the poor with you, but you will not always have me. In pouring this ointment on my body she has done it to prepare me for burial. Truly, I say to you, wherever this gospel is preached in the whole world, what she has done will be told in memory of her."

Then one of the twelve, who was called Judas Iscariot, went to the chief priests and said, "What will you give me if I deliver him to you?" And they paid him thirty pieces of silver. And from that moment he sought an opportunity to betray him.

Now on the first day of Unleavened Bread the disciples asked Jesus, "Where will you have us prepare for you to eat the passover?" He said, "Go into the city to a certain one, and say to him, 'The Teacher says, My time is at hand; I will keep the passover at your house with my disciples.' " And the disciples did as Jesus had directed them.

When it was evening he sat at table with the twelve disciples. As they were eating, he said, "Truly, I say to you, one of you will betray me." They were very sorrowful, and said to him one after another, "Is it I, Lord?" He answered, "He who has dipped his hand in the dish with me, will betray me. The Son of man goes as it is written of him, but woe to that man by whom the Son of man is betrayed! It would have been better for that man if he had not been born." Judas, who betrayed him, said, "Is it I, Master?" He said to him, "You have said so."

As they were eating, Jesus took bread, and blessed, and broke it, and gave it to the disciples and said, "Take, eat; this is my body." And he took a cup, and when he had given thanks he gave it to them, saying, "Drink of it, all of you; for this is my blood of the covenant, which is poured out for many for the forgiveness of sins. I tell you I shall not drink again of this fruit of the vine until that day when I drink it new with you in my Father's kingdom."

When they had sung a hymn, they went out to the Mount of Olives. Then Jesus said, "You will all fall away because of me this night; for it is written, 'I will strike the shepherd, and the sheep of the flock will be scattered.' But after I am raised up, I will go before you to Galilee."

"Though they all fall away because of you," Peter declared, "I will never fall away."

"Truly, I say to you," Jesus answered, "this very night, before the cock crows, you will deny me three times."

"Even if I must die with you," Peter said, "I will not deny you." And so said all the disciples.

Then Jesus went with them to a place called Gethsemane. "Sit here," he said, "while I go yonder and pray." Taking with him Peter and the two sons of Zebedee, he began to be troubled. "My soul is very sorrowful," he said, "even to death; remain here, and watch with me." And going a little farther he fell on his face and prayed, "My Father, if it be possible, let this cup pass from me; nevertheless, not as I will, but as thou wilt." Coming to the disciples, he found them sleeping, and he said to Peter, "So, could you not watch with me one hour? Watch and pray that you may not enter into temptation; the spirit indeed is willing, but the flesh is weak."

For the second time he went away and prayed, "My Father, if this cannot pass unless I drink it, thy will be done." And again he came and found them sleeping, for their eyes were heavy. Leaving them, he went away and prayed for the third time, saying the same words. Then he came to the disciples and said, "Are you still sleeping and taking your rest? Behold, the hour is at hand, and the Son of man is betrayed into the hands of sinners. Rise, let us be going; see, my betrayer is at hand."

While he was still speaking, Judas came,

and with him a great crowd with swords and clubs, from the chief priests and the elders. The betrayer had given them a sign, saying, "The one I shall kiss is the man; seize him." And he came up to Jesus and said, "Hail, Master!" And he kissed him. "Friend, why are you here?" Jesus said.

Then they seized Jesus, and one of those who were with Jesus drew his sword, and struck the slave of the high priest, and cut off his ear. "Put your sword back into its place," said Jesus, "for all who take the sword will perish by the sword. Do you think that I cannot appeal to my Father, and he will at once send me more than twelve legions of angels? But how then should the scriptures be fulfilled, that it must be so?" To the crowds he said, "Have you come out as against a robber, with swords and clubs to capture me? Day after day I sat in the temple teaching, and you did not seize me. But all this has taken place, that the scriptures of the prophets might be fulfilled." Then all the disciples forsook him and fled.

They led Jesus to Caiaphas the high priest, where the scribes and the elders had gathered. Peter followed, as far as the courtyard of the high priest, and there he sat with the guards.

Now the chief priests and the whole council sought false testimony against Jesus that they might put him to death, but they found none, though there were many false witnesses. At last two came forward and said, "This fellow said, 'I am able to destroy the temple of God, and to build it in three days.' "

"Have you no answer to make?" asked the high priest. "What is it that these men testify against you?" But Jesus was silent. And the high priest said to him, "I adjure you by the living God, tell us if you are the Christ, the Son of God."

"You have said so," Jesus replied. "But I tell you, hereafter you will see the Son of man seated at the right hand of Power, and coming on the clouds of heaven."

Then the high priest tore his robes, and said, "He has uttered blasphemy. Why do we still need witnesses? You have now heard his blasphemy. What is your judgment?" They answered, "He deserves death." Then they spat in his face, and some slapped him, saying, "Prophesy to us, you Christ! Who is it that struck you?"

Peter was sitting in the courtyard, and a maid said to him, "You also were with Jesus the Galilean." But he denied it before them all, saying, "I do not know what you mean." He went out to the porch, and another maid said to the bystanders, "This man was with Jesus of Nazareth." Again he denied it with an oath, "I do not know the man." After a little while the bystanders said, "Certainly you are also one of them, for your accent betrays you." Then Peter invoked a curse on himself and swore, "I do not know the man." Immediately the cock crowed, and Peter remembered the saying of Jesus, and he went out and wept bitterly.

When morning came, all the chief priests and the elders took counsel against Jesus to put him to death; and they bound him and delivered him to Pilate the governor.

Judas, seeing that Jesus was condemned, repented and brought back the thirty pieces of silver to the chief priests and the elders, saying, "I have sinned in betraying innocent blood." They said, "What is that to us? See to it yourself." Throwing down the pieces of silver in the temple, he departed; and he went and hanged himself. The chief priests, taking the pieces of silver, said, "It is not lawful to put them into the treasury, since they are blood money." So they bought with them the potter's field, to bury strangers in, and it has been called the Field of Blood to this day.

Now Jesus stood before Pilate, who asked, "Are you the King of the Jews?" Jesus answered, "You have said so." But when he was accused by the chief priests and elders, he made no answer. Then Pilate said, "Do you not hear how many things they testify against you?" But he gave no answer, so that Pilate wondered greatly.

Now at the feast Pilate was accustomed to release for the crowd any one prisoner whom they wanted. And they had then a notorious prisoner, called Barabbas. To the crowd Pilate said, "Whom do you want me to release for you, Barabbas or Jesus who is called Christ?" For he knew that it was out of envy that they had delivered him up. Besides, while he was sitting on the judgment seat, his wife sent word to him, "Have nothing to do with that righteous man, for I have suffered much over him today in a dream."

Now the chief priests and the elders persuaded the people to ask for Barabbas and destroy Jesus. The governor again asked, "Which do you want me to release?" They said, "Barabbas," and Pilate asked, "Then what shall I do with Jesus?" They all said, "Let him be crucified." Pilate said, "Why, what evil has he done?" But they shouted all the more, "Let him be crucified."

When Pilate saw that a riot was beginning, he took water and washed his hands before the crowd, saying, "I am innocent of this man's blood." And all the people answered, "His blood be on us and on our children!" Then he released Barabbas, and having scourged Jesus, delivered him to be crucified.

The soldiers took Jesus into the praetorium, before the whole battalion. They stripped him and put on him a scarlet robe and a crown of thorns, and a reed in his right hand. Kneeling, they mocked him, saying, "Hail, King of the Jews!" And they spat upon him, and took the reed and struck him on the head. Then they took off the robe, put his own clothes on him, and led him away to crucify him.

As they went, they came upon a man of Cyrene, Simon by name; this man they compelled to carry his cross. At Golgotha (which means the place of a skull), they offered Jesus wine to drink, mingled with gall; but when he tasted it, he would not drink it. And when they had crucified him, they divided his garments among them by casting lots; then they sat down and kept watch over him there. And over his head they put the charge against him, which read, "This is Jesus the King of the Jews."

Two robbers were crucified with him, one on the right and one on the left. And those who passed by derided him, wagging their heads and saying, "You who would destroy the temple and build it in three days, save yourself! If you are the Son of God, come down from the cross." So also the chief priests, with the scribes and elders, mocked him, saying, "He saved others; he cannot save himself. He is the King of Israel; let him come down now from the cross, and we will believe in him. He trusts in God; let God deliver him now, if he desires him; for he said, 'I am the Son of God.' " And the robbers who were crucified with him also reviled him in the same way.

Now from the sixth hour there was darkness over all the land until the ninth hour. And about the ninth hour Jesus cried with a loud voice, "Eli, Eli, lama sabachthani?" that is, "My God, my God, why hast thou forsaken me?" Some of the bystanders said, "This man is calling Elijah." And one of them at once ran and took a sponge, filled it with vinegar, put it on a reed, and gave it to him to drink. But the others said, "Wait, let us see whether Elijah will come to save him." And Jesus cried again with a loud voice and yielded up his spirit.

And behold, the curtain of the temple was torn in two, from top to bottom; and the earth shook, and the rocks were split; the tombs also were opened, and many bodies of the saints who had fallen asleep were raised, and coming out of the tombs after his resurrection they went into the holy city and appeared to many. When the centurion and those with him, keeping watch, saw the earthquake and what took place, they were filled with awe, and said, "Truly this was the Son of God!"

There were also many women there, looking on from afar, who had followed Jesus from Galilee, ministering to him; among whom were Mary Magdalene, and Mary the mother of James and Joseph, and the mother of the sons of Zebedee.

When it was evening, there came a rich man from Arimathea, named Joseph, who also was a disciple of Jesus. He asked Pilate for the body of Jesus, and Pilate ordered it to be given. Joseph took the body, wrapped it in a clean linen shroud, and laid it in his own new tomb, which he had hewn in the rock; and he rolled a great stone to the door of the tomb, and departed. Mary Magdalene and the other Mary were there, sitting opposite the sepulcher.

Next day, that is, after the day of Preparation, the chief priests and the Pharisees gathered before Pilate and said, "Sir, we remember how that impostor said, while he was still alive, 'After three days I will rise again.' Therefore order the sepulcher to be made secure until the third day, lest his disciples steal him away, and tell the people, 'He has risen from the dead,' and the last fraud will be worse than the first." Pilate said, "You have a guard; go, make it as secure as you can." So they made the sepulcher secure by sealing the stone and setting a guard.

Now after the sabbath, toward the dawn of the first day of the week, Mary Magdalene and the other Mary went to see the sepulcher. And behold, there was a great earthquake; for an angel of the Lord descended from heaven and came and rolled back the stone, and sat upon it. His appearance was like lightning, and his raiment white as snow. And for fear of him the guards trembled and became like dead men.

To the women the angel said, "Do not be afraid; for I know that you seek Jesus who was crucified. He is not here; for he has risen, as he said. Come, see the place where he lay. Then go quickly and tell his disciples that he has risen from the dead, and behold, he is going before you to Galilee; there you will see him. Lo, I have told you." The women departed quickly from the tomb with fear and great joy, and ran to tell his disciples. And behold, Jesus met them and said, "Hail!" And they came up and took hold of his feet and worshiped him. Then Jesus said, "Do not be afraid; go and tell my brethren to go to Galilee, and there they will see me."

While they were going, some of the guard went into the city and told the chief priests all that had taken place. And when they had assembled with the elders and taken counsel, they gave a sum of money to the soldiers and said, "Tell people, 'His disciples came by night and stole him away while we were asleep.' And if this comes to the governor's ears, we will satisfy him and keep you out of trouble." So they took the money and did as they were directed; and this story has been spread among the Jews to this day.

Now the eleven disciples went to Galilee, to the mountain to which Jesus had directed them. And when they saw him they worshiped him; but some doubted.

And Jesus came and said to them, "All authority in heaven and on earth has been given to me. Go therefore and make disciples of all nations, baptizing them in the name of the Father and of the Son and of the Holy Spirit, teaching them to observe all that I have commanded you; and lo, I am with you always, to the close of the age."

THE GOSPEL
ACCORDING TO
MARK

Widely regarded as the earliest of the four Gospels, Mark's account was written within perhaps thirty years of Christ's death and resurrection. Though it is anonymous (the title was added later), ancient tradition ascribes the book to a certain John Mark, a disciple of both Peter and Paul, who is said to have composed it at Rome as a summary of Peter's preaching. The text, in any case, shows considerable knowledge of Palestine and of the Aramaic language spoken there, while its occasional Latinisms suggest Rome's influence.

Originally written in koine, the everyday Greek of the time, Mark's is the least polished of the Gospels, though the author reveals a flair for graphic description. The narrative opens not with the birth of Jesus in Bethlehem but with the preaching of

John the Baptist, who is presented as the fulfillment of prophecy. Following Jesus' baptism and temptation, his messianic ministry begins at once, leading swiftly to the climax—the week of Jesus' passion at Jerusalem culminating in the crucifixion. The brief mention of the young man who runs away after the arrest of Jesus may be the "artist's signature," in which Mark refers to himself.

———

THE BEGINNING OF the gospel of Jesus Christ, the Son of God.

As it is written in Isaiah the prophet, "Behold, I send my messenger before thy face, who shall prepare thy way; the voice of one crying in the wilderness: Prepare the way of the Lord, make his paths straight."

John the baptizer appeared in the wilderness, preaching a baptism of repentance for the forgiveness of sins. There went out to him the people of Judea and Jerusalem, and they were baptized by him in the river

Jordan, confessing their sins. Now John was clothed with camel's hair, and had a leather belt around his waist, and ate locusts and wild honey. "After me," he preached, "comes he who is mightier than I, the thong of whose sandals I am not worthy to untie. I have baptized you with water; he will baptize you with the Holy Spirit."

In those days Jesus came from Nazareth of Galilee and was baptized by John. When he came up out of the water, he saw the heavens opened and the Spirit descending upon him like a dove. And a voice came from heaven, "Thou art my beloved Son; with thee I am well pleased." Then the Spirit drove him into the wilderness, and he was there for forty days, tempted by Satan. He was with the wild beasts, and the angels ministered to him.

After John was arrested, Jesus came into Galilee, preaching, "The time is fulfilled, and the kingdom of God is at hand; repent, and believe in the gospel." Passing along by the Sea of Galilee, he saw Simon and his brother Andrew, who were fishermen, casting a net in the sea. "Follow me," he said, "and I will make you fishers of men." Immediately they left their nets and followed him. Going on a little farther, he saw James and John the sons of Zebedee, in their boat mending the nets. He called them, and they left their father in the boat with the hired servants, and followed him.

They went into Capernaum, and on the sabbath Jesus entered the synagogue and taught. The people were astonished at his teaching, for he taught as one who had authority, not as the scribes. Suddenly a man with an unclean spirit cried out, "What have you to do with us, Jesus of Nazareth? Have you come to destroy us? I know who you are, the Holy One of God." Jesus rebuked him, saying, "Be silent, and come out of him!" The unclean spirit, convulsing the man and crying loudly, came out. All were amazed, so that they questioned, "What is this? A new teaching! With authority he commands even the unclean spirits, and they obey him." From that moment his fame began spreading.

Jesus left the synagogue, and entered the house of Simon and Andrew, with James and John, where Simon's mother-in-law lay

sick with a fever. When they told him of
her, he came and took her by the hand and
lifted her up. The fever left her, and she
served them. That evening they brought to
him all who were sick or possessed with
demons, and the whole city was gathered
about the door. He healed many, and cast
out many demons; but he would not permit the demons to speak, because they
knew him.

Early in the morning he rose and went
to a lonely place, and prayed. Pursuing
him, Simon and the others found him and
said, "Every one is searching for you."

"Let us go on to the next towns," Jesus
said, "that I may preach there also, for that
is why I came out." So, preaching in synagogues and casting out demons, he went
throughout all Galilee.

Once a leper came beseeching him and
kneeling said, "If you will, you can make
me clean." Moved with pity, Jesus
stretched out his hand and touched him. "I
will," he said. "Be clean." Immediately the
leprosy left the man, and he was made
clean. "Say nothing to any one," Jesus
charged him, "but go, show yourself to the

priest, and offer for your cleansing what Moses commanded, for a proof to the people." But the man talked freely and spread the news, so that Jesus could no longer openly enter a town. He stayed in the country, where people came to him from every quarter.

When he returned to Capernaum, it was reported he was at home, and many gathered together, so that there was no room, not even about the door. And they brought a paralytic on a pallet, carried by four men, and when they could not get near him, they made an opening in the roof and let down the pallet with the paralytic. Jesus, seeing their faith, said to the paralytic, "My son, your sins are forgiven." Now some scribes were sitting there, questioning in their hearts, "Why does this man speak thus? It is blasphemy! Who can forgive sins but God alone?"

"Why do you question thus in your hearts?" Jesus said. "Which is easier, to say, 'Your sins are forgiven,' or to say, 'Rise, take up your pallet and walk'? But that you may know that the Son of man has authority on earth to forgive sins"—he said to the paralytic—"I say to you, rise, take up your pallet and go home." The man rose, immediately took up the pallet and departed. They were all amazed and glorified God, saying, "We never saw anything like this!"

Jesus went out again beside the sea, and a crowd gathered, and he taught them. Later, as he walked along, he saw Levi the son of Alphaeus sitting at the tax office, and he said to him, "Follow me." And Levi rose and followed him. And as Jesus sat at table in Levi's house, many tax collectors and sinners were there. The scribes of the Pharisees, when they saw this, said to his disciples, "Why does he eat with tax collectors and sinners?" Jesus heard it and said, "Those who are well have no need of a physician, but those who are sick; I came not to call the righteous, but sinners."

Now John's disciples and the Pharisees were fasting, and people came and said to Jesus, "Why do these fast, but your disciples do not?"

"Can the wedding guests fast while the bridegroom is with them?" Jesus said. "As long as they have the bridegroom with them, they cannot fast. The days will come, when the bridegroom is taken away, and then they will fast. No one sews a piece of unshrunk cloth on an old garment; if he does, the patch tears away from it and a worse tear is made. And no one puts new wine into old wineskins; if he does, the wine will burst the skins. New wine is for fresh skins."

One sabbath Jesus was going through the grainfields, and his disciples plucked heads of grain. "Look," said the Pharisees, "why are they doing what is not lawful on the sabbath?"

"Have you never read what David did," Jesus said, "when he was in need and was hungry, he and those who were with him: how he entered the house of God and ate the bread of the Presence, which it is not lawful for any but the priests to eat, and also gave it to those who were with him? The sabbath was made for man, not man for the sabbath; so the Son of man is lord even of the sabbath."

Again Jesus entered the synagogue, and a man was there who had a withered hand. While the Pharisees watched to see whether he would heal on the sabbath, so that they might accuse him, Jesus said to the man, "Come here." Then he said to the Pharisees, "Is it lawful on the sabbath to do good or to do harm, to save life or to kill?" They were silent, and he looked around at them with anger, grieved at their hardness of heart. "Stretch out your hand," he said to the man. He stretched it out, and it was restored. Then the Pharisees left, and they immediately held counsel with the Herodians, how to destroy him.

Jesus withdrew with his disciples to the sea, and a great multitude came to him. He told his disciples to have a boat ready because of the crowd, for he had healed many, so that all who had diseases pressed upon him. And whenever the unclean spirits beheld him, they fell down and cried, "You are the Son of God." Strictly he ordered them not to make him known. Afterward he went up on the mountain, and called those whom he desired. Then he appointed twelve, to be with him, and to be sent out to preach and have authority to cast out demons. They were: Simon whom he surnamed Peter, James and John the sons of Zebedee whom he surnamed Boanerges (sons of thunder), Andrew, Philip, Bartholomew, Matthew, Thomas, James the son of Alphaeus, Thaddaeus, Simon the Cananaean, and Judas Iscariot, who betrayed him.

Then he went home, and the crowd came together again, so that they could not even eat. When his family heard of this, they went out to seize him, for people were saying, "He is beside himself." And the scribes who came down from Jerusalem said, "He is possessed by Beelzebul, and by the prince of demons he casts out the demons."

"How can Satan cast out Satan?" Jesus asked. "If a kingdom is divided against itself, that kingdom cannot stand. And if a house is divided against itself, that house will not stand. And if Satan has risen up against himself and is divided, he cannot stand, but is coming to an end. Truly, I say to you, all sins will be forgiven the sons of men, and whatever blasphemies they utter, but whoever blasphemes against the Holy Spirit never has forgiveness, but is guilty of an eternal sin"—for the scribes had said, "He has an unclean spirit." The crowd sitting about him said, "Your mother and your brothers are outside, asking for you." He replied, "Who are my mother and my brothers?" Looking around on those who sat about him, he said, "Here are my mother and my brothers! Whoever does the will of God is my brother, and sister, and mother."

Again he taught beside the sea, and a large crowd gathered, so that he got into a boat, and the crowd was on the land. "Listen!" he said. "A sower went out to sow. And some seed fell along the path, and the birds came and devoured it. Other seed fell on rocky ground, where it had not much soil, and immediately it sprang up, and when the sun rose it was scorched, and since it had no root it withered away. Other seed fell among thorns and the thorns choked it, and it yielded no grain. And other seeds fell into good soil and brought forth grain, yielding thirtyfold and sixtyfold and a hundredfold." And he said, "He who has ears to hear, let him hear."

When he was alone, those about him

with the twelve asked him concerning the parables. "To you has been given the secret of the kingdom of God," he said, "but for those outside everything is in parables; so that they may indeed see but not perceive, and may indeed hear but not understand; lest they should turn again, and be forgiven. Do you not understand this parable? How then will you understand all the parables?

"The sower sows the word. These are the ones along the path; when they hear, Satan immediately comes and takes away the word sown in them. These in like manner are the ones sown upon rocky ground, who immediately receive the word with joy; they have no root, but endure for a while; when tribulation or persecution arises on account of the word, they fall away. Others are the ones sown among thorns; they are those who hear the word, but the cares of the world, and the delight in riches and other things, choke the word, and it proves unfruitful. But those that were sown upon the good soil are the ones who hear the word and accept it and bear fruit, thirtyfold and sixtyfold and a hundredfold."

And he said, "Take heed what you hear; the measure you give will be the measure you get, and still more will be given you. For to him who has will more be given; and from him who has not, even what he has will be taken away."

And he said, "The kingdom of God is as if a man should scatter seed upon the ground, and should sleep and rise night and day, and the seed should sprout and grow, he knows not how. The earth produces of itself, first the blade, then the ear, then the full grain in the ear. But when the grain is ripe, at once he puts in the sickle, because the harvest has come."

And he said, "With what can we compare the kingdom of God? It is like a grain of mustard seed, which, when sown upon the ground, is the smallest of all the seeds on earth; yet it grows up and becomes the greatest of all shrubs, and puts forth large branches, so that the birds of the air can make nests in its shade." With many such parables he spoke the word; he did not speak without a parable, but privately to his own disciples he explained everything.

When evening had come, Jesus said, "Let us go across to the other side." They took him in the boat, and a great storm of wind arose, and the waves beat into the boat, so that it was filling. Jesus was in the stern, asleep on the cushion. They woke him and said, "Teacher, do you not care if we perish?" Then he rebuked the wind, and said to the sea, "Peace! Be still!" And the wind ceased, and there was a great calm. "Why are you afraid?" he said. "Have you no faith?"

"Who then is this," they said in awe, "that even wind and sea obey him?"

They came to the other side, to the country of the Gerasenes. When he left the boat, he was met by a man with an unclean spirit, who lived among the tombs. No one could bind him any more, for chains and fetters he wrenched apart, and night and day among the tombs he was crying out, and bruising himself with stones. Seeing Jesus, he ran and worshiped him, crying, "What have you to do with me, Jesus, Son of the Most High God? I adjure you by God, do not torment me." For Jesus had said to him, "Come out of the man, you unclean spirit!"

"What is your name?" Jesus asked.

"My name is Legion," he replied, "for we are many."

Now a great herd of swine was feeding on the hillside, and the demons begged Jesus, "Send us to the swine, let us enter them." So he gave them leave, and the unclean spirits entered the swine, and the herd, numbering about two thousand, rushed down the steep bank into the sea and were drowned. The herdsmen fled, and told it everywhere, and people came to see what had happened. They saw Jesus, and saw the demoniac sitting there, clothed and in his right mind. At this they were afraid, and begged Jesus to depart from their neighborhood. As he was getting into the boat, the man who had been possessed begged that he might be with him. "Go home to your friends," Jesus said, "and tell them how the Lord has had mercy on you." The man went away and proclaimed in the Decapolis region how much Jesus had done for him; and all marveled.

When Jesus had crossed again to the

other side, a great crowd gathered about him. Then there came a ruler of the synagogue, Jairus, who fell at his feet. "My little daughter is at the point of death," he said. "Come and lay your hands on her, that she may live." Jesus went with him, and a great crowd followed. Now in the crowd there was a woman who had had a flow of blood for twelve years, who had suffered much under many physicians, had spent all that she had, and was no better but rather grew worse. She came up behind Jesus and touched his garment. "If I touch even his garments," she said, "I shall be made well." Immediately the hemorrhage ceased, and she felt that she was healed. Perceiving that power had gone forth from him, Jesus turned about. "Who touched my garments?" he asked. His disciples said, "You see the crowd pressing around, yet you say, 'Who touched me?' " Then the woman, in fear and trembling, fell down before him and told him the truth. "Daughter," he said, "your faith has made you well. Go in peace."

While he was speaking, there came from the ruler's house some who said to Jairus,

"Your daughter is dead. Why trouble the Teacher further?" But Jesus said, "Do not fear, only believe." He allowed no one to follow him except Peter, James, and John, and at the ruler's house he saw a tumult, with people weeping and wailing loudly. "Why do you weep?" Jesus asked. "The child is not dead but sleeping." They laughed at him, but he put them all outside, took the child's parents and his disciples, and went in where the child was (she was twelve years old). Taking her by the hand, he said, "Talitha cumi"; which means, "Little girl, I say to you, arise." Immediately the girl got up and walked, and all were overcome with amazement. And Jesus strictly charged them that no one should know this, and told them to give her something to eat.

With his disciples, he went away from there and came to his own country; and on the sabbath he taught in the synagogue. Many who heard him were astonished. "Where did this man get all this?" they said, taking offense at him. "What is the wisdom given to him? What mighty works are wrought by his hands! Is not this the carpenter, the son of Mary and brother of James and Joses and Judas and Simon, and are not his sisters here with us?" Jesus marveled because of their unbelief. "A prophet is not without honor," he said, "except in his own country, and among his own kin, and in his own house." He could do no mighty work there, except that he laid his hands upon a few sick people and healed them.

After that, he went about among the villages teaching. The twelve he sent out two by two, and gave them authority over the unclean spirits. He charged them to take nothing except a staff; no bread, no bag, no money in their belts, to wear sandals and not put on two tunics. "Where you enter a house," he said, "stay there until you leave the place. If any place will not receive you and they refuse to hear you, when you leave shake the dust from your feet for a testimony against them." Thus they went out and preached that men should repent. They cast out many demons, and anointed with oil many that were sick and healed them.

King Herod heard of all this, for Jesus'

name had become known, and he said, "John the baptizer, whom I beheaded, has been raised." For Herod had put John in prison for the sake of Herodias, his brother's wife. Herod had married her, and John had said, "It is not lawful for you to have your brother's wife." Herodias wanted to kill him, but she could not, for Herod feared John, knowing he was a righteous and holy man. But an opportunity came when Herod on his birthday gave a banquet. Herodias' daughter danced, and she pleased Herod and his guests. "Ask me for whatever you wish," the king vowed, "and I will grant it, even half my kingdom." The girl went out and said to her mother, "What shall I ask?"

"The head of John the baptizer," Herodias said. The girl returned and said to the king, "I want you to give me at once the head of John the Baptist on a platter." The king was exceedingly sorry, but because of his oaths and his guests he did not want to break his word. He sent a soldier of the guard, who beheaded John in the prison. The soldier brought the head on a platter, gave it to the girl, and the girl gave it to her mother. When John's disciples heard of this, they took his body and laid it in a tomb.

The apostles returned to Jesus, and told him all that they had done. Now many were coming and going, and they had no leisure even to eat, so Jesus said, "Come away by yourselves to a lonely place and rest a while." They left in a boat, but many saw them and knew where they were going, and they ran there from all the towns and got there first. As Jesus went ashore he saw a great throng, and he had compassion on them because they were like sheep without a shepherd; and he taught them. When it grew late, his disciples said, "This is a lonely place, and the hour is late. Send them into the villages to buy something to eat."

"You give them something to eat," he answered.

"Shall we buy two hundred denarii worth of bread?" they asked.

"How many loaves have you?" he said. When they had found out, they said, "Five, and two fish." He commanded them all to sit down by companies upon the green grass, so they sat down by hundreds and by fifties. Taking the five loaves and the two fish, he looked up to heaven, and blessed, and broke the loaves, and gave them to the disciples to set before the people; and he divided the two fish among them all. And they all ate and were satisfied, and they took up twelve baskets full of broken pieces of bread and fish. Those who ate the loaves were five thousand men.

Immediately Jesus made his disciples get into the boat and go before him to the other side, to Bethsaida, while he dismissed the crowd. Then he went up on the mountain to pray. When evening came, the boat was out on the sea, and he saw that they were making headway painfully, for the wind was against them. About the fourth watch of the night he came to them, walking on the sea. He meant to pass by them, but when they saw him walking on the sea they thought it was a ghost, and they cried out; for all saw him, and were terrified. "Take heart," he said, "it is I; have no fear." He got into the boat with them and the wind ceased. They were utterly astounded, for they did not understand about the loaves, but their hearts were hardened.

They came to land at Gennesaret, and moored to the shore. When they got out of the boat, immediately the people recognized Jesus, and they ran about the whole neighborhood and brought sick people on pallets to any place where they heard he was. Wherever he went, they laid the sick in the market places, and besought him that they might touch even the fringe of his garment; and as many as touched it were made well.

Now when the Pharisees, with some scribes from Jerusalem, met Jesus, they saw that some of his disciples ate with hands defiled, that is, unwashed. (The Pharisees, and all the Jews, do not eat unless they wash their hands and purify themselves, and they have many other traditions, including the washing of cups and pots and vessels of bronze.) "Why do your disciples not live according to the tradition of the elders," they asked, "but eat with hands defiled?"

"Well did Isaiah prophesy of you hypocrites," Jesus said, "as it is written, 'This people honors me with their lips, but their heart is far from me; in vain do they worship me, teaching as doctrines the precepts of men.' You have a fine way of rejecting the commandment of God, in order to keep your tradition! Moses said, 'Honor your father and your mother'; and, 'He who speaks evil of father or mother, let him surely die'; but you say, 'If a man tells his father or his mother, What you would have gained from me is Corban' (given to God), then you no longer permit him to do anything for his father or mother, thus making void the word of God through your tradition. And many such things you do."

And he called the people to him and said, "Hear me, all of you, and understand: There is nothing outside a man which by going into him can defile him. The things which come out of a man are what defile him." Then he left the people, and when he had entered the house his disciples asked him about the saying. "Are you also without understanding?" he said. "Do you not see that whatever goes into a man from outside cannot defile him, since it enters not his heart but his stomach, and so passes on? (Thus he declared all foods clean.) What comes out of a man's heart is what defiles him. For out of the heart of man come evil thoughts, fornication, theft, murder, adultery, coveting, wickedness, deceit, licentiousness, envy, slander, pride, foolishness. All these evil things come from within, and they defile a man."

From there Jesus arose and went to the region of Tyre and Sidon, where he entered a house, and would not have any one know it. But he could not be hid. A woman, whose little daughter was possessed by an unclean spirit, came and fell down at his feet. She was a Greek, a Syrophoenician by birth, and she begged him to cast the demon out of her daughter. "Let the children first be fed," he said, "for it is not right to take the children's bread and throw it to the dogs."

"Yes, Lord," she answered, "yet even the dogs under the table eat the children's crumbs."

"For this saying," he replied, "you may go your way; the demon has left your daughter." The woman went home, and found the child lying in bed, and the demon gone.

Returning from the region of Tyre and Sidon, Jesus went through the region of the Decapolis. And they brought to him a man who was deaf and had an impediment in his speech. Taking the man aside privately, Jesus put his fingers into the man's ears, and he spat and touched his tongue. Looking up to heaven, he sighed and said, "Ephphatha," that is, "Be opened." The man's ears were opened, his tongue was released, and he spoke plainly. Jesus charged the man's friends to tell no one, but they were astonished beyond measure, and they zealously proclaimed it. "He has done all things well," they said; "he even makes the deaf hear and the dumb speak."

In those days, when another great crowd had gathered, and they had nothing to eat, Jesus said to his disciples, "I have compassion on the crowd, because they have been with me now three days, and have nothing to eat. If I send them away hungry, they will faint, for some of them have come a long way."

"How can one feed these men," his disciples said, "with bread here in the desert?"

"How many loaves have you?" he asked.

"Seven," they said. He commanded the crowd to sit on the ground, and he took the seven loaves, and having given thanks he broke them and gave them to his disciples to set before the people. They also had a few small fish. Having blessed them, he commanded that these should be set before the crowd. About four thousand people ate and were satisfied; and they took up the broken pieces left over, seven baskets full. Then Jesus sent them away; and immediately he got into the boat with his disciples, and went to the district of Dalmanutha.

The Pharisees came and argued with Jesus, seeking from him a sign from heaven, to test him. Sighing deeply in his spirit, he said, "Why does this generation seek a sign? Truly, I say to you, no sign shall be given to this generation." He left them, and getting into the boat again, he departed to the other side. Now they had forgotten to bring bread, so that they had only one loaf in the boat. He cautioned them, "Take heed, beware of the leaven of the Pharisees and the leaven of Herod." But they continued to say, "We have no bread."

"Why do you discuss the fact that you have no bread?" Jesus said. "Do you not yet perceive or understand? Are your hearts hardened? Having eyes, do you not see, and having ears, do you not hear? And do you not remember? When I broke the five loaves for the five thousand, how many baskets full of broken pieces did you take up?" They said, "Twelve." "And the seven for the four thousand, how many baskets full of broken pieces did you take up?" They said, "Seven." And he said, "Do you not yet understand?"

When they came to Bethsaida, some people brought to him a blind man. He took the man by the hand, and led him out of the village. When he had spit on his eyes and laid his hands upon him, he asked, "Do you see anything?" The man looked up. "I see men," he said, "but they look like trees, walking." Again he laid his hands upon his eyes; and the man looked intently and saw everything clearly. Jesus sent him away to his home, saying, "Do not even enter the village."

Going with his disciples to the villages of Caesarea Philippi, on the way Jesus asked his disciples, "Who do men say that I am?" They told him, "John the Baptist; and others say, Elijah; and others one of the prophets."

"But who do you say that I am?" he asked.

"You are the Christ," Peter answered. Then Jesus charged them to tell no one about him.

And he began to teach them that the Son of man must suffer many things, and be rejected by the elders and the chief priests and the scribes, and be killed, and after three days rise again. And he said this plainly. Then Peter took him, and began to rebuke him. But Jesus, turning and seeing his disciples, rebuked Peter. "Get behind me, Satan!" he said. "For you are not on the side of God, but of men."

He called to him the multitude with his disciples, and said, "If any man would come after me, let him deny himself and take up his cross and follow me. For whoever would save his life will lose it; and whoever loses his life for my sake and the gospel's will save it. What does it profit a man, to gain the whole world and forfeit his life? What can a man give in return for his life? Whoever is ashamed of me and of my words in this adulterous and sinful generation, of him will the Son of man also be ashamed, when he comes in the glory of his Father with the holy angels. Truly, I say to you, there are some standing here who will not taste death before they see that the kingdom of God has come with power."

After six days Jesus took Peter, James, and John, and led them up a high mountain apart by themselves; and he was transfigured before them. His garments became glistening, intensely white, as no fuller on earth could bleach them. And there appeared Elijah with Moses, talking to Jesus. "Master," said Peter, "it is well that we are here. Let us make three booths, one for you and one for Moses and one for Elijah" (he did not know what else to say, for they were exceedingly afraid). Then a cloud overshadowed them, and a voice came out of the cloud, "This is my beloved Son; listen to him." Suddenly looking around, they no longer saw any one with them but Jesus only. As they were coming down the mountain, he charged them to tell no one what they had seen, until the Son of man should have risen from the dead. So they kept the matter to themselves, questioning what the rising from the dead meant.

"Why do the scribes say that first Elijah must come?" they asked.

"Elijah does come first to restore all things," Jesus said. "And how is it written of the Son of man, that he should suffer many things and be treated with contempt? But I tell you that Elijah has come, and they did to him whatever they pleased, as it is written of him."

When they came to the other disciples, they saw a great crowd about them, and scribes arguing with them. "What are you discussing?" Jesus asked. One of the crowd answered, "Teacher, I brought my son to you, for he has a dumb spirit.

Wherever it seizes him, it dashes him down, and he foams and grinds his teeth and becomes rigid. I asked your disciples to cast it out, and they were not able." Jesus answered, "O faithless generation, how long am I to be with you? How long am I to bear with you? Bring him to me." They brought the boy, and when the spirit saw Jesus it convulsed the boy. He fell on the ground and rolled about, foaming at the mouth. "How long has he had this?" Jesus asked.

"From childhood," said the father, "and it has often cast him into the fire and into the water. If you can do anything, have pity on us and help us."

"If you can!" said Jesus. "All things are possible to him who believes."

Immediately the father cried, "I believe; help my unbelief!" Then Jesus rebuked the unclean spirit, saying, "You dumb and deaf spirit, I command you, come out of him, and never enter him again." Crying out and convulsing the boy terribly, the spirit came out, and the boy was like a corpse. But Jesus took him by the hand and lifted him up, and he arose. Later his disciples asked him privately, "Why could we not cast it out?" And he said, "This kind cannot be driven out by anything but prayer."

From there they passed through Galilee, and he would not have any one know it. For he was teaching his disciples, saying, "The Son of man will be delivered into the hands of men, and they will kill him; and when he is killed, after three days he will rise." But they did not understand the saying, and they were afraid to ask him.

They came to Capernaum, and when he was in the house he asked, "What were you discussing on the way?" They were silent, for they had discussed which of them was the greatest. "If any one would be first," Jesus said, "he must be last of all and servant of all." Then he took a child, and put him in the midst of them, and taking him in his arms, he said, "Whoever receives one such child in my name receives me; and whoever receives me, receives not me but him who sent me."

"Teacher," said John, "we saw a man casting out demons in your name, and we forbade him, because he was not following us."

"Do not forbid him," Jesus said, "for no one who does a mighty work in my name will be able soon after to speak evil of me. For he that is not against us is for us. Truly, I say to you, whoever gives you a cup of water because you bear the name of Christ, will by no means lose his reward. Whoever causes one of these little ones who believe in me to sin, it would be better for him if a great millstone were hung round his neck and he were thrown into the sea. If your hand causes you to sin, cut it off; it is better for you to enter life maimed than with two hands to go to hell. If your eye causes you to sin, pluck it out; it is better for you to enter the kingdom of God with one eye than with two eyes to be thrown into hell, where their worm does not die, and the fire is not quenched."

Leaving Capernaum, Jesus went to the region of Judea, where crowds gathered to him. As his custom was, he taught them, and soon Pharisees came to test him. "Is it lawful for a man to divorce his wife?" they asked. "What did Moses command you?"

he answered. "Moses allowed a man to write a certificate of divorce," they said, "and to put her away."

"For your hardness of heart he wrote you this commandment," Jesus said. "But from the beginning of creation, 'God made them male and female.' 'For this reason a man shall leave his father and mother and be joined to his wife, and the two shall become one flesh.' So they are no longer two but one flesh. What therefore God has joined together, let not man put asunder." In the house the disciples asked about this matter, and he said, "Whoever divorces his wife and marries another, commits adultery against her; and if she divorces her husband and marries another, she commits adultery."

They were bringing children to him, that he might touch them, and the disciples rebuked them. When Jesus saw it he was indignant. "Let the children come to me," he said, "do not hinder them; for to such belongs the kingdom of God. Truly, I say to you, whoever does not receive the kingdom of God like a child shall not enter it."

As he was setting out on his journey to

Jerusalem, a man ran up and knelt before him. "Good Teacher," he asked, "what must I do to inherit eternal life?"

"Why do you call me good?" Jesus said. "No one is good but God alone. You know the commandments: 'Do not kill, Do not commit adultery, Do not steal, Do not bear false witness, Do not defraud, Honor your father and mother.' "

"Teacher," said the man, "all these I have observed from my youth."

Jesus looking upon him loved him. "You lack one thing," he said. "Go, sell what you have, and give to the poor, and you will have treasure in heaven; and come, follow me." At that the man's countenance fell, and he went away sorrowful, for he had great possessions. Jesus looked around and said to his disciples, "How hard it will be for those who have riches to enter the kingdom of God!" The disciples were amazed, but Jesus said again, "Children, how hard it is to enter the kingdom of God! It is easier for a camel to go through the eye of a needle than for a rich man to enter the kingdom of God."

"Then who can be saved?" they asked, exceedingly astonished.

"With men it is impossible," Jesus said, "but not with God; for all things are possible with God."

"Lo," said Peter, "we have left everything and followed you."

"Truly," Jesus said, "there is no one who has left house or brothers or sisters or mother or father or children or lands, for my sake and for the gospel, who will not receive a hundredfold now in this time, houses and brothers and sisters and mothers and children and lands, with persecutions, and in the age to come eternal life. But many that are first will be last, and the last first."

As they were on the road, Jesus began to tell his disciples what was to happen to him. "Behold, we are going up to Jerusalem, and the Son of man will be delivered to the chief priests and the scribes, and they will condemn him to death, and deliver him to the Gentiles. They will mock him, and spit upon him, and scourge him, and kill him; and after three days he will rise."

James and John came forward and said, "Teacher, we want you to do for us whatever we ask of you. Grant us to sit, one at your right hand and one at your left, in your glory."

"You do not know what you are asking," Jesus said. "Are you able to drink the cup that I drink, or to be baptized with the baptism with which I am baptized?"

"We are able," they said.

"The cup that I drink you will drink," Jesus said, "and with the baptism with which I am baptized, you will be baptized. But to sit at my right hand or at my left is not mine to grant; it is for those for whom it has been prepared."

When the ten heard of this request, they were indignant at James and John. Jesus called them to him and said, "You know that those who are supposed to rule over the Gentiles lord it over them, and their great men exercise authority over them. But it shall not be so among you; whoever would be great among you must be your servant, and whoever would be first among you must be slave of all. For the Son of man also came not to be served but to serve, and to give his life as a ransom for many."

They came to Jericho, and as they were leaving, followed by a great multitude, a blind beggar named Bartimaeus was sitting by the roadside. When he heard it was Jesus, he cried out, "Jesus, Son of David, have mercy on me!" Many rebuked him, but he cried out all the more, "Son of David, have mercy on me!" Jesus stopped and said, "Call him." They said to the blind man, "Take heart; rise, he is calling you." Throwing off his mantle, Bartimaeus sprang up and came to Jesus. "Master," he said, "let me receive my sight." Jesus said, "Go your way; your faith has made you well." Immediately he received his sight and followed him on the way.

When they drew near to Jerusalem, Jesus called two of his disciples. "Go into the village opposite you," he said, "and as you enter it you will find a colt tied, on which no one has ever sat; untie it and bring it. If any one says to you, 'Why are you doing this?' say, 'The Lord has need of it and will send it back here immediately.' " They went and found a colt tied at a door, and they untied it. Those who stood there said, "What are you doing?" They told them what Jesus had said, and they let them go.

Bringing the colt to Jesus, they threw their garments on it, and he sat upon it. Many people spread garments on the road, others spread leafy branches, cut from the fields. Those who went before and those who followed cried, "Hosanna! Blessed is he who comes in the name of the Lord! Blessed is the kingdom of our father David that is coming! Hosanna in the highest!" When Jesus entered Jerusalem he went into the temple, where he looked round at everything. Then, as it was late, he went out to Bethany with the twelve.

On the following day, when they came from Bethany, Jesus was hungry. Seeing a fig tree in leaf, he looked to see if he could find anything on it. There was nothing but leaves, for it was not the season for figs. "May no one ever eat fruit from you again," he said. And his disciples heard it.

In Jerusalem he entered the temple and began to drive out those who sold and bought there. He overturned the tables of the money-changers and the seats of those who sold pigeons, and he would not allow any one to carry anything through the temple. "Is it not written," he said, " 'My house shall be called a house of prayer for all the nations'? But you have made it a den of robbers." The chief priests and the scribes heard of this, and they sought to destroy Jesus, for they feared him because the multitude was astonished at his teaching. That evening he and his disciples again went out of the city.

In the morning, as they returned, they saw the fig tree withered away to its roots. "Master, look!" said Peter. "The fig tree you cursed has withered."

"Have faith in God," Jesus answered. "Truly, I say to you, whoever says to this mountain, 'Be taken up and cast into the sea,' and does not doubt in his heart, but believes that what he says will come to pass, it will be done for him. Therefore I tell you, whatever you ask in prayer, believe that you have received it, and it will be yours. And whenever you stand praying, forgive, if you have anything against any one; so that your Father also who is in heaven may forgive you your trespasses."

They came again to Jerusalem, and as Jesus was walking in the temple, the chief priests, the scribes, and the elders came to him and said, "By what authority are you doing these things?"

"I will ask you a question," Jesus said. "Answer me, and I will tell you by what authority I do these things. Was the baptism of John from heaven or from men? Answer me."

They argued with one another, "If we say, 'From heaven,' he will say, 'Why then did you not believe him?' But shall we say, 'From men'?"—they were afraid of the people, for all held that John was a real prophet. So they answered Jesus, "We do not know."

"Neither will I tell you," said Jesus, "by what authority I do these things."

Jesus then began to speak to them in a parable. "A man planted a vineyard, dug a pit for the wine press, then let it out to tenants and went into another country. Later he sent a servant to get from the tenants some of the fruit of the vineyard. They beat him, and sent him away empty-handed. He sent another servant, and they treated him shamefully. He sent another, and him they killed; and so with others, some they beat and some they killed. He had still one other, a beloved son; finally he sent him to them, saying, 'They will respect my son.' But those tenants said, 'This is the heir; come, let us kill him, and the inheritance will be ours.' So they killed him, and cast him out of the vineyard. Now what will the owner of the vineyard do? He will come and destroy the tenants, and give the vineyard to others."

At this the chief priests and the elders wanted to arrest Jesus, for they perceived that he had told the parable against them. But they feared the multitude, so they left him and went away.

Some of the Pharisees and Herodians came to entrap him in his talk. "Teacher," they said, "we know that you are true, and do not regard the position of men, but truly teach the way of God. Is it lawful to pay taxes to Caesar, or not?" Knowing their hypocrisy, Jesus said, "Why put me to the test? Bring me a coin, and let me look at it." They showed him one, and he said, "Whose likeness and inscription is this?" They said, "Caesar's." Jesus said, "Render to Caesar the things that are Caesar's, and to God the things that are God's." And they were amazed at him.

Some of the Sadducees, who say that there is no resurrection, also came to him. "Teacher," they said, "Moses wrote for us that if a man's brother dies and leaves a wife, but leaves no child, the man must take the wife, and raise up children for his brother. There were seven brothers; the first took a wife, and when he died left no children; and the second took her, and died, leaving no children; and the third likewise; and the seven left no children. Last of all the woman also died. In the resurrection whose wife will she be?"

"Is not this why you are wrong," Jesus said, "that you know neither the scriptures nor the power of God? For when they rise from the dead, they neither marry nor are given in marriage, but are like angels in heaven. And as for the dead being raised, have you not read in the book of Moses, in the passage about the bush, how God said, 'I am the God of Abraham, and the God of Isaac, and the God of Jacob'? He is not

God of the dead, but of the living; you are quite wrong."

One of the scribes, seeing that Jesus answered well, asked, "Which commandment is the first of all?" Jesus answered, "The first is, 'Hear, O Israel: The Lord our God, the Lord is one; and you shall love the Lord your God with all your heart, and with all your soul, and with all your mind, and with all your strength.' The second is this, 'You shall love your neighbor as yourself.' There is no other commandment greater than these."

"You are right, Teacher," the scribe said, "you have truly said that he is one, and there is no other but he; and to love him, and to love one's neighbor, is much more than all burnt offerings and sacrifices." When Jesus saw that the scribe answered wisely, he said, "You are not far from the kingdom of God." After that no one dared to ask Jesus any question.

Again he said, "Beware of the scribes, who like to go about in long robes, and to have salutations in the market places and the best seats in the synagogues and the places of honor at feasts, who devour widows' houses and for a pretense make long prayers. They will receive the greater condemnation." Sitting opposite the treasury, he watched the multitude putting in money. Many rich people put in large sums, and a poor widow came, and put in a penny. Jesus said to his disciples, "Truly, I say to you, this poor widow has put in more than all those others. For they all contributed out of their abundance; but she out of her poverty has put in everything she had."

As he came out of the temple, one of his disciples said, "Look, Teacher, what wonderful stones and what wonderful buildings!"

"Do you see these great buildings?" Jesus answered. "There will not be left here one stone upon another, that will not be thrown down."

"When will this be," they asked, "and what will be the sign when these things are all to be accomplished?"

"Take heed that no one leads you astray," Jesus said. "Many will come in my name, saying, 'I am he!' and they will lead many astray. When you hear of wars and rumors of wars, do not be alarmed; this must take place, but the end is not yet. Nation will rise against nation, and kingdom against kingdom; there will be earthquakes in various places, there will be famines; this is but the beginning of the birth-pangs.

"But take heed to yourselves; for they will deliver you up to councils; and you will be beaten in synagogues; and you will stand before governors and kings for my sake, to bear testimony. And the gospel must first be preached to all nations. When they bring you to trial, do not be anxious what you are to say; but say whatever is given you, for it is not you who speak, but the Holy Spirit. Brother will deliver up brother to death, the father his child, children will rise against parents and have them put to death; and you will be hated by all for my name's sake. But he who endures to the end will be saved.

"But when you see the desolating sacrilege set up where it ought not to be, then let those who are in Judea flee to the mountains; let him who is on the housetop not go down to take anything away; let him who is in the field not turn back to take his mantle. Alas for those who are with child and for those who give suck in those days! Pray that it may not happen in winter. For in those days there will be such tribulation as has not been from the beginning of creation until now, and never will be. And if the Lord had not shortened the days, no human being would be saved; but for the sake of the elect, whom he chose, he shortened the days. Then if any one says to you, 'Look, here is the Christ!' or 'Look, there he is!' do not believe it. False Christs and false prophets will arise and show signs and wonders, to lead astray, if possible, the elect. But take heed; I have told you all things beforehand.

"But after that tribulation the sun will be darkened, the moon will not give its light, the stars will be falling from heaven, and the powers in the heavens will be shaken. Then they will see the Son of man coming in clouds with great power and glory, and he will send out the angels, and gather his elect from the ends of the earth to the ends of heaven.

"From the fig tree learn its lesson: as

soon as its branch becomes tender and puts forth its leaves, you know that summer is near. So also, when you see these things taking place, you know that he is near, at the very gates. Truly, I say to you, this generation will not pass away before all these things take place. Heaven and earth will pass away, but my words will not pass away. But of that day or that hour no one knows, not even the angels in heaven, nor the Son, but only the Father. Take heed, watch; for you do not know when the time will come. And what I say to you I say to all: Watch."

It was now two days before the Passover and the feast of Unleavened Bread. The chief priests and the scribes were again seeking how to arrest Jesus by stealth, and kill him; for they said, "Not during the feast, lest there be a tumult of the people."

While he was at Bethany, as he sat at table a woman came with an alabaster flask of pure nard, very costly, and she poured it over his head. Some said indignantly, "Why was the ointment wasted? It might have been sold for more than three hundred denarii, and given to the poor."

"Let her alone," Jesus said. "She has done a beautiful thing to me. You always have the poor with you, and whenever you will, you can do good to them; but you will not always have me. She has anointed my body beforehand for burying. And truly, I say to you, wherever the gospel is preached, what she has done will be told in memory of her."

Then Judas Iscariot, one of the twelve, went to the chief priests in order to betray him. When the chief priests heard this they were glad, and promised to give Judas money. And he sought an opportunity to betray him.

On the first day of Unleavened Bread, when they sacrificed the passover lamb, the disciples asked, "Where will you have us prepare for the passover?" Jesus called two of them and said, "Go into the city, and a man carrying a jar of water will meet you; follow him. Wherever he enters, say to the householder, 'The Teacher says, Where is my guest room, where I am to eat the passover with my disciples?' He will show you a large upper room furnished and ready; there prepare for us."

The disciples went to Jerusalem and found all as Jesus had told them.

That evening he came to the upper room with the twelve. As they were at table, he said, "Truly, I say to you, one of you will betray me; one who is eating with me." They began to be sorrowful, and to say one after another, "Is it I?" He said, "It is one of the twelve, one who is dipping bread into the dish with me. For the Son of man goes as it is written of him, but woe to that man by whom the Son of man is betrayed! It would have been better for that man if he had not been born."

As they were eating, he took bread, and blessed, and broke it, and gave it to them. "Take," he said; "this is my body." And he took a cup, and when he had given thanks he gave it to them, and they all drank of it. "This is my blood of the covenant," he said, "which is poured out for many. Truly, I say to you, I shall not drink again of the fruit of the vine until that day when I drink it new in the kingdom of God."

When they had sung a hymn, they went out to the Mount of Olives, and Jesus said, "You will all fall away; for it is written, 'I will strike the shepherd, and the sheep will be scattered.' But after I am raised up, I will go before you to Galilee."

"Even though they all fall away," Peter said, "I will not."

"Truly, I say to you," Jesus answered, "this very night, before the cock crows twice, you will deny me three times."

"If I must die with you," said Peter vehemently, "I will not deny you." And all said the same.

They went to a place called Gethsemane, and Jesus said, "Sit here, while I pray." Then he took with him Peter, James, and John, and he began to be greatly distressed and troubled. "My soul is very sorrowful," he said, "even to death; remain here, and watch." Going a little farther, he fell on the ground and prayed that, if it were possible, the hour might pass from him. "Abba, Father, all things are possible to thee," he said. "Remove this cup from me; yet not what I will, but what thou wilt." He came and found the three sleeping, and he said to Peter, "Simon, are you asleep? Could you not watch one hour? Watch and pray that you may not enter into temptation; the spirit indeed is willing, but the flesh is weak."

Again he went away and prayed, saying the same words. Again he came and found them sleeping, and they did not know what to answer him. Then he came the third time, and said, "Are you still sleeping and taking your rest? It is enough; the hour has come; the Son of man is betrayed into the hands of sinners. Rise, let us be going; see, my betrayer is at hand."

While he was still speaking, Judas came, and with him a crowd with swords and clubs, from the chief priests and the scribes and the elders. Now the betrayer had given them a sign, saying, "The one I shall kiss is the man; seize him and lead him away under guard." He went up to Jesus at once, said, "Master!" and kissed him. As they seized Jesus, one of those who stood by drew his sword, and struck the slave of the high priest and cut off his ear.

"Have you come out as against a robber, with swords and clubs to capture me?" Jesus asked. "Day after day I was with you in the temple teaching, and you did not seize me. But let the scriptures be fulfilled." Then all the disciples forsook him and fled. And a young man followed him, with nothing but a linen cloth about his body; they seized him, but he left the linen cloth and ran away naked.

They led Jesus to the high priest; and all the chief priests, the elders, and scribes were assembled. Peter had followed at a distance, right into the courtyard of the high priest, and he was sitting with the guards, warming himself at the fire. Now the chief priests and the council sought testimony against Jesus to put him to death; but they found none. Many bore false witness, but their witness did not agree. Others charged, "We heard him say, 'I will destroy this temple that is made with hands, and in three days I will build another, not made with hands.' " Yet not even so did their testimony agree.

"Have you no answer to make?" the high priest asked Jesus. "What is it that these men testify against you?" But Jesus was silent. Again the high priest asked, "Are you the Christ, the Son of the Blessed?"

"I am," Jesus said, "and you will see the Son of man seated at the right hand of Power, and coming with the clouds of heaven."

At this the high priest tore his garments. "Why do we still need witnesses?" he said. "You have heard his blasphemy. What is your decision?" They all condemned him as deserving death. Some began to spit on him, and they covered his face and struck him, saying, "Prophesy!" The guards received him with blows.

Below in the courtyard one of the maids of the high priest saw Peter warming himself. "You also were with the Nazarene, Jesus," she said. But he denied it, saying, "I neither know nor understand what you mean," and he went out into the gateway. The maid saw him and said to the bystanders, "This man is one of them." Again Peter denied it. After a while the bystanders said, "Certainly you are one of them; for you are a Galilean." But he invoked a curse on himself and swore, "I do not know this man of whom you speak." Immediately the cock crowed a second time, and Peter remembered how Jesus had said,

"Before the cock crows twice, you will deny me three times." And he broke down and wept.

As soon as it was morning the chief priests, with the whole council, held a consultation; then they bound Jesus and delivered him to Pilate.

"Are you the King of the Jews?" Pilate asked.

"You have said so," Jesus answered.

The chief priests accused him of many things, and Pilate asked, "Have you no answer to make? See how many charges they bring against you." But Jesus made no further answer, so that Pilate wondered.

Now at the feast Pilate used to release one prisoner for whom the people asked. Among the rebels in prison was a man called Barabbas, who had committed murder. The crowd asked Pilate to do as he usually did. "Do you want me to release for you the King of the Jews?" he asked. (He perceived it was out of envy that the chief priests had delivered Jesus up.) But the chief priests stirred up the crowd to have Barabbas released instead. "What shall I do with the man whom you call the King of the Jews?" Pilate asked.

"Crucify him," they cried out.

"Why, what evil has he done?" asked Pilate. But they shouted all the more, "Crucify him." So Pilate, wishing to satisfy the crowd, released Barabbas. Then, having scourged Jesus, he delivered him to be crucified.

The soldiers led Jesus to the praetorium, where they clothed him in a purple cloak, and put on him a crown of thorns. "Hail, King of the Jews!" they saluted. They struck his head with a reed, and spat upon him, and knelt down in homage. When they had mocked him, they stripped him of the purple cloak, and put his own clothes on him. And they led him out to crucify him.

A passer-by, Simon of Cyrene, who was coming in from the country, was compelled to carry his cross. At the place called Golgotha (the place of a skull) they offered him wine mingled with myrrh, but he did not take it. And at the third hour they crucified him, and divided his garments, casting lots for them. The inscription of the charge against him read, "The King of the Jews."

They also crucified two robbers, one on his right and one on his left. Those who passed by derided him, wagging their heads, saying, "Aha! You who would destroy the temple and build it in three days, save yourself, and come down from the cross!" The chief priests also mocked him. "He saved others," they said; "he cannot save himself. Let the Christ, the King of Israel, come down now from the cross, that we may see and believe." Those who were crucified with him also reviled him. Many women were looking on from afar, among whom were Mary Magdalene, and Mary the mother of James and Joses, and Salome, who, when he was in Galilee, ministered to him; also many other women who came up with him to Jerusalem.

When the sixth hour had come, there was darkness over the whole land until the ninth hour. Then Jesus cried with a loud voice, "Eloi, Eloi, lama sabachthani?" ("My God, my God, why hast thou forsaken me?") Some of the bystanders said, "He is calling Elijah." One ran and, filling a sponge full of vinegar, put it on a reed and gave it to him to drink, saying, "Wait, let us see whether Elijah will come to take him down."

And Jesus uttered a loud cry, and breathed his last. And the curtain of the temple was torn in two, from top to bottom. When the centurion saw that Jesus thus breathed his last, he said, "Truly this man was the Son of God!"

When evening had come, since it was the day of Preparation, the day before the sabbath, Joseph of Arimathea, a respected member of the council, who was also looking for the kingdom of God, went to Pilate and asked for the body of Jesus. Pilate summoned the centurion and asked whether Jesus was already dead. When he learned he was, he granted the body to Joseph. And Joseph bought a linen shroud, and taking Jesus down, wrapped him in the shroud and laid him in a tomb hewn out of the rock. Then he rolled a large stone against the door of the tomb.

Mary Magdalene and Mary the mother of Joses saw where he was laid, and when the sabbath was past, with Salome they bought spices to anoint him. Very early on the first day of the week they went to the tomb when the sun had risen. They were saying, "Who will roll away the stone for us?" and looking up, they saw that the stone was rolled back. Entering the tomb, they saw a young man sitting on the right side, dressed in a white robe, and they were amazed.

"Do not be amazed," he said. "You seek Jesus of Nazareth, who was crucified. He has risen, he is not here; see the place where they laid him. But go, tell his disciples and Peter that he is going before you to Galilee; there you will see him, as he told you."

The women fled from the tomb, for trembling and astonishment had come upon them; and they said nothing to any one, for they were afraid.

Now WHEN JESUS rose early on the first day of the week, he appeared first to Mary Magdalene, from whom he had cast out seven demons. She went and told the others, as they mourned and wept. But when they heard that he was alive, they would not believe it. After this he appeared in another form to two of them, as they were walking into the country. They went back and told the rest, but they did not believe them.

Afterward Jesus appeared to the eleven as they sat at table, and he upbraided them for their unbelief and hardness of heart, because they had not believed those who saw him after he had risen. And he said to them, "Go into all the world and preach the gospel to the whole creation. He who believes and is baptized will be saved; but he who does not believe will be condemned. And these signs will accompany those who believe: in my name they will cast out demons; they will speak in new tongues; they will pick up serpents, and if they drink any deadly thing, it will not hurt them; they will lay their hands on the sick, and they will recover."

So then the Lord Jesus, after he had spoken to them, was taken up into heaven, and sat down at the right hand of God. And they went forth and preached everywhere, while the Lord worked with them and confirmed the message by the signs that attended it. Amen.

THE GOSPEL
ACCORDING TO
LUKE

Not an eyewitness to the life of Jesus, Luke was a physician and a companion of the apostle Paul. His Gospel, taken as a whole, is an eloquent literary composition, showing thoughtful use of material gathered from different sources. Its middle section contains the only record of several of the most beloved of Jesus' parables, including the Good Samaritan and the Prodigal Son. The book is dedicated to a certain Theophilus, probably a Greek or Roman of high rank.

Throughout the narrative Luke emphasizes Jesus' compassion for the needy, the sick, the brokenhearted, and the outcast, and he also stresses Jesus' severity toward the proud and those who put their trust in riches. More so than the other evangelists, Luke insists on the fact that the teachings of Jesus are universal, addressed to all people. He has a remarkable number of references to women, including Elizabeth, the prophetess Anna, and the widow of Nain, and it is Mary, not Joseph (as in Matthew), who plays the principal role in the stories about Jesus' birth. In the ministry of Jesus, Luke assigns a prominent place to both prayer and the action of the Holy Spirit.

———

INASMUCH AS MANY have undertaken to compile a narrative of the things which have been accomplished among us, just as they were delivered to us by those who from the beginning were eyewitnesses and ministers of the word, it seemed good to me also, having followed all things closely for some time past, to write an orderly account for you, most excellent Theophilus, that you may know the truth concerning the things of which you have been informed.

In the days of Herod, king of Judea, there was a priest named Zechariah, and he had a wife named Elizabeth. They were both righteous before God, walking in all the commandments, but they had no child, because Elizabeth was barren, and both were advanced in years.

When Zechariah's division was on duty, it fell to him by lot to enter the temple and burn incense, while the people were praying outside. And there appeared to him an angel standing on the right side of the altar. Fear fell upon Zechariah, but the angel said, "Do not be afraid, for your prayer is heard, and your wife Elizabeth will bear you a son, and you shall call his name John. And many will rejoice at his birth, for he will be great before the Lord, and he will be filled with the Holy Spirit, even from his mother's womb. He will turn many of the sons of Israel to the Lord their God, and he will go before him in the spirit and power of Elijah to make ready for the Lord a people prepared."

"How shall I know this?" said Zechariah. "For I am an old man, and my wife is advanced in years."

"I am Gabriel," the angel answered, "who stand in the presence of God; I was sent to bring you this good news. Behold, you will be silent and unable to speak until the day that these things come to pass, because you did not believe my words."

The people were waiting for Zechariah, and they wondered at his delay. When he came out, he could not speak, and they perceived that he had seen a vision; he made signs to them and remained dumb. When his time of service was ended, he went home. Afterward his wife conceived, and for five months she hid herself, saying, "Thus the Lord has taken away my reproach among men."

In the sixth month the angel Gabriel was sent from God to a city of Galilee named Nazareth, to a virgin betrothed to a man whose name was Joseph, of the house of David; and the virgin's name was Mary. "Hail, O favored one," the angel said, "the Lord is with you!" But Mary was greatly troubled at the saying, and considered what sort of greeting this might be. "Do not be afraid," the angel said, "for you have found favor with God. And behold, you will conceive and bear a son, and you shall call his name Jesus. He will be great, and will be called the Son of the Most High; and the Lord God will give to him the throne of his father David, and he will reign over the house of Jacob for ever; and of his kingdom there will be no end."

"How shall this be," Mary said, "since I have no husband?"

"The Holy Spirit will come upon you," the angel answered, "and the power of the Most High will overshadow you; therefore the child to be born will be called holy, the Son of God. Behold, your kinswoman Elizabeth in her old age has also conceived a son; and this is the sixth month with her who was called barren. For with God nothing will be impossible."

"Behold, I am the handmaid of the Lord," said Mary; "let it be to me according to your word." And the angel departed from her.

In those days Mary arose and went into the hill country, to the house of Zechariah. When Elizabeth heard the greeting of Mary, the babe leaped in her womb, and she was filled with the Holy Spirit. "Blessed are you among women," she exclaimed, "and blessed is the fruit of your womb! And why is this granted me, that the mother of my Lord should come to me? For behold, at your greeting the babe in my womb leaped for joy. And blessed is she who believed that there would be a fulfilment of what was spoken to her from the Lord."

"My soul magnifies the Lord," Mary said, "and my spirit rejoices in God my Savior, for he has regarded the low estate of his handmaiden. Henceforth all generations will call me blessed; for he who is mighty has done great things for me, and holy is his name. His mercy is on those who fear him from generation to generation. He has shown strength with his arm, he has scattered the proud in the imagination of their hearts, he has put down the mighty from their thrones, and exalted those of low degree; he has filled the hungry with good things, and the rich he has sent empty away. He has helped his servant Israel, in remembrance of his mercy, as he spoke to our fathers, to Abraham and to his posterity for ever." And Mary remained with Elizabeth about three months, then returned to her home.

Now when the time came, Elizabeth gave birth to a son. On the eighth day they came to circumcise the child; and they would have named him Zechariah after his father, but his mother said, "He shall be called John." They said, "None of your kindred is called by this name," and they made signs to his father, inquiring what he would have him called. He asked for a writing tablet, and wrote, "His name is John," and they all marveled. Immediately Zechariah's tongue was loosed, and he spoke, blessing God. Fear came on all their neighbors, and these things were talked about through the hill country of Judea; and all who heard them said, "What then will this child be?"

Then Zechariah was filled with the Holy Spirit, and he prophesied: "Blessed be the Lord God of Israel, for he has visited and redeemed his people, and has raised up a horn of salvation for us in the house of his servant David, as he spoke by the mouth of his holy prophets from of old. And you, child, will be called the prophet of the Most High; for you will go before the Lord to prepare his ways, to give knowledge of salvation to his people in the forgiveness of their sins, through the tender mercy of our God, when the day shall dawn upon us from on high to give light to those who sit in darkness and in the shadow of death, to guide our feet into the way of peace." And the child grew and became strong in spirit, and he was in the wilderness till the day of his manifestation to Israel.

In those days a decree went out from Caesar Augustus that all the world should be enrolled. This was the first enrollment, when Quirinius was governor of Syria, and all went to be enrolled, each to his own city. Joseph also went up from Nazareth to the city of David, which is called Bethlehem, because he was of the house and lineage of David, to be enrolled with Mary, his betrothed, who was with child. While they were there she gave birth to her first-born son and wrapped him in swaddling cloths, and laid him in a manger, because there was no place for them in the inn.

In that region there were shepherds keeping watch over their flock by night, and an angel appeared, and the glory of the Lord shone around them, and they were filled with fear. "Be not afraid," the angel said, "for behold, I bring you good news of a great joy which will come to all the people; for to you is born this day in the city of David a Savior, who is Christ the Lord. And this will be a sign; you will find a babe wrapped in swaddling cloths and lying in a manger." Suddenly there was with the angel a multitude of the heavenly host praising God and saying, "Glory to God in the highest, and on earth peace among men with whom he is pleased!"

When the angels went away into heaven, the shepherds said, "Let us go over to Bethlehem and see this thing that has happened, which the Lord has made known to us." They went with haste, and found Mary and Joseph, and the babe lying in a manger. And they made known the saying which had been told them concerning this child, and all who heard it wondered. But Mary kept all these things, pondering them in her heart. When, at the end of eight days, the child was circumcised, he was called Jesus, the name given by the angel before he was conceived in the womb.

At the time for purification according to

the law of Moses, they brought the child up to Jerusalem to present him to the Lord, and to offer a sacrifice according to the law, "a pair of turtledoves, or two young pigeons." Now there was a man in Jerusalem, Simeon, who was righteous and devout. It had been revealed to him by the Holy Spirit that he should not die before he had seen the Lord's Christ. Now, inspired by the Spirit, he came into the temple; and when the parents brought in the child Jesus, he took him in his arms and blessed God and said, "Lord, now lettest thou thy servant depart in peace, according to thy word; for mine eyes have seen thy salvation which thou hast prepared in the presence of all peoples, a light for revelation to the Gentiles, and for glory to thy people Israel."

The child's father and mother marveled at what was said about him; and Simeon blessed them and said to Mary, "Behold, this child is set for the fall and rising of many in Israel, and for a sign that is spoken against (and a sword will pierce through your own soul also), that thoughts out of many hearts may be revealed."

There was also a prophetess, Anna, who was of a great age, having lived with her husband seven years from her virginity, and as a widow till she was eighty-four. She did not depart from the temple, worshiping with fasting and prayer night and day. Coming up at that very hour, she gave thanks to God, and spoke of the child to all who were looking for the redemption of Jerusalem. And when Joseph and Mary had performed everything according to the law, they returned to Nazareth. And the child grew and became strong, filled with wisdom; and the favor of God was upon him.

Now his parents went to Jerusalem every year for the Passover, and when Jesus was twelve years old, they went up according to custom. As they were returning, Jesus stayed behind in Jerusalem, and his parents, supposing him to be in the company, went a day's journey. When they sought him among their kinsfolk and acquaintances and did not find him, they returned to Jerusalem. After three days they found him in the temple, sitting among the teachers, listening and asking questions; and all who heard him were amazed at his understanding and his answers. When they saw him they were astonished; and his mother said, "Son, why have you treated us so? Behold, your father and I have been looking for you anxiously."

"How is it that you sought me?" Jesus answered. "Did you not know that I must be in my Father's house?" They did not understand this saying, but he went down with them to Nazareth, and was obedient to them; and his mother kept all these things in her heart.

IN THE FIFTEENTH year of the reign of Tiberius Caesar, Pontius Pilate being governor of Judea, and Herod being tetrarch of Galilee, in the high-priesthood of Annas and Caiaphas, the word of God came to John the son of Zechariah in the wilderness. And he went into all the region about the Jordan, preaching a baptism of repentance for the forgiveness of sins. As it is written in the book of Isaiah the prophet, "The voice of one crying in the wilderness: Prepare the way of the Lord, make his paths straight. Every valley shall be filled, and every mountain and hill shall be brought low, and the crooked shall be made straight, and the rough ways shall be made smooth; and all flesh shall see the salvation of God."

To the multitudes that came to be baptized by him John said, "You brood of vipers! Who warned you to flee from the wrath to come? Bear fruits that befit repentance, and do not begin to say to yourselves, 'We have Abraham as our father'; for I tell you, God is able from these stones to raise up children to Abraham."

The multitudes asked him, "What then shall we do?" And he answered, "He who has two coats, let him share with him who has none; and he who has food, let him do likewise." Tax collectors also came to be baptized, and said, "Teacher, what shall we do?" And he said, "Collect no more than is appointed you." Soldiers also asked, "And we, what shall we do?" And he said, "Rob no one by violence or by false accusation, and be content with your wages."

Now all the people questioned in their hearts concerning John, whether he were the Christ. "I baptize you with water," he answered, "but he who is mightier than I is coming, the thong of whose sandals I am not worthy to untie; he will baptize you with the Holy Spirit and with fire. His winnowing fork is in his hand, to clear his threshing floor, and to gather the wheat into his granary, but the chaff he will burn with unquenchable fire."

So John preached good news to the people. But Herod the tetrarch, who had been reproved by John for Herodias, his brother's wife, and for other evil things, shut up John in prison.

Now when all the people were baptized, and when Jesus also had been baptized and was praying, the heaven was opened, and the Holy Spirit descended upon him as a dove, and a voice came from heaven, "Thou art my beloved Son; with thee I am well pleased." When he began his ministry, Jesus was about thirty years of age.

Full of the Holy Spirit, Jesus returned from the Jordan, and was led by the Spirit for forty days in the wilderness, tempted by the devil. He ate nothing, and when those days were ended he was hungry. The devil said to him, "If you are the Son of

God, command this stone to become bread."

"It is written," Jesus answered, " 'Man shall not live by bread alone.' "

The devil took him up and showed him all the kingdoms of the world in a moment of time, and said, "To you I will give all this, for it has been delivered to me, and I give it to whom I will. If you will worship me, it shall all be yours."

"It is written," Jesus answered, " 'You shall worship the Lord your God, and him only shall you serve.' "

Then the devil took him to Jerusalem and set him on the pinnacle of the temple, and said, "If you are the Son of God, throw yourself down from here; for it is written, 'He will give his angels charge of you, to guard you,' and 'On their hands they will bear you up, lest you strike your foot against a stone.' "

"It is said," Jesus answered, " 'You shall not tempt the Lord your God.' "

When the devil had ended every temptation, he departed until an opportune time. And Jesus returned in the power of the Spirit into Galilee, and a report concerning him went out through all the surrounding country. And he taught in their synagogues, being glorified by all.

At Nazareth, where he had been brought up, he went to the synagogue on the sabbath. He stood up to read, and there was given to him the book of the prophet Isaiah. Opening the book, he read: "The Spirit of the Lord is upon me, because he has anointed me to preach good news to the poor. He has sent me to proclaim release to the captives and recovering of sight to the blind, to set at liberty those who are oppressed, to proclaim the acceptable year of the Lord."

Closing the book, he gave it back to the attendant and sat down; and the eyes of all in the synagogue were fixed on him. "Today," he said, "this scripture has been fulfilled in your hearing." All spoke well of him, and wondered at the gracious words which proceeded out of his mouth; and they said, "Is not this Joseph's son?"

"Doubtless," Jesus said, "you will quote to me this proverb, 'Physician, heal yourself; what we have heard you did at Capernaum, do here also in your own country.'

Truly, I say to you, no prophet is acceptable in his own country. But in truth, I tell you, there were many widows in Israel in the days of Elijah, when there came a great famine over the land; and Elijah was sent to none of them but only to Zarephath in Sidon, to a woman who was a widow. And there were many lepers in Israel in the time of the prophet Elisha; and none of them was cleansed but only Naaman the Syrian."

At this, all in the synagogue were filled with wrath. They rose up and put Jesus out of the city, and led him to the brow of a hill, that they might throw him down headlong. But he passed through the midst of them, and he went away to Capernaum, where he stayed at Simon Peter's house.

Now when the sun was setting, the sick were brought to him, and he laid his hands on every one of them and healed them. Demons also came out of many, crying, "You are the Son of God!" But he would not allow them to speak, because they knew that he was the Christ. When it was day he departed into a lonely place, and the people came to him and would have kept him from leaving, but he said, "I must preach the good news of the kingdom of God to the other cities also; for I was sent for this purpose." And he went preaching in the synagogues of Judea.

While he was standing by the lake of Gennesaret, the people pressed upon him to hear the word of God. Getting into Simon's boat, he asked him to put out a little from the land; then he sat down and taught the people from the boat. When he had ceased speaking, he said to Simon, "Put out into the deep and let down your nets for a catch."

"Master," Simon answered, "we toiled all night and took nothing! But at your word I will let down the nets." When they had done this, they enclosed a great shoal of fish; and as their nets were breaking, they beckoned to their partners in another boat to come and help them. They came and filled both boats, so that they began to sink. When Simon Peter saw it, he fell down at Jesus' knees. "Depart from me," he said, "for I am a sinful man, O Lord." He and all that were with him were astonished at the catch of fish, and so also were

James and John, sons of Zebedee, who were his partners. "Do not be afraid," Jesus said; "henceforth you will be catching men." And when they had landed, they left everything and followed him.

After this, Jesus went on and saw a tax collector, named Levi, sitting at the tax office. "Follow me," he said. And Levi left everything and followed him. Later Levi made Jesus a great feast in his house, with a large company of tax collectors and others at table. And the Pharisees murmured against his disciples, saying, "Why do you eat and drink with tax collectors and sinners?"

"Those who are well have no need of a physician," Jesus answered, "but those who are sick; I have not come to call the righteous, but sinners to repentance."

"The disciples of John fast often and offer prayers," the Pharisees said, "and so do our disciples, but yours eat and drink."

"Can you make wedding guests fast while the bridegroom is with them?" Jesus asked. "The days will come, when the bridegroom is taken away from them, and then they will fast." Then he told them a parable: "No one tears a piece from a new garment and puts it upon an old garment; if he does, he will tear the new, and the piece from the new will not match the old. And no one puts new wine into old wineskins; if he does, the new wine will burst the skins and it will be spilled, and the skins will be destroyed. But new wine must be put into fresh wineskins. And no one after drinking old wine desires new; for he says, 'The old is good.' "

In these days he went out to the mountain, and all night he continued in prayer. When it was day, he called his disciples, and chose from them twelve, whom he named apostles: Simon, whom he named Peter, Andrew his brother, James and John, Philip, Bartholomew, Matthew, Thomas, James the son of Alphaeus, Simon who was called the Zealot, Judas the son of James, and Judas Iscariot, who became a traitor. Then he came down with them and stood on a level place, with a great crowd of his disciples and a great multitude of people who came to hear him and to be healed. All sought to touch him, for power came forth from him and healed them all.

Lifting up his eyes on his disciples, he said: "Blessed are you poor, for yours is the kingdom of God. Blessed are you that hunger now, for you shall be satisfied. Blessed are you that weep now, for you shall laugh. Blessed are you when men hate you, and when they exclude you and revile you on account of the Son of man! Rejoice in that day, and leap for joy, for behold, your reward is great in heaven; for so their fathers did to the prophets. But woe to you that are rich, for you have received your consolation. Woe to you that are full now, for you shall hunger. Woe to you that laugh now, for you shall mourn and weep. Woe to you, when all men speak well of you, for so their fathers did to the false prophets.

"But I say to you that hear, Love your enemies, do good to those who hate you, bless those who curse you, pray for those who abuse you. To him who strikes you on the cheek, offer the other also; and from him who takes away your coat do not withhold even your shirt. Give to every one who begs from you; and of him who takes away your goods do not ask them again. And as you wish that men would do to you, do so to them.

"If you love those who love you, what credit is that to you? For even sinners love those who love them. And if you do good to those who do good to you, what credit is that to you? For even sinners do the same. And if you lend to those from whom you hope to receive, what credit is that to you? Even sinners lend to sinners, to receive as much again. But love your enemies, and do good, and lend, expecting nothing in return; and your reward will be great, and you will be sons of the Most High; for he is kind to the ungrateful and the selfish. Be merciful, even as your Father is merciful. Judge not, and you will not be judged; condemn not, and you will not be condemned; forgive, and you will be forgiven; give, and it will be given to you; good measure, pressed down, shaken together, running over, will be put into your lap. For the measure you give will be the measure you get back.

"No good tree bears bad fruit, nor again does a bad tree bear good fruit; for each tree is known by its own fruit. For figs are not gathered from thorns, nor are grapes picked from a bramble bush. The good man out of the good treasure of his heart produces good, and the evil man out of his evil treasure produces evil; for out of the abundance of the heart his mouth speaks. Why do you call me 'Lord, Lord,' and not do what I tell you? Every one who hears my words and does them is like a man building a house, who dug deep, and laid the foundation upon rock; and when a flood arose, the stream broke against that house, and could not shake it. But he who hears my words and does not do them is like a man who built a house on the ground without a foundation; against which the stream broke, and immediately it fell, and the ruin of that house was great."

After this, Jesus entered Capernaum. Now a centurion had a slave who was dear to him and who was at the point of death. When he heard of Jesus, he sent elders of the Jews asking him to come and heal his slave. "He is worthy to have you do this for him," the elders said, "for he loves our nation, and he built us our synagogue."

Jesus went with them, followed by a multitude, and when he was not far from the house, the centurion sent friends to say, "Lord, do not trouble yourself, for I am not worthy to have you come under my roof; therefore I did not presume to come to you. But say the word, and let my servant be healed. For I am a man set under authority, with soldiers under me; and I say to one, 'Go,' and he goes; and to another, 'Come,' and he comes; and to my slave, 'Do this,' and he does it." At this, Jesus marveled, and he said to the multitude, "I tell you, not even in Israel have I found such faith." When those who had been sent returned to the house, they found the slave well.

Soon afterward Jesus went with his disciples to a city called Nain. As he drew near, a man who had died was being carried out, the only son of his mother, and she was a widow; and a large crowd was with her. The Lord had compassion on her and said, "Do not weep." He touched the bier, and the bearers stood still, and he said, "Young man, I say to you, arise." The dead man sat up and began to speak,

and Jesus gave him to his mother. Fear
seized them all, and they glorified God,
saying, "A great prophet has arisen among
us!" and "God has visited his people!"
The report of this spread through all the
surrounding country.

The disciples of John the Baptist told
him of all these things, and he sent two of
them to the Lord to ask, "Are you he who
is to come, or shall we look for another?"
In that hour Jesus cured many of diseases
and plagues and evil spirits, and on many
that were blind he bestowed sight. "Go
and tell John," he answered, "what you
have seen and heard: the blind receive
their sight, the lame walk, lepers are
cleansed, and the deaf hear, the dead are
raised up, the poor have good news
preached to them. And blessed is he who
takes no offense at me."

When the messengers had gone, Jesus
began to speak to the crowds concerning
John: "What did you go out into the wilderness to behold? A reed shaken by the
wind? What then did you go out to see? A
man clothed in soft clothing? Behold,
those who are gorgeously appareled and

live in luxury are in kings' courts. What then did you go out to see? A prophet? Yes, I tell you, and more than a prophet. This is he of whom it is written, 'Behold, I send my messenger before thy face, who shall prepare thy way before thee.' I tell you, among those born of women none is greater than John; yet he who is least in the kingdom of God is greater than he. To what then shall I compare the men of this generation? They are like children sitting in the market place and calling to one another, 'We piped to you, and you did not dance; we wailed, and you did not weep.' For John the Baptist has come eating no bread and drinking no wine; and you say, 'He has a demon.' The Son of man has come eating and drinking; and you say, 'Behold, a glutton and a drunkard, a friend of tax collectors and sinners!' Yet wisdom is justified by all her children."

One of the Pharisees, named Simon, asked Jesus to eat with him, and he took his place at table. A woman of the city, a sinner, when she learned where Jesus was, brought an alabaster flask of ointment, and coming up behind him, she began to weep and to wet his feet with her tears, and she wiped them with her hair, and kissed his feet, and anointed them. Now when the Pharisee saw this, he said to himself, "If this man were a prophet, he would have known what sort of woman this is who is touching him."

"Simon," said Jesus, "I have something to say to you. A certain creditor had two debtors; one owed five hundred denarii, and the other fifty. When they could not pay, he forgave them both. Now which of them will love him more?"

"The one, I suppose," Simon answered, "to whom he forgave more."

"Do you see this woman?" Jesus said, turning toward her. "I entered your house, you gave me no water for my feet, but she has wet my feet with her tears and wiped them with her hair. You gave me no kiss, but from the time I came in she has not ceased to kiss my feet. You did not anoint my head with oil, but she has anointed my feet with ointment. Therefore I tell you, her sins, which are many, are forgiven, for she loved much; but he who is forgiven little, loves little." Then he said to the woman, "Your sins are forgiven." Those at table with him began to say among themselves, "Who is this, who even forgives sins?" To the woman Jesus said, "Your faith has saved you; go in peace."

Soon afterward he went on through cities and villages, bringing the good news of the kingdom of God. The twelve were with him, and also some women who had been healed of evil spirits and infirmities: Mary, called Magdalene, from whom seven demons had gone out, and Joanna, the wife of Chuza, Herod's steward, and Susanna, and many others, who provided for them out of their means. And when a great crowd came to him, he said, "A sower went out to sow his seed; and as he sowed, some fell along the path, and was trodden under foot, and the birds of the air devoured it. And some fell on the rock; and as it grew up, it withered away, because it had no moisture. And some fell among thorns; and the thorns grew with it and choked it. And some fell into good soil and grew, and yielded a hundredfold. He who has ears to hear, let him hear."

When his disciples asked him what this

meant, he said, "To you it has been given to know the secrets of the kingdom of God; but for others they are in parables, so that seeing they may not see, and hearing they may not understand. Now the parable is this: The seed is the word of God. The ones along the path are those who have heard; then the devil comes and takes away the word from their hearts. The ones on the rock are those who, when they hear the word, receive it with joy; but these have no root, they believe for a while and in time of temptation fall away. As for what fell among the thorns, they are those who hear, but as they go on their way they are choked by the cares and riches and pleasures of life, and their fruit does not mature. What fell in the good soil are those who, hearing the word, hold it fast in an honest and good heart, and bring forth fruit with patience.

"No one after lighting a lamp covers it with a vessel, or puts it under a bed, but on a stand, that those who enter may see the light. For nothing is hid that shall not be made manifest, nor anything secret that shall not be known and come to light.

Take heed then how you hear; for to him who has will more be given, and from him who has not, even what he thinks that he has will be taken away."

Then his mother and his brothers came to him, but they could not reach him for the crowd. He was told, "Your mother and your brothers are outside, desiring to see you." But he said, "My mother and my brothers are those who hear the word of God and do it."

One day he got into a boat with his disciples, saying, "Let us go across to the other side of the lake." As they sailed he fell asleep, and a storm of wind came down, and the boat was filling with water. "Master, Master," they said, waking him, "we are perishing!" He awoke and rebuked the wind and the raging waves, and they ceased, and there was a calm. "Where is your faith?" he asked. And they were afraid, and they marveled, saying, "Who then is this, that he commands even wind and water, and they obey him?"

Afterward Jesus called the twelve together and gave them power over all demons and to cure diseases, and he sent them out to preach the kingdom of God. "Take nothing for your journey," he said, "no staff, nor bag, nor bread, nor money; and do not have two tunics. Whatever house you enter, stay there, and from there depart. Wherever they do not receive you, when you leave that town shake off the dust from your feet as a testimony against them." So they departed and went through the villages, preaching the gospel and healing everywhere.

Now Herod the tetrarch heard of all that was done by Jesus, and he was perplexed, because it was said by some that John had been raised from the dead, by some that Elijah had appeared, and by others that one of the old prophets had risen. Herod said, "John I beheaded; but who is this about whom I hear such things?" And he sought to see Jesus.

On their return the apostles told Jesus what they had done. Then he withdrew with them to a city called Bethsaida, and the crowds followed, and he welcomed them and spoke of the kingdom of God, and cured those who had need of healing.

Now the day began to wear away, and

the twelve came and said, "Send the crowd into the villages to lodge and get provisions, for we are here in a lonely place."

"You give them something to eat," Jesus said.

"We have no more than five loaves and two fish," they said, "unless we are to go and buy food for all these people." (There were about five thousand men.)

"Make them sit down," he said, "in companies, about fifty each." They did so; then taking the five loaves and the two fish, Jesus looked up to heaven, and blessed and broke them, and gave them to the disciples to set before the crowd. All ate and were satisfied, and they took up what was left over, twelve baskets of broken pieces.

Now it happened that as Jesus was praying, the disciples were with him; and he asked them, "Who do the people say that I am?"

"John the Baptist," they answered, "but others say, Elijah; and others, that one of the old prophets has risen."

"But who do you say that I am?" he asked.

"The Christ of God," Peter answered.

Then he commanded them strictly to tell this to no one. "The Son of man must suffer many things," he said, "and be rejected by the elders and chief priests and scribes, and be killed, and on the third day be raised." And he said to all, "If any man would come after me, let him deny himself and take up his cross daily and follow me. For whoever would save his life will lose it; and whoever loses his life for my sake, he will save it. For what does it profit a man if he gains the whole world and loses or forfeits himself? For whoever is ashamed of me and of my words, of him will the Son of man be ashamed when he comes in his glory. But I tell you truly, there are some standing here who will not taste death before they see the kingdom of God."

About eight days after this he took with him Peter and John and James, and went up on the mountain to pray. As he was praying, the appearance of his countenance was altered, and his raiment became dazzling white. And behold, two men talked with him, Moses and Elijah, who appeared in glory and spoke of his departure, which he was to accomplish at Jerusalem. Peter and the others were heavy with sleep, and when they wakened they saw his glory and the two men who stood with him. As the men were parting from him, Peter said, "Master, it is well that we are here; let us make three booths, one for you and one for Moses and one for Elijah." Then a cloud came and overshadowed them; and they were afraid as they entered the cloud. And a voice came out of the cloud: "This is my Son, my Chosen; listen to him!" When the voice had spoken, Jesus was found alone, and the disciples kept silence and told no one in those days anything of what they had seen.

When they had come down from the mountain, Jesus said to his disciples, "Let these words sink into your ears: the Son of man is to be delivered into the hands of men." But they did not understand this saying, and it was concealed from them, that they should not perceive it; and they were afraid to ask him about it. Then an argument arose among them as to which was the greatest. When Jesus perceived the thought of their hearts, he took a child and put him by his side, and said, "Whoever receives this child in my name receives me, and whoever receives me receives him who sent me; for he who is least among you all is the one who is great."

When the days drew near for him to be received up, he set his face to go to Jerusalem. And he sent messengers ahead, who entered a village of the Samaritans to make ready for him; but the people would not receive him because his face was set toward Jerusalem. Then his disciples James and John said, "Lord, do you want us to bid fire come down from heaven and consume them?" But he rebuked them; and they went on to another village. As they were walking, a man said to him, "I will follow you wherever you go." And Jesus said to him, "Foxes have holes, and birds of the air have nests; but the Son of man has nowhere to lay his head." To another he said, "Follow me." The man said, "Lord, let me first go and bury my father." But Jesus said, "Leave the dead to bury their own dead; but as for you, go and proclaim the kingdom of God." Another said, "I will follow you, Lord; but let me first say farewell to those at my home." And Jesus said, "No one who puts his hand to the plow and looks back is fit for the kingdom of God."

After this the Lord appointed seventy others, and sent them on ahead of him, two by two, into every town and place where he himself was about to come. "The harvest is plentiful," he said to them, "but the laborers are few; pray therefore the Lord of the harvest to send out laborers into his harvest. Go your way; behold, I send you out as lambs in the midst of wolves. Carry no purse, no bag, no sandals; and salute no one on the road. Whatever house you enter, first say, 'Peace be to this house!' And if a son of peace is there, your peace shall rest upon him; but if not, it shall return to you. Remain in the same house, eating and drinking what they provide, for the laborer deserves his wages; do not go from house to house. Whenever you enter a town and they receive you, eat what is set before you; heal the sick in it and say to them, 'The kingdom of God has come near to you.' But whenever they do not receive you, go into the streets and say, 'Even the dust of your town that clings to our feet, we wipe off against you; nevertheless, know that the kingdom of God has come near.' I tell you, it shall be more tolerable on that day for Sodom than for that town.

"Woe to you, Chorazin! woe to you, Bethsaida! for if the mighty works done in you had been done in Tyre and Sidon, they would have repented long ago, sitting in sackcloth and ashes. But in the judgment it shall be more tolerable for Tyre and Sidon than for you. And you, Capernaum, will you be exalted to heaven? You shall be brought down to Hades." To the seventy he said, "He who hears you hears me, and he who rejects you rejects me, and he who rejects me rejects him who sent me."

Afterward the seventy returned with joy, saying, "Lord, even the demons are subject to us in your name!" And he said to them, "I saw Satan fall like lightning from heaven. Behold, I have given you authority to tread upon serpents and scorpions, and over all the power of the enemy; and nothing shall hurt you. Nevertheless, do not rejoice in this, that the spirits are subject to you; but rejoice that your names are written in heaven."

In that same hour he rejoiced in the Holy Spirit and said, "I thank thee, Father, Lord of heaven and earth, that thou hast hidden these things from the wise and understanding and revealed them to babes; yea, Father, for such was thy gracious will. All things have been delivered to me by my Father; and no one knows who the Son is except the Father, or who the Father is except the Son and any one to whom the Son chooses to reveal him." Turning to the disciples, he said, "Blessed are the eyes which see what you see! For I tell you that many prophets and kings desired to see what you see, and did not see it, and to hear what you hear, and did not hear it."

Another time a lawyer stood up to put him to the test. "Teacher," he said, "what shall I do to inherit eternal life?"

"What is written in the law?" Jesus asked. "How do you read?"

"You shall love the Lord your God," the lawyer answered, "with all your heart, and with all your soul, and with all your strength, and with all your mind; and your neighbor as yourself."

"You have answered right," Jesus said; "do this, and you will live." But the lawyer, desiring to justify himself, said, "And who is my neighbor?"

"A man was going down from Jerusalem to Jericho," Jesus replied, "and he fell among robbers, who stripped him and beat him and left him half dead. Now a priest was going down that road; and when he saw him he passed by on the other side. So likewise a Levite, when he saw him, passed by. But a Samaritan came to where he was, and when he saw him he had compassion, and bound up his wounds, pouring on oil and wine. Then he brought him to an inn, and he gave two denarii to the innkeeper, saying, 'Take care of him; and whatever more you spend, I will repay you when I come back.' Which of these three, do you think, proved neighbor to the man who fell among the robbers?"

"The one who showed mercy on him," the lawyer said.

"Go and do likewise," said Jesus.

As they went on their way, he entered a village, and a woman named Martha received him into her house. She had a sister called Mary, who sat at the Lord's feet and listened to his teaching. But Martha was distracted with much serving, and she said, "Lord, do you not care that my sister has left me to serve alone? Tell her to help me." But the Lord answered, "Martha, Martha, you are anxious and troubled about many things; one thing is needful. Mary has chosen the good portion, which shall not be taken away from her."

He was praying in a certain place, and when he ceased, one of his disciples said, "Lord, teach us to pray, as John taught his disciples." And he said to them, "When you pray, say:

"Father, hallowed be thy name. Thy kingdom come. Give us each day our daily bread; and forgive us our sins, for we ourselves forgive every one who is indebted to us; and lead us not into temptation."

And he said to them, "Which of you who has a friend will go to him at midnight and say to him, 'Friend, lend me three loaves; for a friend of mine has arrived on a journey, and I have nothing to set before him'; and he will answer from within, 'Do not bother me; the door is now shut, and my children are with me in bed; I cannot get up and give you anything'? I tell you, though he will not get up and give him anything because he is his friend, yet because of his importunity he will rise and give him whatever he needs. And I tell you, ask, and it will be given you; seek, and you will find; knock, and it will be opened to you. For every one who asks receives, and he who seeks finds, and to him who knocks it will be opened. What father among you, if his son asks for an egg, will give him a scorpion? If you then, who are evil, know how to give good gifts to your children, how much more will the heavenly Father give the Holy Spirit to those who ask him!"

Once he was casting out a demon that was dumb, and when the dumb man spoke, the people marveled. But some said, "He casts out demons by Beelzebul, the prince of demons." Others, to test him, sought a sign from heaven. Knowing their thoughts, Jesus said, "Every kingdom divided against itself is laid waste, and a divided household falls. And if Satan also is divided against himself, how will his kingdom stand? You say that I cast out demons by Beelzebul. If I do, by whom do your sons cast them out? They shall be your judges. But if it is by the finger of God that I cast out demons, then the kingdom of God has come upon you. He who is not with me is against me, and he who does not gather with me scatters.

"When the unclean spirit has gone out of a man, that spirit passes through waterless places seeking rest; and finding none he says, 'I will return to my house.' When he comes he finds it swept and put in order. Then he brings seven other spirits more evil than himself, and they dwell there; and the last state of that man becomes worse than the first." As he said this, a woman in the crowd raised her voice and said, "Blessed is the womb that bore you, and the breasts that you sucked!" But he said, "Blessed rather are those who hear the word of God and keep it!"

When the crowds were increasing, he

began to say, "This generation is an evil generation; it seeks a sign, but no sign shall be given to it except the sign of Jonah. For as Jonah became a sign to the men of Nineveh, so will the Son of man be to this generation. The queen of the South will arise at the judgment with the men of this generation and condemn them; for she came from the ends of the earth to hear the wisdom of Solomon, and behold, something greater than Solomon is here. The men of Nineveh will arise at the judgment with this generation and condemn it; for they repented at the preaching of Jonah, and behold, something greater than Jonah is here. No one after lighting a lamp puts it under a bushel, but on a stand, that those who enter may see. Your eye is the lamp of your body; when your eye is sound, your whole body is full of light; but when it is not sound, your body is full of darkness."

A Pharisee asked him to dine, so he went in and sat at table. The Pharisee was astonished to see that he did not wash before dinner, and the Lord said, "You Pharisees cleanse the outside of the cup, but inside you are full of extortion and wickedness. You fools! Did not he who made the outside make the inside also? But give for alms those things which are within; and behold, everything is clean for you. But woe to you Pharisees! for you tithe mint and rue and every herb, and neglect justice and the love of God; these you ought to have done, without neglecting the others. You love the best seat in the synagogues and salutations in the market places. Woe to you! for you are like graves which are not seen, and men walk over them without knowing it." As he went away from there, the scribes and the Pharisees began to press him hard, to provoke him to speak of many things, lying in wait for him, to catch at something he might say.

In the meantime, when so many thousands of the multitude had gathered together that they trod upon one another, he said to his disciples, "Beware of the leaven of the Pharisees, which is hypocrisy. Nothing is covered up that will not be revealed, or hidden that will not be known. Whatever you have whispered in private rooms shall be proclaimed upon the housetops. I tell you, my friends, do not fear those who kill the body, and after that have no more that they can do. But fear him who, after he has killed, has power to cast into hell; yes, I tell you, fear him! Are not five sparrows sold for two pennies? And not one of them is forgotten before God. Why, even the hairs of your head are all numbered. Fear not; you are of more value than many sparrows.

"I tell you, every one who acknowledges me before men, the Son of man will acknowledge before the angels of God; but he who denies me before men will be denied before the angels of God. Every one who speaks a word against the Son of man will be forgiven; but he who blasphemes against the Holy Spirit will not be forgiven. And when they bring you before synagogues and the authorities, do not be anxious how you are to answer, for the Holy Spirit will teach you in that very hour what you ought to say."

One of the multitude said, "Teacher, bid my brother divide the inheritance with me." But he replied, "Who made me a judge over you?" And he said to them, "Take heed, and beware of all covetousness; for a man's life does not consist in the abundance of his possessions." Then he told them a parable: "The land of a rich man brought forth plentifully; and he thought, 'What shall I do, for I have nowhere to store my crops? I will pull down my barns, and build larger ones, and I will say to my soul, you have ample goods laid up for many years; take your ease, eat, drink, be merry.' But God said to him, 'Fool! This night your soul is required of you; and the things you have prepared, whose will they be?' So is he who lays up treasure for himself, and is not rich toward God."

Then to his disciples he said, "Do not be anxious about your life, what you shall eat, nor about your body, what you shall put on. For life is more than food, and the body more than clothing. Consider the ravens; they neither sow nor reap, they have neither storehouse nor barn, and yet God feeds them. Of how much more value are you than the birds! And which of you by being anxious can add a cubit to his span of life? If then you are not able to do as small a thing as that, why are you anxious about the rest?

"Consider the lilies, how they grow; they neither toil nor spin; yet I tell you, even Solomon in all his glory was not arrayed like one of these. But if God so clothes the grass which is alive in the field today and tomorrow is thrown into the oven, how much more will he clothe you, O men of little faith! And do not seek what you are to eat and what you are to drink, nor be of anxious mind. For all the nations of the world seek these things; and your Father knows that you need them. Instead, seek his kingdom, and these things shall be yours as well.

"Fear not, little flock, for it is your Father's good pleasure to give you the kingdom. Sell your possessions, and give alms; provide yourselves with purses that do not grow old, with a treasure in the heavens that does not fail, where no thief approaches and no moth destroys. For where your treasure is, there will your heart be also. Let your lamps be burning, and be like men who are waiting for their master to come home from the feast, so that they may open to him at once. Blessed are those servants whom the master finds awake when he comes. You also must be ready; for the Son of man is coming at an unexpected hour."

"Lord," Peter asked, "are you telling this for us or for all?"

"Who then is the faithful and wise steward," said the Lord, "whom his master will set over his household, to give them food at the proper time? Blessed is that servant whom his master when he comes will find so doing. Truly, I say to you, he will set him over all his possessions. But if that servant says to himself, 'My master is delayed in coming,' and begins to beat the servants, and to eat and get drunk, the master will come when he does not expect him, and will punish him, and put him with the unfaithful. Every one to whom much is given, of him will much be required; and of him to whom men commit much they will demand the more.

"I came to cast fire upon the earth; and would that it were already kindled! I have a baptism to be baptized with; and how I am constrained until it is accomplished! Do you think that I have come to give peace on earth? No, I tell you, but rather division; for henceforth in one house there will be five divided, three against two and two against three."

He also said to the multitudes, "When you see a cloud rising in the west, you say at once, 'A shower is coming'; and so it happens. And when you see the south wind blowing, you say, 'There will be scorching heat'; and it happens. You hypocrites! You know how to interpret the appearance of earth and sky; but why do you not know how to interpret the present time?"

There were some present who told him of the Galileans whose blood Pilate had mingled with their sacrifices. "Do you think," he answered, "that these Galileans were worse sinners than all the other Galileans, because they suffered thus? I tell you, No; but unless you repent you will all likewise perish." And he told this parable: "A man had a fig tree planted in his vineyard; and he came seeking fruit on it and found none. And he said to the vinedresser,

'Lo, these three years I have come seeking fruit on this fig tree, and I find none. Cut it down; why should it use up the ground?' And the vinedresser answered, 'Let it alone, sir, this year also, till I dig about it and put on manure. And if it bears fruit next year, well and good; but if not, you can cut it down.' "

Now he was teaching in one of the synagogues on the sabbath. And there was a woman who had had a spirit of infirmity for eighteen years; she was bent over and could not fully straighten herself. When Jesus saw her, he laid his hands upon her and said, "Woman, you are freed from your infirmity." Immediately she was made straight, and she praised God. But the ruler of the synagogue, indignant because Jesus had healed on the sabbath, said to the people, "There are six days on which work ought to be done; come on those days and be healed, and not on the sabbath day."

"You hypocrites!" the Lord answered. "Does not each of you on the sabbath untie his ox or his ass from the manger, and lead it away to water it? And ought not this woman be loosed from this bond on the sabbath day?" At this, all his adversaries were put to shame, and all the people rejoiced.

As he went through towns and villages, teaching, and journeying toward Jerusalem, some one asked, "Lord, will those who are saved be few?"

"Strive to enter by the narrow door," he replied, "for many will seek to enter and will not be able. When once the householder has shut the door, you will stand outside and knock, saying, 'Lord, open to us.' He will answer you, 'I do not know where you come from.' Then you will say, 'We ate and drank in your presence, and you taught in our streets.' But he will say, 'I tell you, I do not know where you come from; depart from me, all you workers of iniquity!' There you will weep and gnash your teeth, when you see Abraham and Isaac and Jacob and all the prophets in the kingdom of God and you yourselves thrust out. And men will come from east and west, and from north and south, and sit at table in the kingdom of God. And behold, some are last who will be first, and some are first who will be last."

At that very hour some Pharisees came, and said to him, "Get away from here, for Herod wants to kill you."

"Go and tell that fox," he said, " 'Behold, I cast out demons and perform cures today and tomorrow, and the third day I finish my course. Nevertheless, I must go on my way, for it cannot be that a prophet should perish away from Jerusalem.' O Jerusalem, Jerusalem, killing the prophets and stoning those who are sent to you! How often would I have gathered your children together as a hen gathers her brood under her wings, and you would not! Behold, your house is forsaken. And I tell you, you will not see me until you say, 'Blessed is he who comes in the name of the Lord!' "

One sabbath when he went to dine at the house of a Pharisee, they were watching him, and there was a man there who had dropsy. "Is it lawful," Jesus asked, "to heal on the sabbath, or not?" But they were silent. Then he took the man and healed him, and he said, "Which of you, having a son or an ox that has fallen into a well, will not immediately pull him out on a sabbath day?" And they could not reply to this.

Now when he marked how those invited chose the places of honor, he told a parable: "When you are invited to a feast, do not sit down in a place of honor, lest a more eminent man than you be invited, and he who invited you will come and say, 'Give place to this man,' and then you will begin with shame to take the lowest place. But when you are invited, sit in the lowest place, so that your host may say, 'Friend, go up higher'; then you will be honored in the presence of all who sit at table. For every one who exalts himself will be humbled, and he who humbles himself will be exalted." He said also to the Pharisee who had invited him, "When you give a banquet, do not invite your friends or brothers or kinsmen or rich neighbors, lest they invite you in return, and you be repaid. But invite the poor, the maimed, the lame, the blind, and you will be blessed, because they cannot repay you. You will be repaid at the resurrection of the just."

When one of those at table heard this,

he said, "Blessed is he who shall eat bread
in the kingdom of God!"

"A man once gave a great banquet,"
Jesus said to him, "and invited many. He
sent his servant to say to those invited,
'Come; for all is now ready.' But they all
began to make excuses. The first said, 'I
have bought a field, and I must go and see
it; I pray you, have me excused.' Another
said, 'I have bought five yoke of oxen, and
I go to examine them; I pray you, have me
excused.' Another said, 'I have married a
wife, and therefore I cannot come.' When
the servant reported this, the householder
in anger said, 'Go out quickly to the streets
and lanes of the city, and bring in the poor
and maimed and blind and lame.' And the
servant said, 'Sir, what you commanded
has been done, and still there is room.'
And the master said, 'Go out to the high-
ways and hedges, and compel people to
come in, that my house may be filled. For I
tell you, none of those who were invited
shall taste my banquet.' "

Now great multitudes accompanied Jesus; and he turned and said, "If any one
comes to me and does not hate his own

father and mother and wife and children and brothers and sisters, yes, and even his own life, he cannot be my disciple. Whoever does not bear his own cross and come after me, cannot be my disciple. For which of you, desiring to build a tower, does not first sit down and count the cost? Otherwise, when he has laid a foundation, and is not able to finish, all who see it begin to mock him, saying, 'This man began to build, and was not able to finish.' So therefore, whoever of you does not renounce all that he has cannot be my disciple."

Now the tax collectors and sinners were all drawing near to hear him. And the Pharisees and the scribes murmured, "This man receives sinners and eats with them." So he told them this parable: "What man of you, having a hundred sheep, if he has lost one of them, does not leave the ninety-nine in the wilderness, and go after the one which is lost, until he finds it? And when he has found it, he lays it on his shoulders, rejoicing, and he calls together his friends, saying, 'Rejoice with me, for I have found my sheep which was lost.' Just so, I tell you, there will be more joy in heaven over one sinner who repents than over ninety-nine righteous persons who need no repentance."

And he said, "There was a man who had two sons; and the younger said, 'Father, give me the share of property that falls to me.' And he divided his living between them. Not many days later, the younger son gathered all he had and took his journey into a far country, and there he squandered his property in loose living. And when he had spent everything, a great famine arose, and he began to be in want. So he joined himself to one of the citizens of that country, who sent him into his fields to feed swine. And he would gladly have fed on the pods that the swine ate; and no one gave him anything. But when he came to himself he said, 'How many of my father's hired servants have bread enough and to spare, but I perish here with hunger! I will arise and go to my father, and I will say to him, "Father, I have sinned against heaven and before you; I am no longer worthy to be called your son; treat me as one of your hired servants." ' And he arose and came to his father. But while he was yet at a distance, his father saw him and had compassion, and ran and embraced him and kissed him. And the son said to him, 'Father, I have sinned against heaven and before you; I am no longer worthy to be called your son.' But the father said to his servants, 'Bring quickly the best robe, and put it on him; and put a ring on his hand, and shoes on his feet; and bring the fatted calf and kill it, and let us eat and make merry; for this my son was dead, and is alive again; he was lost, and is found.' And they began to make merry.

"Now his elder son was in the field; and as he came near to the house, he heard music and dancing. And he called a servant and asked what this meant. And he said, 'Your brother has come, and your father has killed the fatted calf, because he has received him safe and sound.' But he was angry and refused to go in. His father came out and entreated him, but he answered, 'Lo, these many years I have served you, and I never disobeyed your command; yet you never gave me a kid, that I might make merry with my friends. But when this son of yours came, who has devoured your living with harlots, you killed for him the fatted calf!' And he said to him, 'Son, you are always with me, and all that is mine is yours. It was fitting to make merry, for this your brother was dead, and is alive; he was lost, and is found.' "

Jesus also said to the disciples, "There was a rich man who had a steward, and charges were brought to him that this man was wasting his goods. And he called him and said, 'Turn in the account of your stewardship, for you can no longer be steward.' And the steward said to himself, 'What shall I do? I am not strong enough to dig, and I am ashamed to beg. I have decided what to do, so that people may receive me into their houses.' Summoning his master's debtors one by one, he said to the first, 'How much do you owe my master?' He said, 'A hundred measures of oil.' And he said, 'Take your bill, and sit down quickly and write fifty.' Then he said to another, 'And how much do you owe?' He said, 'A hundred measures of wheat.' He said, 'Take your bill, and write eighty.' The master commended the dishonest steward for his shrewdness; for the sons of this world are more shrewd in dealing with their own generation than the sons of light. And I tell you, make friends for yourselves by means of unrighteous mammon, so that when it fails they may receive you into the eternal habitations.

"He who is faithful in very little is faithful in much; he who is dishonest in very little is dishonest in much. If then you have not been faithful in the unrighteous mammon, who will entrust to you the true riches? And if you have not been faithful in that which is another's, who will give you that which is your own? No servant can serve two masters; for either he will hate the one and love the other, or he will be devoted to the one and despise the other. You cannot serve God and mammon."

And he said, "There was a rich man who feasted sumptuously every day. And at his gate lay a poor man named Lazarus, full of sores, who desired to be fed with what fell from the rich man's table; moreover, the dogs came and licked his sores. The poor man died and was carried by the angels to Abraham's bosom. The rich man also died and was buried; and in Hades, being in torment, he lifted up his eyes, and saw Abraham far off and Lazarus in his bosom. And he called out, 'Father Abraham, have mercy upon me, and send Lazarus to dip the end of his finger in water and cool my tongue; for I am in anguish in this flame.' But Abraham said, 'Son, remember that you in your lifetime received your good things, and Lazarus in like manner evil things; but now he is comforted here, and you are in anguish. And besides all this, between us and you a great chasm has been fixed, in order that those who would pass from here to you may not be able, and none may cross from there to us.' And the rich man said, 'Then I beg you, father, to send him to my father's house, for I have five brothers, so that he may warn them, lest they also come into this place of torment.' But Abraham said, 'They have Moses and the prophets; let them hear them.' And he said, 'No, father Abraham; but if some one goes to them from the dead, they will repent.' Abraham said to him, 'If they do not hear Moses and the prophets, neither will they be convinced if some one should rise from the dead.' "

And Jesus said to his disciples, "Temptations to sin are sure to come; but woe to him by whom they come! It would be better for him if a millstone were hung round his neck and he were cast into the sea, than that he should cause one of these little ones to sin. Take heed to yourselves; if your brother sins, rebuke him, and if he repents, forgive him; and if he sins against you seven times in the day, and turns to you seven times, and says, 'I repent,' you must forgive him."

On the way to Jerusalem he entered a village, where he was met by ten lepers who stood at a distance and lifted up their voices and said, "Jesus, Master, have mercy on us."

"Go and show yourselves to the priests," he said.

As they went they were cleansed, and one of them, a Samaritan, turned back, praising God with a loud voice; and he fell on his face at Jesus' feet, giving him thanks. "Were not ten cleansed?" Jesus asked. "Where are the nine? Was no one found to return and give praise to God except this foreigner? Rise and go your way; your faith has made you well."

Being asked by the Pharisees when the kingdom of God was coming, Jesus answered them, "The kingdom of God is not coming with signs to be observed; nor will they say, 'Lo, here it is!' or 'There!' for behold, the kingdom of God is in the midst of you."

And to the disciples he said, "The days are coming when you will desire to see one of the days of the Son of man, and you will not see it. And they will say to you, 'Lo, there!' or 'Lo, here!' Do not go, do not follow them. For as the lightning flashes and lights up the sky from one side to the other, so will the Son of man be in his day. But first he must suffer many things and be rejected by this generation. As it was in the days of Noah, so will it be in the days of the Son of man. They ate, they drank, they married, they were given in marriage, until the day when Noah entered the ark, and the flood came and destroyed them all. Likewise as it was in the days of Lot—they ate, they drank, they bought, they sold,

they planted, they built, but on the day
when Lot went out from Sodom fire and
sulphur rained from heaven and destroyed
them all—so will it be on the day when the
Son of man is revealed. On that day, let
him who is on the housetop, with his
goods in the house, not come down to take
them away; and likewise let him who is in
the field not turn back. Remember Lot's
wife. Whoever seeks to gain his life will
lose it, but whoever loses his life will preserve it. I tell you, in that night there will
be two in one bed; one will be taken and
the other left. There will be two women
grinding together; one will be taken and
the other left." The disciples said to him,
"Where, Lord?" And he said, "Where the
body is, there the eagles will be gathered
together."

And he told them a parable, to the effect
that they ought always to pray and not lose
heart. "In a certain city," he said, "there
was a judge who neither feared God nor
regarded man; and there was a widow in
that city who kept coming to him and saying, 'Vindicate me against my adversary.'
For a while he refused; but afterward he

said to himself, 'Because this widow bothers me, I will vindicate her, or she will wear me out by her continual coming.' Hear what the unrighteous judge says. And will not God vindicate his elect, who cry to him day and night? I tell you, he will vindicate them speedily. Nevertheless, when the Son of man comes, will he find faith on earth?"

He also told this parable to some who trusted in themselves that they were righteous and despised others: "Two men went up into the temple to pray, one a Pharisee and the other a tax collector. The Pharisee prayed thus, 'God, I thank thee that I am not like other men, extortioners, unjust, adulterers, or even like this tax collector. I fast twice a week, I give tithes of all that I get.' But the tax collector, standing far off, would not even lift up his eyes to heaven, but beat his breast, saying, 'God, be merciful to me a sinner!' I tell you, this man went down to his house justified rather than the other; for every one who exalts himself will be humbled, but he who humbles himself will be exalted."

Now they were bringing even infants to him that he might touch them; and when the disciples saw it, they rebuked them. But Jesus called them to him, saying, "Let the children come to me, for to such belongs the kingdom of God. Truly, I say to you, whoever does not receive the kingdom of God like a child shall not enter it."

And a ruler asked him, "Good Teacher, what shall I do to inherit eternal life?"

"Why do you call me good?" Jesus said. "No one is good but God alone. You know the commandments: 'Do not commit adultery, Do not kill, Do not steal, Do not bear false witness, Honor your father and mother.' "

"All these I have observed from my youth," said the ruler.

"One thing you still lack," Jesus replied. "Sell all that you have and distribute to the poor, and you will have treasure in heaven; and come, follow me." But when the ruler heard this he became sad, for he was very rich. Jesus looking at him said, "How hard it is for those who have riches to enter the kingdom of God! For it is easier for a camel to go through the eye of a needle than for a rich man to enter the kingdom of God."

"Then who can be saved?" asked those who heard this saying.

"What is impossible with men," Jesus said, "is possible with God."

"Lo, we have left our homes," said Peter, "and followed you."

"Truly, I say to you," Jesus replied, "there is no man who has left house or wife or brothers or parents or children, for the sake of the kingdom of God, who will not receive manifold more in this time, and in the age to come eternal life."

Now taking the twelve, Jesus said to them, "Behold, we are going up to Jerusalem, and everything that is written of the Son of man by the prophets will be accomplished. For he will be delivered to the Gentiles, and will be mocked and shamefully treated and spit upon; they will scourge him and kill him, and on the third day he will rise." But this saying was hid from them, and they did not grasp what was said.

When he was passing through Jericho, a man named Zacchaeus, a chief tax collector, sought to see who Jesus was, but could not, on account of the crowd and because he was small of stature. So he ran ahead and climbed a sycamore tree. When Jesus came to the place, he looked up and said, "Zacchaeus, make haste and come down; for I must stay at your house today." He came down, and received him joyfully; and all murmured, "He has gone in to be the guest of a man who is a sinner." Then Zacchaeus stood and said, "Behold, Lord, the half of my goods I give to the poor, and if I have defrauded any one of anything, I restore it fourfold."

"Today salvation has come to this house," Jesus said, "since he also is a son of Abraham. For the Son of man came to seek and to save the lost."

Jesus then proceeded to tell a parable, because he was near Jerusalem, and because the people supposed that the kingdom of God was to appear immediately: "A nobleman went into a far country to receive a kingdom and then return. Calling ten of his servants, he gave them ten pounds, and said, 'Trade with these till I come.' But his citizens hated him and sent an embassy after him, saying, 'We do not want this man to reign over us.' When he returned, having received the kingdom, he called his servants, that he might know what they had gained. The first said, 'Lord, your pound has made ten pounds more.' And he said, 'Well done, good servant! Because you have been faithful in a very little, you shall have authority over ten cities.' And the second said, 'Lord, your pound has made five pounds.' And he said, 'And you are to be over five cities.' Then another came, saying, 'Lord, here is your pound, which I kept laid away in a napkin; for I was afraid of you, because you are a severe man; you take up what you did not lay down, and reap what you did not sow.' The nobleman said, 'I will condemn you out of your own mouth, you wicked servant! You knew that I was a severe man. Why then did you not put my money into the bank, and I should have collected it with interest?' And he said to those who stood by, 'Take the pound from him, and give it to him who has the ten pounds. I tell you, that to every one who has will more be given; but from him who has not, even what he has will be taken away. But as for these enemies of mine, who did not want me to reign over them, bring them here and slay them before me.' "

After this, Jesus went on ahead, going up to Jerusalem. Near Bethany, at the mount that is called Olivet, he told two of the disciples, "Go into the village opposite, where on entering you will find a colt tied, on which no one has ever yet sat; untie it and bring it here. If any one asks you, 'Why are you untying it?' you shall say this, 'The Lord has need of it.' " Those who were sent found it as he had told them, and as they were untying the colt, its owners said, "Why are you untying the colt?" They said, "The Lord has need of it." And they brought it to Jesus, and throwing their garments on the colt they set Jesus upon it. As he rode along, they spread garments on the road and the whole multitude of the disciples began to rejoice and praise God with a loud voice for all the mighty works that they had seen. "Blessed is the King," they said, "who comes in the name of the Lord!

Peace in heaven and glory in the highest!" Some of the Pharisees in the multitude said, "Teacher, rebuke your disciples." But he answered, "I tell you, if these were silent, the very stones would cry out."

When he drew near and saw the city he wept over it. "Would that even today you knew the things that make for peace!" he said. "But now they are hid from your eyes. For the days shall come upon you, when your enemies will cast up a bank about you and surround you, and hem you in on every side, and dash you to the ground, you and your children within you, and they will not leave one stone upon another, because you did not know the time of your visitation." In the city he entered the temple and began to drive out those who sold, saying to them, "It is written, 'My house shall be a house of prayer'; but you have made it a den of robbers."

While he was teaching daily in the temple, the chief priests and the scribes and the principal men of the people sought to destroy him. But they did not find anything they could do, for all the people hung upon his words. Then one day the chief priests and the scribes with the elders came up. "Tell us by what authority you do these things," they said, "or who it is that gave you this authority."

"I also will ask you a question," he answered. "Now tell me, was the baptism of John from heaven or from men?" They discussed it with one another, saying, "If we say, 'From heaven,' he will say, 'Why did you not believe him?' But if we say, 'From men,' all the people will stone us; for they are convinced that John was a prophet." So they answered that they did not know whence it was. And Jesus said to them, "Neither will I tell you by what authority I do these things."

And he told the people this parable: "A man planted a vineyard, and let it out to tenants, and went into another country. When the time came he sent a servant to the tenants, that they should give him some of the fruit, but the tenants beat him and sent him away empty-handed. He sent another servant, and him also they treated shamefully and sent away empty-handed. He sent yet a third, and this one they wounded and cast out. Then the owner of the vineyard said, 'I will send my beloved son; it may be they will respect him.' But when the tenants saw the son, they said to themselves, 'This is the heir; let us kill him, that the inheritance may be ours.' And they cast him out of the vineyard and killed him. What then will the owner of the vineyard do? He will come and destroy those tenants, and give the vineyard to others."

When the people heard this, they said, "God forbid!" But he looked at them and said, "What then is this that is written: 'The very stone which the builders rejected has become the head of the corner'? Every one who falls on that stone will be broken to pieces; but when it falls on any one it will crush him."

At that very hour the scribes and the chief priests tried to lay hands on him, for they perceived that he had told this parable against them; but they feared the people. So they watched him, and sent spies, who pretended to be sincere, that they might take hold of what he said, so as to deliver him up to the governor. They asked, "Teacher, we know that you speak and teach rightly, and show no partiality, but truly teach the way of God. Is it lawful for us to give tribute to Caesar, or not?" But he perceived their craftiness, and said, "Show me a coin. Whose likeness and inscription has it?" They said, "Caesar's." He said to them, "Then render to Caesar the things that are Caesar's, and to God the things that are God's." Marveling at his answer, they were silent.

There came to him some Sadducees, those who say that there is no resurrection. "Teacher," they said, "Moses wrote for us that if a man's brother dies, having a wife but no children, the man must take the wife and raise up children for his brother. Now there were seven brothers; the first took a wife, and died without children; and the second and the third took her, and likewise all seven left no children and died. Afterward the woman also died. In the resurrection, therefore, whose wife will the woman be? For the seven had her as wife."

"The sons of this age," Jesus answered, "marry and are given in marriage; but those who are accounted worthy to attain to that age and to the resurrection from the dead neither marry nor are given in marriage, for they are equal to angels and are sons of God, being sons of the resurrection. But that the dead are raised, even Moses showed, in the passage about the bush, where he calls the Lord the God of Abraham and the God of Isaac and the God of Jacob. Now he is not God of the dead, but of the living; for all live to him."

And in the hearing of all the people he said to his disciples, "Beware of the scribes, who like to go about in long robes, and love salutations in the market places and the best seats in the synagogues and the places of honor at feasts, who devour widows' houses and for a pretense make long prayers. They will receive the greater condemnation."

While some were speaking of the temple, how it was adorned with noble stones and offerings, Jesus said, "As for these things, the days will come when there shall not be left here one stone upon another." And they asked him, "Teacher, when will this be, and what will be the sign when this is about to take place?"

"Take heed that you are not led astray," he said, "for many will come in my name, saying, 'I am he!' and, 'The time is at hand!' Do not go after them. And when you hear of wars and tumults, do not be terrified; for this must first take place, but the end will not be at once. Nation will rise against nation, and kingdom against kingdom; there will be great earthquakes, and in various places famines and pestilences; and there will be terrors and great signs from heaven. But before all this they will persecute you, delivering you up to the synagogues and prisons, and you will be brought before kings and governors for my name's sake. This will be a time for you to bear testimony. Settle it therefore in your minds, not to meditate beforehand how to answer; for I will give you a mouth and wisdom, which none of your adversaries will be able to withstand. You will be delivered up even by parents and brothers and kinsmen and friends, and some of you they will put to death; you will be hated by all for my name's sake. But not a hair of your head will perish. By your endurance you will gain your lives.

"But when you see Jerusalem surrounded by armies, then know that its desolation has come near. Then let those who are in Judea flee to the mountains, and let those who are inside the city depart, and let not those who are out in the country enter it; for these are days of vengeance, to fulfil all that is written. Alas for those who are with child and for those who give suck in those days! For great distress shall be upon the earth and wrath upon this people; they will fall by the edge of the sword, and be led captive among all nations; and Jerusalem will be trodden down by the Gentiles, until the times of the Gentiles are fulfilled. And there will be signs in sun and moon and stars, and upon the earth distress of nations in perplexity at the roaring of the sea and the waves, men fainting with fear and with foreboding of what is coming on the world; for the powers of the heavens will be shaken. And then they will see the Son of man coming in a cloud with power and great glory. Now when these things begin to take place, look up, because your redemption is drawing near.

"Look at the fig tree, and all the trees;

as soon as they come out in leaf, you know that summer is near. So also, when you see these things taking place, you know that the kingdom of God is near. Truly, I say to you, this generation will not pass away till all has taken place. Heaven and earth will pass away, but my words will not pass away. But take heed to yourselves lest your hearts be weighed down with dissipation and drunkenness and cares of this life, and that day come upon you suddenly like a snare; for it will come upon all who dwell upon the face of the whole earth. But watch at all times, praying that you may have strength to escape all these things, and to stand before the Son of man."

Now the feast of Unleavened Bread drew near, which is called the Passover. And the chief priests and the scribes were seeking how to put him to death; for they feared the people. Then Satan entered into Judas called Iscariot, one of the twelve. He conferred with the chief priests and officers how he might betray Jesus, and they were glad, and engaged to give him money. So he sought an opportunity to betray him in the absence of the multitude.

The day of Unleavened Bread came, on which the passover lamb had to be sacrificed, and Jesus told Peter and John, "Go and prepare the passover for us, that we may eat it."

"Where will you have us prepare it?" they asked.

"When you have entered the city," he said, "a man carrying a jar of water will meet you; follow him into the house which he enters, and tell the householder, 'The Teacher says to you, Where is the guest room, where I am to eat the passover with my disciples?' And he will show you a large upper room furnished; there make ready." They went and found it as he had told them; and they prepared the passover.

Now when the hour came, he sat at table with the apostles. "I have earnestly desired," he said, "to eat this passover with you before I suffer; for I tell you I shall not eat it until it is fulfilled in the kingdom of God." Then he took a cup, and when he had given thanks he said, "Take this, and divide it among yourselves; for I tell you that from now on I shall not drink of the fruit of the vine until the kingdom of God comes." And he took bread, and when he had given thanks he broke it and gave it to them. "This is my body," he said, "which is given for you. Do this in remembrance of me." Likewise he took the cup after supper, saying, "This cup which is poured out for you is the new covenant in my blood. But behold, the hand of him who betrays me is with me on the table. For the Son of man goes as it has been determined; but woe to that man by whom he is betrayed!" And they began to question one another, which of them it was that would do this.

A dispute also arose among them, which of them was to be regarded as the greatest. And he said to them, "The kings of the Gentiles exercise lordship over them. But not so with you; rather let the greatest among you become as the youngest, and the leader as one who serves. Which is the greater, one who sits at table, or one who serves? Is it not the one who sits at table? But I am among you as one who serves. You have continued with me in my trials; and I assign to you, as my Father assigned to me, a kingdom, that you may eat and drink at my table in my kingdom, and sit on thrones judging the twelve tribes of Israel.

"Simon, Simon, behold, Satan demanded to have you, that he might sift you like wheat, but I have prayed for you that your faith may not fail; and when you have turned again, strengthen your brethren."

"Lord," said Peter, "I am ready to go with you to prison and to death."

"I tell you, Peter," Jesus said, "the cock will not crow this day, until you three times deny that you know me."

And he said to them, "When I sent you out with no purse or bag or sandals, did you lack anything?" They said, "Nothing." He said to them, "But now, let him who has a purse take it, and likewise a bag. And let him who has no sword sell his mantle and buy one. For I tell you that this scripture must be fulfilled in me, 'And he was reckoned with transgressors'; for what is written about me has its fulfilment." And they said, "Look, Lord, here are two swords." And he said to them, "It is enough."

After this, taking his disciples he went,

as was his custom, to the Mount of Olives. Withdrawing about a stone's throw, he knelt down and prayed, "Father, if thou art willing, remove this cup from me; nevertheless not my will, but thine, be done."

Then there appeared to him an angel from heaven, strengthening him. And being in an agony he prayed more earnestly; and his sweat became like great drops of blood falling down upon the ground. When he rose, he came to the disciples and found them sleeping for sorrow, and he said, "Why do you sleep? Rise and pray that you may not enter into temptation."

While he was still speaking, there came a crowd, with Judas leading them. He drew near to Jesus to kiss him, but Jesus said, "Judas, would you betray the Son of man with a kiss?" When those about him saw what would follow, one of them drew a sword and struck the slave of the high priest and cut off his right ear. But Jesus said, "No more of this!" He touched the slave's ear and healed him. To the chief priests and officers he said, "Have you come out as against a robber, with swords and clubs? When I was with you day after day in the temple, you did not lay hands on me. But this is your hour, and the power of darkness."

Then they seized him and led him away to the high priest's house. At a distance, Peter followed, and in the courtyard he sat down among the guards and servants at the fire. Then a maid, gazing at him, said, "This man also was with him."

"Woman, I do not know him," Peter said. A little later some one else saw him and said, "You also are one of them."

"Man, I am not," said Peter. After an interval of about an hour still another insisted, "Certainly this man also was with him; for he is a Galilean."

"Man," said Peter, "I do not know what you are saying." And immediately, while he was still speaking, the cock crowed. And the Lord turned and looked at Peter, and Peter remembered how he had said to him, "Before the cock crows today, you will deny me three times." And he went out and wept bitterly.

Now the men who were holding Jesus mocked him and beat him; they also blindfolded him and asked, "Prophesy! Who is it that struck you?" And they spoke many other words against him, reviling him.

When day came, the elders, the chief priests, and the scribes assembled in council. "If you are the Christ," they said to Jesus, "tell us."

"If I tell you," he replied, "you will not believe. But from now on the Son of man shall be seated at the right hand of the power of God."

"Are you the Son of God, then?" they all asked.

"You say that I am," he answered.

"What further testimony do we need?" they said. "We have heard it ourselves from his own lips."

Then the whole company of them arose, and brought him before Pilate, and they began to accuse him. "We found this man perverting our nation," they said, "and forbidding us to give tribute to Caesar, and saying that he himself is Christ a king."

"Are you the King of the Jews?" Pilate asked.

"You have said so," Jesus answered.

"I find no crime in this man," Pilate said to the chief priests and the multitudes. But they were urgent, saying, "He stirs up the people, teaching throughout all Judea, from Galilee even to this place."

When Pilate heard this, he asked whether Jesus was a Galilean, and when he learned that he was, he sent him to Herod, who was then in Jerusalem. Herod was glad to see Jesus, for he had long desired to meet him, and he was hoping to see some sign done by him. So he questioned him at length, but Jesus made no answer. The chief priests and the scribes stood by, vehemently accusing him. And Herod with his soldiers treated him with contempt and mocked him; then, arraying him in gorgeous apparel, he sent him back to Pilate.

Calling together the chief priests and the rulers and the people, Pilate said, "You brought me this man as one who was perverting the people; and after examining him before you, behold, I did not find this man guilty of any of your charges against him; neither did Herod, for he sent him back to us. Behold, nothing deserving death has been done by him; I will therefore chastise him and release him." Now he was obliged to release one man to them at the festival.

But they all cried out together, "Away with this man, and release to us Barabbas" (a man who had been arrested for insurrection and murder). Pilate addressed them once more, desiring to release Jesus; but they shouted, "Crucify, crucify him!"

"Why, what evil has he done?" Pilate asked. "I have found in him no crime deserving death; I will therefore chastise him and release him."

But they were urgent, demanding with loud cries that he should be crucified. And their voices prevailed. So Pilate gave sentence that their demand should be granted. He released Barabbas, whom they asked for, but Jesus he delivered up to their will.

As they led him away, they seized one Simon of Cyrene, who was coming in from the country, and laid the cross on him, to carry it behind Jesus. A great multitude followed, with many women who bewailed and lamented him. But Jesus, turning to them, said, "Daughters of Jerusalem, do not weep for me, but weep for yourselves and for your children. For behold, the days are coming when they will say, 'Blessed are the barren, and the wombs that never bore, and the breasts that never gave suck!' Then they will say to the mountains, 'Fall on us'; and to the hills, 'Cover us.' For if they do this when the wood is green, what will happen when it is dry?"

Two others, who were criminals, were led away to be put to death with him. When they came to the place called The Skull, there they crucified him, and the criminals, one on the right and one on the left. "Father, forgive them," Jesus said, "for they know not what they do." And they cast lots to divide his garments.

The people stood by, watching, but the rulers scoffed, "He saved others; let him save himself, if he is the Christ of God, his Chosen One!" The soldiers also mocked him, offering him vinegar, and saying, "If you are the King of the Jews, save yourself!" There was also an inscription over him, "This is the King of the Jews."

One of the criminals railed at him, saying, "Are you not the Christ? Save yourself and us!" But the other rebuked him, "Do you not fear God, since you are under the same sentence of condemnation? And we indeed justly; for we are receiving the due reward of our deeds; but this man has done nothing wrong." And he said, "Jesus, remember me when you come into your kingdom."

Jesus replied, "Truly, I say to you, today you will be with me in Paradise."

It was now about the sixth hour, and the sun's light failed, and there was darkness over the whole land until the ninth hour; and the curtain of the temple was torn in two. Then Jesus cried with a loud voice, "Father, into thy hands I commit my spirit!" And he breathed his last. Now when the centurion saw what had taken place, he praised God, and said, "Certainly this man was innocent!" And the multitudes, when they saw what had taken place, returned home beating their breasts. And all his acquaintances and the women who had followed him from Galilee stood at a distance and saw these things.

Now it was the day of Preparation, and the sabbath was beginning. A man named Joseph, of Arimathea, a member of the council, a righteous man who had not consented to their deed, went to Pilate and asked for the body of Jesus. Then he took it down and wrapped it in a linen shroud, and laid it in a rock-hewn tomb, where no one had yet been laid. The women followed, and saw the tomb, and how his body was laid; then they returned home, and prepared spices and ointments.

On the sabbath the women rested according to the commandment. But on the first day of the week, at early dawn, they went to the tomb, taking the spices. They found the stone rolled away from the tomb, but when they went in they did not find the body. While they were perplexed about this, behold, two men stood by them in dazzling apparel, and the women, frightened, bowed their faces to the ground.

"Why do you seek the living among the dead?" the men asked. "He is not here, but has risen. Remember how he told you, while he was still in Galilee, that the Son of man must be delivered into the hands of sinful men, and be crucified, and on the third day rise." The women remembered, and returning from the tomb they told all this to the eleven and the rest. Now it was

Mary Magdalene and Joanna and Mary the mother of James and the other women with them who told this to the apostles; but these words seemed an idle tale, and they did not believe them. But Peter ran to the tomb and, stooping and looking in, he saw the linen cloths by themselves; and he went home wondering at what had happened.

That very day two of the disciples were going to a village named Emmaus, and while they walked, Jesus himself drew near and went with them. But their eyes were kept from recognizing him. "What is this conversation," Jesus asked, "which you are holding with each other?" They stood still, looking sad. Then one, Cleopas, answered, "Are you the only visitor to Jerusalem who does not know the things that have happened there?"

"What things?" Jesus asked.

"Concerning Jesus of Nazareth," they answered, "who was a prophet mighty in deed and word, and how our chief priests delivered him up to be crucified. Moreover, some of our women were at the tomb early in the morning and did not find his body. They came back saying they had seen angels, who said that he was alive. Some of us went to the tomb, and found it just as the women had said."

"O foolish men," said Jesus, "and slow of heart to believe all that the prophets have spoken! Was it not necessary that the Christ should suffer these things and enter into his glory?" And beginning with Moses and all the prophets, he interpreted in the scriptures the things concerning himself.

As they drew near to Emmaus, Jesus appeared to be going further, but they said, "Stay with us, for the day is now far spent." So he stayed, and when he was at table he took the bread and blessed, and broke it, and gave it to them. And their eyes were opened and they recognized him; and he vanished out of their sight. "Did not our hearts burn within us," they said, "while he talked to us on the road?" That same hour they returned to Jerusalem, and they found the eleven and the others gathered together, who said, "The Lord has risen indeed, and has appeared to Simon!" Then the two told what had happened on the road, and how he was known to them in the breaking of the bread.

As they were saying this, Jesus himself stood among them and said, "Peace to you!" Startled and frightened, they supposed that they saw a spirit. "Why are you troubled," Jesus asked, "and why do questionings rise in your hearts? See my hands and my feet, that it is I myself; handle me, and see; for a spirit has not flesh and bones as you see that I have." Still they disbelieved for joy, and wondered. "Have you anything here to eat?" he asked. They gave him a piece of broiled fish, and he ate before them.

Then he said to them, "These are my words which I spoke to you, while I was still with you, that everything written about me in the law of Moses and the prophets and the psalms must be fulfilled." He opened their minds to understand the scriptures, and he said, "Thus it is written, that the Christ should suffer and on the third day rise from the dead, and that repentance and forgiveness of sins should be preached in his name to all nations, beginning from Jerusalem. You are witnesses of these things. And behold, I send the promise of my Father upon you; but stay in the city, until you are clothed with power from on high."

Then he led them out as far as Bethany, and lifting up his hands he blessed them. While he blessed them, he parted from them, and was carried up into heaven. And they returned to Jerusalem with great joy, and were continually in the temple blessing God.

THE GOSPEL
ACCORDING TO
JOHN

A strong and early tradition assigns the authorship of the fourth Gospel, produced near the close of the first century, to the aged apostle John. Whether the book was written directly by John, or indirectly (his teachings may have been edited by another), the church has accepted it as an authoritative supplement to the story of Jesus' ministry given by the other evangelists. Often called a "spiritual" Gospel, John's narrative attempts to go behind and beyond the physical events of Jesus' ministry in an effort to explain his divine origin. This purpose may be readily seen in the magnificent prologue, where John briefly treats the significance of the Incarnation.

In his narrative John recounts just seven of Jesus' miracles, which he calls "signs," each of them intended to convey a definite meaning. He also provides a number of long and pithy discourses of Jesus, dealing with such topics as the need to be born again, and the spiritual life of the believer. In these discourses Jesus' teachings are often set forth in symbols, all drawn from common experience (bread, water, light, darkness, shepherd, door), which help to make the meaning vivid and memorable.

IN THE BEGINNING was the Word, and the Word was with God, and the Word was God. He was in the beginning with God; all things were made through him, and without him was not anything made that was made. In him was life, and the life was the light of men. The light shines in the darkness, and the darkness has not overcome it.

There was a man sent from God, whose name was John. He came for testimony, to bear witness to the light, that all might believe through him. He was not the light, but came to bear witness to the light.

The true light that enlightens every man was coming into the world. He was in the world, and the world was made through him, yet the world knew him not. He came to his own home, and his own people received him not. But to all who received him, who believed in his name, he gave power to become children of God; who were born, not of blood nor of the will of the flesh nor of the will of man, but of God.

And the Word became flesh and dwelt among us, full of grace and truth; we have beheld his glory, glory as of the only Son from the Father. And from his fulness have we all received, grace upon grace. For the law was given through Moses; grace and truth came through Jesus Christ. No one has ever seen God; the only Son, who is in the bosom of the Father, he has made him known.

THIS IS THE testimony of John, when the Pharisees in Jerusalem sent priests and Levites to Bethany beyond the Jordan, where John was baptizing, to ask him, "Who are you?"

"I am not the Christ," he confessed.

"What then?" they asked. "Are you Elijah or the prophet?"

"I am not," he answered.

"Then who are you?" they said. "Let us have an answer for those who sent us. What do you say about yourself?"

"I am the voice," he said, "of one crying in the wilderness, 'Make straight the way of the Lord,' as the prophet Isaiah said."

"Then why are you baptizing," they asked, "if you are neither the Christ, nor Elijah, nor the prophet?"

"I baptize with water," John answered, "but among you stands one whom you do not know, even he who comes after me, the thong of whose sandal I am not worthy to untie."

The next day John saw Jesus coming toward him. "Behold, the Lamb of God," he said, "who takes away the sin of the world! This is he of whom I said, 'After me comes a man who ranks before me, for he was before me.' I myself did not know him; but for this I came baptizing with water, that he might be revealed to Israel. I saw the Spirit descend as a dove from heaven, and it remained on him. Now he who sent me to baptize with water said, 'He on whom you see the Spirit descend and remain, this is he who baptizes with the Holy Spirit.' And I have seen and have borne witness that this is the Son of God."

The next day again John was with two of his disciples, and he looked at Jesus as he walked, and said, "Behold, the Lamb of God!" The disciples heard him, and they followed Jesus. Jesus turned and saw them. "What do you seek?" he asked. "Rabbi, where are you staying?" they said. "Come and see," he said. They came and they stayed with him that day, for it was about the tenth hour. One of the two was Andrew, Simon Peter's brother. He went to his brother and said, "We have found the Messiah," and he brought him to Jesus, who looked at him, and said, "So you are Simon the son of John? You shall be called Cephas" (which means Peter).

The next day Jesus decided to go to Galilee. He found Philip, and said, "Follow me." Now Philip was from Bethsaida, the city of Andrew and Peter. Philip found Nathanael, and said, "We have found him of whom Moses in the law and also the prophets wrote, Jesus of Nazareth, the son of Joseph."

"Can anything good come out of Nazareth?" Nathanael asked. Philip said, "Come and see."

Jesus saw Nathanael coming. "Behold," he said, "an Israelite indeed, in whom is no guile!"

"How do you know me?" Nathanael asked.

"Before Philip called you," Jesus answered, "when you were under the fig tree, I saw you."

"Rabbi, you are the Son of God!" Nathanael answered. "You are the King of Israel!"

"Because," said Jesus, "I said to you, I saw you under the fig tree, do you believe? You shall see greater things than these. Truly, I say to you, you will see heaven opened, and the angels of God ascending and descending upon the Son of man."

On the third day there was a marriage at Cana in Galilee, and the mother of Jesus was there; Jesus also was invited, with his disciples. When the wine gave out, the mother of Jesus said, "They have no wine."

"O woman," he said, "what have you to do with me? My hour has not yet come."

His mother said to the servants, "Do whatever he tells you." Now six stone jars were standing there, for the Jewish rites of purification, each holding twenty or thirty gallons. "Fill the jars with water," Jesus said. They filled them to the brim, and he said, "Draw some out, and take it to the steward." When the steward tasted the water now become wine, and did not know where it came from (though the servants knew), the steward called the bridegroom. "Every man serves the good wine first," he said, "and when men have drunk freely, then the poor wine; but you have kept the good wine until now." This first of his signs Jesus did at Cana, and manifested his glory; and his disciples believed in him.

The Passover of the Jews was at hand, and Jesus went up to Jerusalem. In the temple he found those who were selling oxen and sheep and pigeons, and the money-changers at their business. Making a whip of cords, he drove them all, with the sheep and oxen, out of the temple, and he poured out the coins of the money-changers and overturned their tables. He told those who sold pigeons, "Take these things away; you shall not make my Father's house a house of trade." His disciples remembered that it was written, "Zeal for thy house will consume me." The Jews then said, "What sign have you to show us for doing this?"

"Destroy this temple," he said, "and in three days I will raise it up."

"It has taken forty-six years to build this temple," the Jews said, "and will you raise it up in three days?" But he spoke of the temple of his body. When therefore he was raised from the dead, his disciples remembered he had said this; and they believed the scripture and the word which Jesus had spoken.

While he was in Jerusalem, many believed in his name when they saw the signs which he did; but Jesus did not trust himself to them, because he himself knew what was in man. Now there was a Pharisee named Nicodemus, who came to Jesus by night. "Rabbi," he said, "we know that you are a teacher from God; for no one can do these signs, unless God is with him."

"Truly, truly, I say to you," Jesus answered, "unless one is born anew, he cannot see the kingdom of God."

"How can a man be born when he is old?" Nicodemus asked. "Can he enter a second time into his mother's womb and be born?"

"Truly, truly, I say to you," said Jesus, "unless one is born of water and the Spirit, he cannot enter the kingdom of God. That which is born of the flesh is flesh, and that which is born of the Spirit is spirit. Do not marvel that I said to you, 'You must be born anew.' The wind blows where it wills, and you hear the sound of it, but you do not know whence it comes or whither it goes; so it is with every one who is born of the Spirit."

"How can this be?" Nicodemus asked.

"Are you a teacher of Israel," Jesus replied, "and yet you do not understand this? Truly, I say to you, we speak of what we know, and bear witness to what we have seen; but you do not receive our testimony. If I have told you earthly things and you do not believe, how can you believe if I tell you heavenly things? No one has ascended into heaven but he who descended from heaven, the Son of man. And as Moses lifted up the serpent in the wilderness, so must the Son of man be lifted up, that whoever believes in him may have eternal life."

For God so loved the world that he gave his only Son, that whoever believes in him should not perish but have eternal life. God sent the Son into the world, not to condemn, but that the world might be saved through him. He who believes in him is not condemned; he who does not believe is condemned already. The light has come into the world, and men loved darkness rather than light, for every one who does evil hates the light, lest his deeds should be exposed. But he who does what is true comes to the light, that it may be clearly seen that his deeds have been wrought in God.

After this, Jesus and his disciples went into the land of Judea; there he remained with them and baptized (though Jesus himself did not baptize, but only his disciples). John also was baptizing at Aenon near Salim, because there was much water there; for John had not yet been put in prison.

Now a discussion arose between John's disciples and a Jew over purifying. They came to John, and said, "Rabbi, he who was with you beyond the Jordan, to whom you bore witness, here he is, baptizing, and all are going to him."

"No one can receive anything," John answered, "except what is given him from heaven. You yourselves bear me witness, that I said, I am not the Christ, but I have been sent before him. He who has the bride is the bridegroom; the friend of the bridegroom, who stands and hears him, rejoices greatly at the bridegroom's voice; therefore this joy of mine is now full. He must increase, but I must decrease."

He who is of the earth belongs to the earth, and of the earth he speaks; he who comes from heaven is above all. He bears witness to what he has seen and heard, yet no one receives his testimony; he who receives his testimony sets his seal to this, that God is true. He whom God has sent utters the words of God, for it is not by measure that he gives the Spirit; the Father loves the Son, and has given all things into his hand. He who believes in the Son has eternal life; he who does not obey the Son shall not see life, but the wrath of God rests upon him.

Now when Jesus knew that the Pharisees had heard that he was making more disciples than John, he left Judea for Galilee. Passing through Samaria, he came to a town called Sychar, near the field that Jacob gave to his son Joseph. Jacob's well was there, and Jesus, wearied with his journey, sat down beside it while his disciples went into the town to buy food. It was about noon.

There came a woman from the town to draw water, and Jesus asked her for a drink. "How is it," the woman asked, "that you, a Jew, ask a drink of me, a woman of Samaria?" (Jews have no dealings with Samaritans.)

"If you knew the gift of God," Jesus answered, "and who it is that asks for a drink, you would ask him, and he would give you living water."

"Sir, you have nothing to draw with," said the woman, "and the well is deep; where do you get that living water? Are you greater than our father Jacob, who gave us the well?"

"Every one who drinks of this water will thirst again," replied Jesus, "but whoever drinks of the water that I shall give him will never thirst. It will become in him a spring of water welling up to eternal life."

"Sir, give me this water," said the woman, "that I may not thirst, nor come here to draw."

"Go, call your husband," said Jesus, "and come here."

"I have no husband," answered the woman.

"You are right, for you have had five husbands," Jesus said, "and he whom you now have is not your husband."

"Sir, I perceive that you are a prophet," said the woman. "Our fathers worshiped on this mountain, but you say that in Jerusalem is the place where men ought to worship."

"Woman, believe me," said Jesus, "the hour is coming when neither on this mountain nor in Jerusalem will you worship the Father. You worship what you do not know; we worship what we know, for salvation is from the Jews. But the hour is coming, and now is, when the true worshipers will worship the Father in spirit and truth, for such the Father seeks to worship him. God is spirit, and those who worship him must worship in spirit and truth."

"I know that the Messiah is coming," said the woman. "When he comes, he will show us all things."

Then Jesus said, "I who speak to you am he."

Just then his disciples came. They marveled that he was talking with a woman, but they said nothing. The woman, forgetting her water jar, hurried into the town and said to the people, "Come, see a man who told me all that I ever did. Can this be the Christ?" Many believed the woman's testimony and went out to meet him.

Meanwhile the disciples besought him, saying, "Rabbi, eat." But he said, "I have food to eat of which you do not know." So the disciples said to one another, "Has any one brought him food?"

"My food is to do the will of him who sent me," said Jesus, "and to accomplish his work. Do you not say, 'There are yet four months, then comes the harvest'? Lift up your eyes, and see how the fields are already white for harvest. He who reaps receives wages, and gathers fruit for eternal life, so that sower and reaper may rejoice together. For here the saying holds true, 'One sows and another reaps.' I sent you to reap that for which you did not labor; others have labored, and you have entered into their labor."

When the people from the town came to him, they asked him to stay with them; and he stayed there two days. And many more believed because of his word. They said to the woman, "It is no longer because of your words that we believe, for we have heard for ourselves, and we know that this is indeed the Savior of the world."

After the two days he departed to Galilee, and he came again to Cana. Now at

Capernaum there was an official whose son was at the point of death. When he heard that Jesus was nearby, he went and begged him to come down and heal his son. "Unless you see signs and wonders," Jesus said, "you will not believe."

"Sir," the official said, "come down before my child dies."

"Go," said Jesus, "your son will live."

The man believed, and as he was going down, his servants met him and told him that his son was living. He asked the hour when he began to mend. "Yesterday at the seventh hour," they said. The father knew that was the hour when Jesus had said, "Your son will live." This was now the second sign that Jesus did when he had come from Judea to Galilee.

After this there was a feast of the Jews, and Jesus went up to Jerusalem. Now there is in Jerusalem a pool (in Hebrew called Bethzatha), which has five porticoes. In these lay a multitude of invalids, blind, lame, paralyzed. One man there had been ill for thirty-eight years, and when Jesus saw him and knew he had been there a long time, he said, "Do you want to be healed?"

"Sir," he answered, "I have no man to put me into the pool when the water is troubled; while I am going another steps down before me."

"Rise," said Jesus, "take up your pallet, and walk." At once the man was healed, and he took up his pallet and walked.

Now that day was the sabbath. So the Jews said to the man, "It is the sabbath, it is not lawful for you to carry your pallet." But he answered, "The man who healed me told me to do so." They asked, "Who is the man?" Now he did not know who it was, for Jesus had withdrawn. Afterward Jesus found him in the temple, and said, "See, you are well! Sin no more, that nothing worse befall you." The man went and told the Jews that it was Jesus; and this was why the Jews persecuted him, because he did this on the sabbath. But Jesus answered them, "My Father is working still, and I am working." Then the Jews sought all the more to kill him, because he not only broke the sabbath but also called God his own Father, making himself equal with God.

Jesus said to the Jews, "The Son can do

nothing of his own accord, but only what he sees the Father doing; for whatever he does, the Son does likewise. For the Father loves the Son, and shows him all that he is doing; and greater works than these will he show, that you may marvel. As the Father raises the dead, so also the Son gives life to whom he will. The Father judges no one, but has given all judgment to the Son, that all may honor the Son, even as they honor the Father. He who does not honor the Son does not honor the Father who sent him. He who hears my word and believes him who sent me, has eternal life; he does not come into judgment, but has passed from death to life. Truly, truly, I say to you, the hour is coming, and now is, when the dead will hear the voice of the Son of God, and those who hear will live. Do not marvel at this; for the hour is coming when all who are in the tombs will hear his voice and come forth, those who have done good, to the resurrection of life, and those who have done evil, to the resurrection of judgment.

"I can do nothing on my own authority; as I hear, I judge; and my judgment is just, because I seek not my own will but the will of him who sent me. If I bear witness to myself, my testimony is not true; there is another who bears witness to me, and I know that the testimony which he bears to me is true. You sent to John, and he has borne witness to the truth. Not that the testimony which I receive is from man; but I say this that you may be saved. He was a shining lamp, and you were willing to rejoice in his light. But my testimony is greater than that of John; for the works which the Father has granted me to accomplish, these very works I am doing, bear witness that the Father has sent me. And the Father has himself borne witness to me. His voice you have never heard, his form you have never seen; and you do not have his word abiding in you, for you do not believe him whom he has sent.

"You search the scriptures, because you think that in them you have eternal life; and it is they that bear witness to me; yet you refuse to come to me. I do not receive glory from men. But I know that you have not the love of God within you. I have come in my Father's name, and you do not receive me; if another comes in his own name, him you will receive. How can you believe, who receive glory from one another and do not seek the glory that comes from the only God? Do not think that I shall accuse you to the Father; it is Moses who accuses you, on whom you set your hope. If you believed Moses, you would believe me, for he wrote of me. But if you do not believe his writings, how will you believe my words?"

After this, Jesus went to the other side of the Sea of Galilee, and a multitude followed him. He went up on the mountain with his disciples, and saw the multitude. "How are we to buy bread," he said to Philip, "that these people may eat?" This he said to test him, for he himself knew what he would do.

"Two hundred denarii," said Philip, "would not buy enough bread for each of them to get a little." Andrew, Simon Peter's brother, said, "There is a lad here who has five barley loaves and two fish; but what are they among so many?"

"Make the people sit down," said Jesus. Now there was much grass in the place;

so the men sat down, in number about five thousand. Jesus then took the loaves, and when he had given thanks, he distributed them; so also the fish, as much as they wanted. When they had eaten their fill, he told his disciples, "Gather up the fragments left over, that nothing may be lost," and they filled twelve baskets with fragments from the five loaves. When the people saw this, they said, "This is indeed the prophet who is to come into the world!" Perceiving that they were about to take him by force to make him king, Jesus withdrew to the mountain by himself.

When evening came, his disciples got into a boat and started across to Capernaum. It was now dark, and the sea rose because a strong wind was blowing. When they had rowed three or four miles, they saw Jesus walking on the sea and drawing near to the boat.

They were frightened, but he said, "It is I; do not be afraid." Then they were glad to take him into the boat, and immediately the boat was at the land to which they were going.

Next day the people on the other side of

the sea saw that there had been only one boat there, and that Jesus had not entered it, but that his disciples had gone away alone. However, other boats came near the place, so the people got into the boats and went to Capernaum, seeking Jesus.

When they found him on the other side, they said, "Rabbi, when did you come here?"

"Truly, truly," Jesus answered, "you seek me, not because you saw signs, but because you ate your fill of the loaves. Do not labor for the food which perishes, but for the food which endures to eternal life, which the Son of man will give to you; for on him has God the Father set his seal."

"What must we do," they said, "to be doing the works of God?"

"This is the work of God," Jesus answered, "that you believe in him whom he has sent."

"Then what sign do you do," they said, "that we may see, and believe you? What work do you perform? Our fathers ate the manna in the wilderness; as it is written, 'He gave them bread from heaven to eat.'"

"It was not Moses who gave you the bread from heaven," Jesus said. "My Father gives you the true bread from heaven. For the bread of God is that which comes down from heaven, and gives life to the world."

"Lord," they said, "give us this bread always."

"I am the bread of life," said Jesus. "He who comes to me shall not hunger, and he who believes in me shall never thirst. But I said that you have seen me and yet do not believe. All that the Father gives me will come to me; and him who comes to me I will not cast out. For I have come down from heaven, not to do my own will, but the will of him who sent me, that I should lose nothing he has given me. For this is the will of my Father, that every one who sees the Son and believes in him should have eternal life; and I will raise him up at the last day."

The Jews then murmured at him because he said, "I am the bread which came down from heaven." They asked, "Is not this Jesus, the son of Joseph, whose father and mother we know? How does he now say, 'I have come down from heaven'?"

"Do not murmur among yourselves," Jesus answered. "No one can come to me unless the Father draws him. It is written in the prophets, 'And they shall all be taught by God.' Every one who has learned from the Father comes to me. Not that any one has seen the Father except him who is from God. Your fathers ate the manna in the wilderness, and they died. I am the bread of life which comes down from heaven that a man may eat of it and not die. I am the living bread which came down from heaven; if any one eats of this bread, he will live for ever; and the bread which I shall give for the life of the world is my flesh."

The Jews disputed among themselves, saying, "How can this man give us his flesh to eat?"

"Truly," Jesus said, "unless you eat the flesh of the Son of man and drink his blood, you have no life in you; he who eats my flesh and drinks my blood has eternal life, and I will raise him up at the last day. For my flesh is food indeed, and my blood is drink indeed. He who eats my flesh and drinks my blood abides in me, and I in him. As the living Father sent me, and I live because of the Father, so he who eats me will live because of me."

Many of his disciples, when they heard this, said, "This is a hard saying; who can listen to it?" But Jesus, knowing that his disciples murmured, said, "Do you take offense at this? Then what if you were to see the Son of man ascending where he was before? It is the spirit that gives life, the flesh is of no avail; the words that I have spoken to you are spirit and life. But there are some of you that do not believe." For Jesus knew from the first who those were that did not believe, and who it was that would betray him. "This is why I told you," he said, "that no one can come to me unless it is granted him by the Father."

After this many of his disciples drew back and no longer went about with him. "Do you also wish to go away?" Jesus said to the twelve.

"Lord," Simon Peter answered, "to whom shall we go? You have the words of eternal life; and we have believed, and have come to know, that you are the Holy One of God."

"Did I not choose you, the twelve," Jesus answered, "and one of you is a devil?" He spoke of Judas the son of Simon Iscariot, for he, one of the twelve, was to betray him.

After this, Jesus went about in Galilee, but not in Judea, because the Jews sought to kill him. Now the Jews' feast of Tabernacles was at hand, so his brothers said to him, "Leave here and go to Judea, that your disciples may see the works you are doing. For no man works in secret if he seeks to be known openly. If you do these things, show yourself to the world." For even his brothers did not believe in him. "My time has not yet come," Jesus said, "but your time is always here. The world cannot hate you, but it hates me because I testify of it that its works are evil. Go to the feast yourselves; I am not going up to this feast, for my time has not yet fully come." But after his brothers had gone up, then he also went, not publicly but in private.

The Jews were looking for him at the

feast, and there was much muttering about him among the people. While some said, "He is a good man," others said, "No, he is leading the people astray." Yet for fear of the Jews no one spoke openly of him. About the middle of the feast Jesus went into the temple and taught. The Jews marveled, saying, "How is it that this man has learning, when he has never studied?"

"My teaching is not mine," Jesus answered them, "but his who sent me; if any man's will is to do his will, he shall know whether the teaching is from God or whether I am speaking on my own authority. He who speaks on his own authority seeks his own glory; but he who seeks the glory of him who sent him is true, and in him there is no falsehood. Did not Moses give you the law? Yet none of you keeps the law. Why do you seek to kill me?"

"You have a demon!" the people answered. "Who is seeking to kill you?"

"I did one deed," Jesus answered, "and you all marvel at it. Moses gave you circumcision (not that it is from Moses, but from the fathers), and you circumcise a man upon the sabbath. If on the sabbath a man receives circumcision, so that the law of Moses may not be broken, are you angry with me because on the sabbath I made a man's whole body well? Do not judge by appearances, but judge with right judgment."

Some of the people of Jerusalem said, "Is not this the man whom they seek to kill? And here he is, speaking openly, and they say nothing to him! Can it be that the authorities really know that this is the Christ? Yet we know where this man comes from; and when the Christ appears, no one will know where he comes from." So Jesus proclaimed, as he taught in the temple, "You know me, and you know where I come from? But I have not come of my own accord; he who sent me is true, and him you do not know. I know him, for I come from him, and he sent me." So they sought to arrest him; but no one laid hands on him, because his hour had not yet come. Yet many of the people believed in him. "When the Christ appears," they said, "will he do more signs than this man has done?"

The Pharisees heard the crowd thus

muttering about him, and the chief priests and Pharisees sent officers to arrest him. Jesus then said, "I shall be with you a little longer, and then I go to him who sent me; you will seek me and you will not find me; where I am you cannot come."

"Where does this man intend to go," the Jews said, "that we shall not find him? Does he intend to go to the Dispersion among the Greeks and teach the Greeks? What does he mean?"

On the last day of the feast, the great day, Jesus stood up, and proclaimed, "If any one thirst, let him come to me and drink. He who believes in me, as the scripture has said, 'Out of his heart shall flow rivers of living water.'" Now this he said about the Spirit, which those who believed in him were to receive; for as yet the Spirit had not been given, because Jesus was not yet glorified. When they heard these words, some people said, "This is really the prophet," or, "This is the Christ." But some said, "Is the Christ to come from Galilee? Has not the scripture said that the Christ is descended from David, and comes from Bethlehem, the village where

David was?" So there was a division among the people over him. Some wanted to arrest him, but no one laid hands on him.

The officers then went back to the chief priests and Pharisees, who asked, "Why did you not bring him?"

"No man ever spoke like this man!" they answered.

"Are you led astray," the Pharisees said, "you also? Have any of the authorities believed in him? But this crowd, who do not know the law, are accursed." Nicodemus, who had gone to him before, and who was one of them, said, "Does our law judge a man without first giving him a hearing and learning what he does?"

"Are you from Galilee too?" they replied. "Search and you will see that no prophet is to rise from Galilee."

Early in the morning Jesus came again to the temple, and he sat down and taught, and the scribes and the Pharisees brought a woman caught in adultery. "Teacher, this woman has been caught in the act of adultery," they said. "Now in the law Moses commanded us to stone such. What do you say about her?" This they said to test him, that they might have some charge to bring against him. Jesus bent down and wrote with his finger on the ground. When they continued to ask him, he stood up, and said, "Let him who is without sin among you be the first to throw a stone at her." And once more he bent down and wrote with his finger on the ground. Then they went away, one by one, beginning with the eldest, and Jesus was left alone with the woman standing before him.

Jesus looked up, and said, "Woman, where are they? Has no one condemned you?"

"No one, Lord," she said.

"Neither do I condemn you," Jesus said. "Go, and do not sin again."

Jesus again spoke to the people, saying, "I am the light of the world; he who follows me will not walk in darkness, but will have the light of life."

"You are bearing witness to yourself," the Pharisees said. "Your testimony is not true."

"Even if I do bear witness to myself," Jesus answered, "my testimony is true, for

I know whence I have come and whither I am going, but you do not know whence I come or whither I am going. You judge according to the flesh, I judge no one. Yet even if I do judge, my judgment is true, for it is not I alone that judge, but I and he who sent me. In your law it is written that the testimony of two men is true; I bear witness to myself, and the Father who sent me bears witness to me."

"Where is your Father?" they asked.

"You know neither me nor my Father," Jesus answered. "If you knew me, you would know my Father also." These words he spoke in the temple; but no one arrested him, because his hour had not yet come.

Again he said to the Jews, "I go away, and you will seek me and die in your sin; where I am going, you cannot come."

"Will he kill himself," they asked, "since he says, 'Where I am going, you cannot come'?"

"You are from below," he said, "I am from above; you are of this world, I am not of this world. I told you that you would die in your sins, for you will die in your sins unless you believe that I am he."

"Who are you?" they asked.

"Even what I have told you from the beginning," he replied. "I have much to say about you and much to judge; but he who sent me is true, and I declare to the world what I have heard from him." They did not understand that he spoke to them of the Father, so Jesus said, "When you have lifted up the Son of man, then you will know that I am he, and that I do nothing on my own authority but speak as the Father taught me." As he spoke thus, many of the Jews believed in him, and Jesus said to them, "If you continue in my word, you are truly my disciples, and you will know the truth, and the truth will make you free."

"We are descendants of Abraham," they said, "and have never been in bondage to any one. How is it that you say, 'You will be made free'?"

"Truly," said Jesus, "every one who commits sin is a slave to sin. The slave does not continue in the house for ever; the son continues for ever. So if the Son makes you free, you will be free indeed. I know that you are descendants of Abraham; yet you seek to kill me, because my word finds no place in you. I speak of what I have seen with my Father, and you do what you have heard from your father."

"Abraham is our father," they said.

"If you were Abraham's children," Jesus said, "you would do what Abraham did, but now you seek to kill me, a man who has told you the truth which I heard from God; this is not what Abraham did. You do what your father did."

"We were not born of fornication," they said. "We have one Father, even God."

"If God were your Father," Jesus said, "you would love me, for I came forth from God; I came not of my own accord, but he sent me. Why do you not understand what I say? It is because you cannot bear to hear my word. You are of your father the devil, and your will is to do your father's desires. He was a murderer from the beginning, and has nothing to do with the truth, because there is no truth in him. When he lies, he speaks according to his own nature, for he is a liar and the father of lies. But, because I tell the truth, you do not believe me. Which of you convicts me of sin? If I tell the truth, why do you not believe me? He who is of God hears the words of God; the reason why you do not hear them is that you are not of God."

"Are we not right," the Jews asked, "in saying that you are a Samaritan and have a demon?"

"I have not a demon," Jesus answered, "but I honor my Father, and you dishonor me. Yet I do not seek my own glory; there is One who seeks it and he will be the judge. Truly, truly, I say to you, if any one keeps my word, he will never see death."

"Now we know that you have a demon," they said. "Abraham died, as did the prophets; and you say, 'If any one keeps my word, he will never taste death.' Are you greater than our father Abraham, who died? And the prophets died! Who do you claim to be?"

"If I glorify myself," Jesus answered, "my glory is nothing; it is my Father who glorifies me, of whom you say that he is your God. But you have not known him; I know him. If I said, I do not know him, I should be a liar like you; but I do know

him and I keep his word. Your father
Abraham rejoiced that he was to see my
day; he saw it and was glad."

"You are not yet fifty years old," they
said, "and have you seen Abraham?"

"Truly, truly, I say to you," Jesus replied, "before Abraham was, I am." Then
they took up stones to throw at him; but
Jesus hid himself, and went out of the
temple.

As he passed by, he saw a man blind
from birth, and his disciples asked, "Rabbi,
who sinned, this man or his parents, that
he was born blind?"

"It was not that this man sinned," Jesus
said, "or his parents, but that the works of
God might be made manifest in him. We
must work the works of him who sent me,
while it is day; night comes, when no one
can work. As long as I am in the world, I
am the light of the world." Then he spat
on the ground and made clay and anointed
the man's eyes, saying, "Go, wash in the
pool of Siloam." So he went and washed
and came back seeing. Those who knew
the man said to him, "How were your eyes
opened?" He told them, and they brought

him to the Pharisees; now it was a sabbath day when Jesus opened the man's eyes. The Pharisees asked him how he had received his sight, and he said, "He put clay on my eyes, and I washed, and I see." Some of the Pharisees said, "This man is not from God, for he does not keep the sabbath." But others said, "How can a man who is a sinner do such signs?" There was a division among them, so they asked the blind man, "What do you say about him, since he has opened your eyes?" He said, "He is a prophet."

The Jews did not believe that the man had been blind until they called his parents, and asked, "Is this your son, who you say was born blind? How then does he now see?"

"We know that this is our son," they answered, "and that he was born blind; but how he now sees we do not know, nor do we know who opened his eyes. Ask him; he is of age, he will speak for himself." They said this out of fear, for the Jews had agreed that if any one should confess Jesus to be Christ, he was to be put out of the synagogue.

A second time they called the man who had been blind. "Give God the praise," they said; "we know that this man is a sinner."

"Whether he is a sinner," said the man, "I do not know; one thing I know, that though I was blind, now I see."

"What did he do to you?" they asked. "How did he open your eyes?"

"I have told you already," he said, "and you would not listen. Why do you want to hear it again? Do you too want to become his disciples?"

"You are his disciple," they said, reviling him, "but we are disciples of Moses. We know that God has spoken to Moses, but as for this man, we do not know where he comes from."

"Why, this is a marvel!" he replied. "You do not know where he comes from, yet he opened my eyes. We know God does not listen to sinners, but if any one is a worshiper of God and does his will, God listens to him. Never since the world began has it been heard that any one opened the eyes of a man born blind. If this man were not from God, he could do nothing."

"You were born in utter sin," they answered, "and would you teach us?" And they cast him out.

Jesus heard that they had cast the man out, and having found him he said, "Do you believe in the Son of man?"

"Who is he, sir," he asked, "that I may believe in him?"

"You have seen him," Jesus said, "and it is he who speaks to you."

"Lord," he said, "I believe"; and he worshiped him.

"For judgment I came into this world," Jesus said, "that those who do not see may see, and that those who see may become blind." Some of the Pharisees nearby heard this, and they said, "Are we also blind?"

"If you were blind," Jesus said, "you would have no guilt; but now that you say, 'We see,' your guilt remains. Truly, truly, I say to you, he who does not enter the sheepfold by the door but climbs in by another way, that man is a thief and a robber; but he who enters by the door is the shepherd. The sheep hear his voice, and he calls his own sheep by name and leads them out. A stranger they will not follow, for they do not know the voice of strangers." They did not understand what he was saying, so he again said to them, "I am the door of the sheepfold; if any one enters by me, he will be saved, and will go in and out and find pasture. The thief comes only to steal and destroy; I came that they may have life, and have it abundantly. I am the good shepherd. The good shepherd lays down his life for the sheep. He who is a hireling, whose own the sheep are not, sees the wolf coming and leaves the sheep, and the wolf snatches them and scatters them. I am the good shepherd; I know my own and my own know me, as the Father knows me and I know the Father; and I lay down my life for the sheep. And I have other sheep that are not of this fold; I must bring them also, and they will heed my voice. So there shall be one flock, one shepherd. For this reason the Father loves me, because I lay down my life, that I may take it again. No one takes it from me, but I lay it down of my own accord. I have power to lay it down, and I have power to take it again; this charge I have received from my Father."

Because of these words, there was again a division among the Jews. Many of them said, "He has a demon, and he is mad; why listen to him?" Others said, "These are not the sayings of one who has a demon. Can a demon open the eyes of the blind?"

It was the feast of the Dedication at Jerusalem; it was winter, and Jesus was walking in the temple, in the portico of Solomon. So the Jews gathered round him, and said, "How long will you keep us in suspense? If you are the Christ, tell us plainly."

"I told you," Jesus answered, "and you do not believe. The works that I do in my Father's name, they bear witness to me; but you do not believe, because you do not belong to my sheep. My sheep hear my voice, and I know them, and they follow me; and I give them eternal life, and they shall never perish, and no one shall snatch them out of my hand. My Father, who has given them to me, is greater than all, and no one is able to snatch them out of the Father's hand. I and the Father are one."

The Jews took up stones again to stone him. "I have shown you many good works from the Father," Jesus said. "For which of these do you stone me?"

"It is not for a good work that we stone you," they answered, "but for blasphemy; because you, being a man, make yourself God."

Jesus answered, "Is it not written in your law, 'I said, you are gods'? If he called them gods to whom the word of God came (and scripture cannot be broken), do you say of him whom the Father consecrated and sent into the world, 'You are blaspheming,' because I said, 'I am the Son of God'? If I am not doing the works of my Father, then do not believe me; but if I do them, even though you do not believe me, believe the works, that you may know and understand that the Father is in me and I am in the Father." Again they tried to arrest him, but he escaped from their hands.

Now a certain man was ill, Lazarus of Bethany, the brother of Mary and her sister Martha. The sisters sent to Jesus, saying, "Lord, he whom you love is ill." But when Jesus heard it he said, "This illness is not unto death; it is for the glory of God, so that the Son of God may be glorified by means of it." He stayed two days longer where he was, then he said to the disciples, "Let us go into Judea again."

"Rabbi," the disciples said, "the Jews were but now seeking to stone you, and are you going there again?"

"Are there not twelve hours in the day?" Jesus answered. "If any one walks in the day, he does not stumble, because he sees the light of this world. But if any one walks in the night, he stumbles, because the light is not in him." Then he said, "Our friend Lazarus has fallen asleep, but I go to awake him out of sleep." He spoke of death, but the disciples thought that he meant taking rest in sleep. Then Jesus told them plainly, "Lazarus is dead; and for your sake I am glad that I was not there, so that you may believe. But let us go to him." Thomas, called the Twin, said, "Let us also go, that we may die with him."

When Jesus came to Bethany he found that Lazarus had already been in the tomb four days. Bethany was near Jerusalem, about two miles off, and many of the Jews had come to console Martha and Mary. When Martha heard that Jesus was coming, she went and met him. "Lord, if you had been here," she said, "my brother would not have died. Even now I know that whatever you ask from God, God will give you."

"Your brother will rise again," said Jesus.

"I know that he will rise again in the resurrection at the last day," Martha replied.

"I am the resurrection and the life," Jesus said. "He who believes in me, though he die, yet shall he live, and whoever lives and believes in me shall never die. Do you believe this?"

"Yes, Lord," she said, "I believe that you are the Christ, the Son of God, he who is coming into the world." Martha then went and called her sister, saying quietly, "The Teacher is here and is calling for you." Mary rose quickly, and when the Jews in the house saw her go out, they followed, supposing that she was going to the tomb. She came to Jesus and fell at his feet, saying, "Lord, if you had been here, my brother would not have died." When Jesus saw her weeping, and also the Jews, he was deeply moved in spirit and troubled. "Where have you laid him?" he asked. They said, "Lord, come and see." Then Jesus wept, so the Jews said, "See how he loved him!" But some said, "Could not he who opened the eyes of the blind man have kept this man from dying?"

Jesus, deeply moved again, came to the tomb; it was a cave, and a stone lay upon it. "Take away the stone," he said.

"Lord," said Martha, "by this time there will be an odor, for he has been dead four days."

"Did I not tell you," said Jesus, "that if you would believe you would see the glory of God?" They took away the stone, and Jesus lifted up his eyes and said, "Father, I thank thee that thou hast heard me. I knew that thou hearest me always, but I have said this on account of the people standing by, that they may believe that thou didst send me." Then he cried with a loud voice, "Lazarus, come out." The dead man came out, his hands and feet bound and his face wrapped with a cloth. Jesus said, "Unbind him, and let him go."

Many of the Jews who had come with Mary believed in him, but some went to the Pharisees and told what Jesus had done. So the chief priests and the Pharisees gathered the council, and said, "What are we to do? For this man performs many signs. If we let him go on thus, every one will believe in him, and the Romans will come and destroy both our holy place and our nation." But one of them, Caiaphas, who was high priest that year, said, "You know nothing at all; you do not understand that it is expedient for you that one man should die for the people, and that the whole nation should not perish." Thus he prophesied that Jesus should die for the nation, and not for the nation only, but to gather into one the children of God who are scattered abroad. So from that day on they took counsel how to put him to death. Jesus therefore no longer went about openly, but went to the country near the wilderness, to a town called Ephraim;

and there he stayed with the disciples.

Now the Passover was at hand, and many went up to Jerusalem to purify themselves. They were looking for Jesus and saying to one another, "What do you think? That he will not come to the feast?" Now the chief priests and the Pharisees had given orders that if any one knew where he was, he should let them know, so that they might arrest him.

Six days before the Passover, Jesus came to Bethany, where they made him a supper. Martha served, and Lazarus was one of those at table with him. Mary took a pound of costly ointment of pure nard and anointed the feet of Jesus and wiped his feet with her hair; and the house was filled with the fragrance. But Judas Iscariot said, "Why was this ointment not sold for three hundred denarii and given to the poor?" Not that he cared for the poor, but he was a thief, and as he had the money box he used to take what was put into it. "Let her alone," Jesus said, "let her keep it for the day of my burial. The poor you always have with you, but you do not always have me."

When the Jews learned that he was there, they came, not only on account of Jesus but also to see Lazarus. So the chief priests planned to put Lazarus also to death, because on account of him many of the Jews were believing in Jesus. The next day a great crowd who had come to the feast heard that Jesus was coming to Jerusalem. They took palm branches and went to meet him, crying, "Hosanna! Blessed is he who comes in the name of the Lord, even the King of Israel!" The Pharisees then said, "You see that you can do nothing; look, the whole world has gone after him." And Jesus found a young ass and sat upon it; as it is written, "Fear not, daughter of Zion; behold, your king is coming, sitting on an ass's colt!" His disciples did not understand this at first; but when Jesus was glorified, then they remembered that this had been written of him and had been done to him.

Now among those at the feast were some Greeks. These said to Philip, "Sir, we wish to see Jesus." Philip and Andrew went and told Jesus, and Jesus said, "The hour has come for the Son of man to be glorified. Truly, truly, I say to you, unless a grain of wheat falls into the earth and dies, it remains alone; but if it dies, it bears much fruit. He who loves his life loses it, and he who hates his life in this world will keep it for eternal life. If any one serves me, he must follow me; and where I am, there shall my servant be also; if any one serves me, the Father will honor him. Now is my soul troubled. And what shall I say? 'Father, save me from this hour'? No, for this purpose I have come to this hour. Father, glorify thy name."

Then a voice came from heaven, "I have glorified it, and I will glorify it again." The crowd heard it and said that it had thundered. Others said, "An angel has spoken to him."

"This voice has come for your sake," Jesus said, "not for mine. Now is the judgment of this world, now shall the ruler of this world be cast out; and I, when I am lifted up from the earth, will draw all men to myself." He said this to show by what death he was to die, but the crowd answered, "We have heard from the law that the Christ remains for ever. How can you

say that the Son of man must be lifted up?
Who is this Son of man?"

"The light is with you for a little
longer," Jesus said. "Walk while you have
the light, lest the darkness overtake you;
he who walks in the darkness does not
know where he goes. While you have the
light, believe in the light, that you may
become sons of light." Then he departed
and hid himself from them. Though he had
done many signs, yet they did not believe
in him; it was so that the word spoken by
the prophet Isaiah might be fulfilled:
"Lord, who has believed our report, and to
whom has the arm of the Lord been revealed?" Therefore they could not believe.
For Isaiah again said, "He has blinded
their eyes and hardened their heart, lest
they should see with their eyes and perceive with their heart, and turn for me to
heal them." Isaiah said this because he saw
his glory and spoke of him.

Nevertheless, many even of the authorities did believe in him, but they did not
confess it, lest they should be put out of
the synagogue: for they loved the praise of
men more than the praise of God.

Then Jesus cried out, "He who believes in me, believes not in me but in him who sent me. And he who sees me sees him who sent me. I have come as light into the world, that whoever believes in me may not remain in darkness. If any one hears my sayings and does not keep them, I do not judge him; for I did not come to judge the world but to save the world. He who rejects me has a judge; the word that I have spoken will be his judge on the last day. For I have not spoken on my own authority; the Father has given me commandment what to speak, and I know that his commandment is eternal life. What I say, I say as the Father has bidden me."

Before the feast of the Passover, when Jesus knew that his hour had come to depart to the Father, having loved his own, he loved them to the end. During supper, when the devil had already put it into the heart of Judas Iscariot to betray him, Jesus rose, laid aside his garments, and girded himself with a towel. He poured water into a basin, and began to wash the disciples' feet, and to wipe them with the towel. He came to Peter, who said, "Lord, do you wash my feet?"

"What I am doing," Jesus answered, "you do not know now, but afterward you will understand."

"You shall never wash my feet," Peter said.

"If I do not wash you," said Jesus, "you have no part in me."

"Lord," said Peter, "not my feet only but also my hands and my head!"

"He who has bathed," Jesus said, "does not need to wash, except for his feet, but he is clean all over; and you are clean, but not every one of you." He knew who was to betray him; that was why he said, "You are not all clean."

When he had washed their feet and resumed his place, he said, "Do you know what I have done to you? You call me Teacher and Lord; and you are right, for so I am. If I then, your Lord and Teacher, have washed your feet, you also ought to wash one another's feet, for I have given you an example. A servant is not greater than his master; nor is he who is sent greater than he who sent him. If you know these things, blessed are you if you do them. I am not speaking of you all; I know whom I have chosen; it is that the scripture may be fulfilled, 'He who ate my bread has lifted his heel against me.' I tell you this now, before it takes place, that when it does take place you may believe that I am he. Truly, truly, I say to you, he who receives any one whom I send receives me; and he who receives me receives him who sent me." Then he was troubled in spirit, and testified, "Truly, truly, I say to you, one of you will betray me."

The disciples looked at one another, uncertain of whom he spoke. One of his disciples, whom Jesus loved, was lying close to his breast, so Peter beckoned to him, and said, "Tell us who it is of whom he speaks." The disciple asked, "Lord, who is it?"

"It is he," answered Jesus, "to whom I shall give this morsel when I have dipped it," and he gave it to Judas Iscariot. Then Satan entered into Judas, and Jesus said to him, "What you are going to do, do quickly." No one at the table knew why he said this to him. Some thought that, because Judas had the money box, Jesus was telling him to buy what was needed for the feast, or that he should give something to the poor. After receiving the morsel, Judas immediately went out; and it was night.

"Now is the Son of man glorified," Jesus said, "and in him God is glorified; if God is glorified in him, God will also glorify him in himself, and at once. Little children, yet a little while I am with you. You will seek me; and as I said to the Jews, 'Where I am going you cannot come.' A new commandment I give to you, that you love one another, even as I have loved you. By this all men will know that you are my disciples, if you have love for one another."

"Lord, where are you going?" Peter asked.

"Where I am going," Jesus answered, "you cannot follow me now; but you shall follow afterward."

"Lord, why cannot I follow you now?" said Peter. "I will lay down my life for you."

"Will you lay down your life for me?" Jesus replied. "Truly, truly, I say to you, the cock will not crow, till you have denied me three times.

"Let not your hearts be troubled; believe in God, believe also in me. In my Father's house are many rooms; if it were not so, would I have told you that I go to prepare a place for you? And when I go and prepare a place for you, I will come again and will take you to myself, that where I am you may be also. And you know the way where I am going."

"Lord," said Thomas, "we do not know where you are going; how can we know the way?"

"I am the way, and the truth, and the life," Jesus said; "no one comes to the Father, but by me. If you had known me, you would have known my Father also; henceforth you know him and have seen him."

"Lord," said Philip, "show us the Father, and we shall be satisfied."

"Have I been with you so long, and yet you do not know me, Philip?" Jesus said. "He who has seen me has seen the Father. The words that I say to you I do not speak on my own authority; but the Father who dwells in me does his works. Believe me that I am in the Father and the Father in me; or else believe me for the sake of the works themselves. He who believes in me will also do the works that I do; and greater works than these will he do, because I go to the Father. Whatever you ask in my name, I will do it, that the Father may be glorified in the Son. If you love me, you will keep my commandments. And I will pray the Father, and he will give you another Counselor, to be with you for ever, even the Spirit of truth, whom the world cannot receive, because it neither sees him nor knows him; you know him, for he dwells with you, and will be in you. I will not leave you desolate; I will come to you. Yet a little while, and the world will see me no more, but you will see me; because I live, you will live also. In that day you will know that I am in my Father, and you in me, and I in you. He who keeps my commandments loves me; and he who loves me will be loved by my Father, and I will love him and manifest myself to him."

"Lord," said Judas (not Iscariot), "how

is it that you will manifest yourself to us, and not to the world?"

"If a man loves me," answered Jesus, "he will keep my word, and my Father will love him, and we will make our home with him. These things I have spoken to you, while I am still with you. But the Counselor, the Holy Spirit, whom the Father will send in my name, he will teach you all things, and bring to your remembrance all that I have said to you. Peace I leave with you; my peace I give to you; not as the world gives do I give to you. Let not your hearts be troubled, neither let them be afraid. You heard me say to you, 'I go away, and I will come to you.' If you loved me, you would have rejoiced, because I go to the Father; for the Father is greater than I. I have told you before it takes place, so that when it does take place, you may believe. I will no longer talk much with you, for the ruler of this world is coming. He has no power over me; but I do as the Father has commanded me, so that the world may know that I love the Father.

"I am the true vine, and my Father is the vinedresser. Every branch of mine that bears no fruit, he takes away, and every branch that does bear fruit he prunes, that it may bear more fruit. As the branch cannot bear fruit by itself, unless it abides in the vine, neither can you, unless you abide in me. I am the vine, you are the branches. Apart from me you can do nothing. If you abide in me, and my words abide in you, ask whatever you will, and it shall be done for you. By this my Father is glorified, that you bear much fruit, and so prove to be my disciples. As the Father has loved me, so have I loved you. If you keep my commandments, you will abide in my love, just as I have kept my Father's commandments and abide in his love. These things I have spoken to you, that my joy may be in you, and that your joy may be full.

"This is my commandment, that you love one another as I have loved you. Greater love has no man than this, that he lay down his life for his friends. You are my friends if you do what I command. No longer do I call you servants, for the servant does not know what his master is doing; but all that I have heard from my Father I have made known to you. You did not choose me, but I chose you and appointed you, that you should go and bear fruit and that your fruit should abide; so that whatever you ask the Father in my name, he may give it to you. This I command you, to love one another.

"If the world hates you, know that it has hated me before it hated you. If you were of the world, the world would love its own; because you are not of the world, because I chose you out of the world, therefore the world hates you. Remember that I said to you, 'A servant is not greater than his master.' If they persecuted me, they will persecute you. But this they will do on my account, because they do not know him who sent me. He who hates me hates my Father also. If I had not done among them the works which no one else did, they would not have sin; but now they have seen and hated both me and my Father. It is to fulfil the word that is written in their law, 'They hated me without a cause.' But when the Counselor comes, the Spirit of truth, who proceeds from the Father, he will bear witness to me. And you also are witnesses, because you have been with me from the beginning.

"I have said all this to keep you from falling away. They will put you out of the synagogues; indeed, the hour is coming when whoever kills you will think he is offering service to God. And they will do this because they have not known the Father, nor me. But I have said these things to you, that when their hour comes you may remember that I told you of them. I did not say these things to you from the beginning, because I was with you. But now I am going to him who sent me, and because I have said these things, sorrow has filled your hearts. Nevertheless, it is to your advantage that I go away, for if I do not go, the Counselor will not come to you; but if I go, I will send him. When he comes, he will convince the world concerning sin and righteousness and judgment: concerning sin, because they do not believe in me; concerning righteousness, because I go to the Father, and you will see me no more; concerning judgment, because the ruler of this world is judged.

"I have yet many things to say to you, but you cannot bear them now. When the

Spirit of truth comes, he will guide you into all the truth; for he will not speak on his own authority, but whatever he hears he will speak, and he will declare to you the things to come. He will glorify me, for he will take what is mine and declare it to you. All that the Father has is mine; therefore I said that he will take what is mine and declare it to you. A little while, and you will see me no more; again a little while, and you will see me."

Some of his disciples said to one another, "What is this that he says? We do not know what he means."

Jesus knew that they did not understand, so he said, "Truly, truly, I say to you, you will weep and lament, but the world will rejoice; you will be sorrowful, but your sorrow will turn into joy. When a woman is in travail she has sorrow, because her hour has come; but when she is delivered of the child, she no longer remembers the anguish, for joy that a child is born into the world. So you have sorrow now, but I will see you again and your hearts will rejoice, and no one will take your joy from you. In that day you will ask nothing of me, but if you ask anything of the Father, he will give it to you in my name; ask, and you will receive, that your joy may be full. I have said this to you in figures; the hour is coming when I shall no longer speak in figures but tell you plainly of the Father. The Father himself loves you, because you loved me and believed that I came from him. I came from the Father and have come into the world; again, I am leaving the world and going to the Father."

"Ah, now you are speaking plainly," the disciples said, "not in any figure! Now we know that you know all things, and need none to question you; by this we believe that you came from God."

"Do you now believe?" Jesus said. "The hour is coming, indeed it has come, when you will be scattered, every man to his home, and will leave me alone; yet I am not alone, for the Father is with me. I have said this to you, that in me you may have peace. In the world you have tribulation; but be of good cheer, I have overcome the world."

Jesus then lifted up his eyes to heaven, and said, "Father, the hour has come; glorify thy Son that the Son may glorify thee, since thou hast given him power over all flesh, to give eternal life to all whom thou hast given him. And this is eternal life, that they know thee the only true God, and Jesus Christ whom thou hast sent. I glorified thee on earth, having accomplished the work which thou gavest me to do; and now, Father, glorify thou me in thy own presence with the glory which I had with thee before the world was made.

"I have manifested thy name to the men whom thou gavest me out of the world, and they have kept thy word. Now they know that everything is from thee; for I have given them the words which thou gavest me, and they know in truth that I came from thee, that thou didst send me. I am praying for them, not for the world, but for those whom thou hast given me. All mine are thine, and thine are mine, and I am glorified in them. Holy Father, keep them in thy name that they may be one, even as we are one. While I was with them, I guarded them in thy name, and none of them is lost but the son of perdition, that the scripture might be fulfilled.

But now I am coming to thee; and these things I speak in the world, that they may have my joy fulfilled in themselves. The world has hated them because they are not of the world. I do not pray that thou shouldst take them out of the world, but that thou shouldst keep them from the evil one. Sanctify them in the truth; thy word is truth. As thou didst send me into the world, so I have sent them into the world. And for their sake I consecrate myself, that they also may be consecrated in truth.

"I do not pray for these only, but also for those who believe in me through their word, that they may all be one. The glory which thou hast given me I have given to them, that they may be one even as we are one, I in them and thou in me, that they may become perfectly one, so that the world may know that thou hast sent me and hast loved them even as thou hast loved me. Father, I desire that they also may be with me where I am, to behold my glory which thou hast given me before the foundation of the world. O righteous Father, the world has not known thee, but I have known thee; and these know that thou hast sent me. I made known to them thy name, and I will make it known, that the love with which thou hast loved me may be in them, and I in them."

When Jesus had spoken these words, he went with his disciples across the Kidron valley to a garden, which they entered. Judas Iscariot also knew the place (for Jesus often met there with his disciples), so he procured a band of soldiers from the chief priests and the Pharisees, and went there with lanterns and weapons. Jesus, knowing all that was to befall him, came forward and said, "Whom do you seek?"

"Jesus of Nazareth," they answered.

"I am he," Jesus said.

At this they drew back and fell to the ground. Again he asked, "Whom do you seek?"

"Jesus of Nazareth," they said again.

"I told you that I am he," said Jesus. "If you seek me, let these men go." This was to fulfil the word which he had spoken, "Of those whom thou gavest me I lost not one."

Then Peter, having a sword, drew it and struck the high priest's slave (whose name was Malchus) and cut off his right ear. "Put your sword into its sheath," Jesus said. "Shall I not drink the cup which the Father has given me?" Then the soldiers seized Jesus and bound him, and they led him to Annas, the father-in-law of Caiaphas.

Peter and another disciple followed Jesus. As this other disciple was known to the high priest, he entered the court along with Jesus, while Peter stood outside. So the other disciple spoke to the maid who kept the door, and brought Peter in. The maid said to Peter, "Are not you also one of this man's disciples?" He said, "I am not." Now the soldiers had made a charcoal fire, and Peter stood with them, warming himself.

The high priest then questioned Jesus about his disciples and his teaching. "I have spoken openly to the world," Jesus answered. "I have always taught in synagogues and in the temple, where all Jews come together; I have said nothing secretly. Why do you ask me? Ask those who have heard me." At this, one of the officers struck Jesus with his hand, saying,

"Is that how you answer the high priest?"

"If I have spoken wrongly," said Jesus, "bear witness to the wrong; but if I have spoken rightly, why do you strike me?" Annas then sent him bound to Caiaphas the high priest.

Now Peter was standing and warming himself. Some said to him, "Are not you also one of his disciples?" He denied it, and said, "I am not." One of the servants of the high priest, a kinsman of the man whose ear Peter had cut off, asked, "Did I not see you in the garden with him?" Peter again denied it; and at once a cock crowed.

Early in the morning they led Jesus from the house of Caiaphas to the praetorium. The Jews themselves did not enter the praetorium, that they might not be defiled, but might eat the passover, so Pilate went out to them. "What accusation do you bring against this man?" he asked.

"If this man were not an evildoer," they answered, "we would not have handed him over."

"Take him yourselves," said Pilate, "and judge him by your own law."

"It is not lawful for us to put any man to death," they said. This was to fulfil the word which Jesus had spoken to show by what death he was to die. Pilate entered the praetorium, called Jesus, and said, "Are you the King of the Jews?"

"Do you say this of your own accord," asked Jesus, "or did others say it to you about me?"

"Am I a Jew?" Pilate answered. "Your own nation and the chief priests have handed you over to me; what have you done?"

"My kingship is not of this world," Jesus answered. "If my kingship were of this world, my servants would fight, that I might not be handed over to the Jews; but my kingship is not from the world."

"So you are a king?" Pilate asked.

"You say that I am a king," Jesus replied. "For this I was born, and for this I have come into the world, to bear witness to the truth. Every one who is of the truth hears my voice."

"What is truth?" Pilate asked. Then he went out to the Jews again, and told them, "I find no crime in him. But you have a custom that I should release one man for you at the Passover; will you have me release for you the King of the Jews?" They cried out, "Not this man, but Barabbas!" Now Barabbas was a robber.

Then Pilate took Jesus and scourged him. And the soldiers plaited a crown of thorns, and put it on his head, and arrayed him in a purple robe. "Hail, King of the Jews!" they said, and struck him with their hands. Pilate went out again, and said to the crowd, "See, I am bringing him out to you, that you may know that I find no crime in him." Wearing the crown of thorns and the purple robe, Jesus came out.

"Behold the man!" Pilate said.

When the chief priests and the officers saw him, they cried out, "Crucify him, crucify him!"

"Take him yourselves," said Pilate, "and crucify him, for I find no crime in him."

"We have a law," the Jews answered, "and by that law he ought to die, because he has made himself the Son of God." When Pilate heard this, he was the more afraid; he entered the praetorium, and said to Jesus, "Where are you from?" But Jesus gave no answer. Pilate therefore said, "You will not speak to me? Do you not know that I have power to release you, and power to crucify you?"

"You would have no power over me," Jesus answered, "unless it had been given you from above; therefore he who delivered me to you has the greater sin."

Upon this, Pilate sought to release him, but the Jews cried out, "If you release this man, you are not Caesar's friend; every one who makes himself a king sets himself against Caesar." Then Pilate brought Jesus out and sat on the judgment seat at a place called The Pavement. Now it was the day of Preparation of the Passover, about the sixth hour. Pilate said to the Jews, "Behold your King!"

"Away with him," they cried out, "away with him, crucify him!"

"Shall I crucify your King?" Pilate asked.

"We have no king but Caesar," the chief priests answered. Then Pilate handed him over to be crucified.

They took Jesus, and he went out, bearing his own cross, to the place of the skull, called in Hebrew, Golgotha. There they crucified him, and with him two others, one on either side. Pilate also put a title on the cross in Hebrew, Latin, and Greek; it read, "Jesus of Nazareth, the King of the Jews." Many of the Jews read this title, for Golgotha was near the city, and the chief priests said to Pilate, "Do not write, 'The King of the Jews,' but, 'This man said, I am King of the Jews.' "

"What I have written," Pilate answered, "I have written."

The soldiers then took his garments and made four parts, one for each soldier. But the tunic was without seam, woven from top to bottom; so they said, "Let us not tear it, but cast lots for it." This was to fulfil the scripture, "They parted my garments among them, and for my clothing they cast lots."

Standing by the cross were his mother, and his mother's sister, Mary the wife of Clopas, and Mary Magdalene. When Jesus saw his mother, and the disciple whom he loved standing near, he said to his mother, "Woman, behold, your son!" Then he said to the disciple, "Behold, your mother!" From that hour the disciple took her to his own home.

After this, Jesus, knowing that all was now finished, said (to fulfil the scripture), "I thirst." A bowl full of vinegar stood there; so they put a sponge full of the vinegar on a reed and held it to his mouth. When Jesus had received the vinegar, he said, "It is finished"; and he bowed his head and gave up his spirit.

Since it was the day of Preparation, in order to prevent the bodies from remaining on the cross on the sabbath, the Jews asked Pilate that their legs might be broken, and that they might be taken away. So the soldiers broke the legs of the two who had been crucified with him. When they came to Jesus and saw that he was already dead, they did not break his legs, but a soldier pierced his side with a spear, and at once there came out blood and water. He who saw it has borne witness—his testimony is true, and he knows that he tells the truth—that you also may believe. For these things took place that the scriptures might be fulfilled, "Not a bone of him shall be broken," and, "They shall look on him whom they have pierced."

After this, Joseph of Arimathea, who was a secret disciple of Jesus, asked Pilate for the body, and Pilate gave him leave. Nicodemus, who had come to Jesus by night, brought a mixture of myrrh and aloes, about a hundred pounds' weight; then they bound the body of Jesus in linen cloths with the spices, as is the burial custom of the Jews. Now there was a garden nearby, and in it a new tomb where no one had ever been laid. There they laid Jesus.

Now on the first day of the week Mary Magdalene came to the tomb while it was still dark, and saw that the stone had been taken away. She ran to Peter and the other disciple, the one whom Jesus loved, and said, "They have taken the Lord out of the tomb, and we do not know where they have laid him." Peter then ran with the other disciple to the tomb, but the other disciple reached the tomb first. Stooping to look in, he saw the linen cloths lying there, but he did not go in. Then Peter came and went into the tomb, and he saw the linen cloths lying, and the napkin, which had been on Jesus' head, rolled up in a place by itself. Then the other disciple went in, and he saw and believed; for as yet they did not know the scripture, that he must rise from the dead. Then the two went home.

But Mary Magdalene stood weeping outside the tomb. She stooped to look in, and saw two angels in white sitting where the body of Jesus had lain, one at the head and one at the feet. "Woman," they said, "why are you weeping?"

"Because they have taken away my Lord," she said, "and I do not know where they have laid him." Then she turned and saw Jesus standing, but she did not know that it was he.

"Woman, why are you weeping?" Jesus said. "Whom do you seek?"

Supposing him to be the gardener, she said, "Sir, if you have carried him away, tell me where you have laid him, and I will take him away."

"Mary," said Jesus. She turned and said in Hebrew, "Rabboni!" (which means Teacher).

"Do not hold me," Jesus said, "for I have not yet ascended to the Father; but go to my brethren and say to them, I am ascending to my Father and your Father, to my God and your God." She went and said to the disciples, "I have seen the Lord," and she told them that Jesus had said these things to her.

That evening, the doors being shut where the disciples were, for fear of the Jews, Jesus came and stood among them. "Peace be with you," he said, and he showed them his hands and his side. Then the disciples were glad, and Jesus said, "As the Father has sent me, even so I send you." He breathed on them, and said, "Receive the Holy Spirit. If you forgive the sins of any, they are forgiven; if you retain the sins of any, they are retained."

Now Thomas, one of the twelve, called the Twin, was not there when Jesus came. So the other disciples told him, "We have seen the Lord." But he said, "Unless I see in his hands the print of the nails, and place my finger in the mark of the nails, and place my hand in his side, I will not believe." Eight days later the disciples were again in the house, and Thomas was with them. The doors were shut, but Jesus came and stood among them, and said, "Peace be with you." Then he said to Thomas, "Put your finger here, and see my hands; and put out your hand, and place it in my side; do not be faithless, but believing." Thomas answered, "My Lord and my God!"

"Have you believed because you have seen me?" Jesus said. "Blessed are those who have not seen and yet believe."

Now Jesus did many other signs in the presence of the disciples, which are not written in this book; but these are written that you may believe that Jesus is the Christ, the Son of God, and that believing, you may have life in his name.

AFTER THIS, JESUS revealed himself again to the disciples by the Sea of Galilee, in this way. Some of them were together, and Peter said, "I am going fishing." They all went out in the boat, but that night they caught nothing. As day was breaking, Jesus stood on the beach; yet the disciples did not know him. "Children," he said, "have you any fish?"

"No," they answered.

"Cast the net on the right side of the boat," he said, "and you will find some." They cast it, and now they were not able to haul it in, for the quantity of fish. That disciple whom Jesus loved said to Peter, "It is the Lord!" When Peter heard this, he sprang into the sea, but the others came in the boat, dragging the net full of fish.

On land, they saw a charcoal fire, with fish lying on it. "Bring some of the fish you caught," Jesus said. Peter hauled the net ashore, full of large fish, a hundred and fifty-three of them, and although there were so many, the net was not torn.

"Come and have breakfast," Jesus said. Now none of the disciples dared ask, "Who are you?" They knew it was the Lord. Jesus gave them some bread, and so with the fish. This was now the third time that Jesus was revealed to the disciples after he was raised from the dead.

When they had finished breakfast, Jesus said to Peter, "Simon, son of John, do you love me more than these?"

"Yes, Lord," said Peter, "you know that I love you."

"Feed my lambs," Jesus said. A second

time he said to him, "Simon, son of John, do you love me?"

"Yes, Lord," said Peter, "you know that I love you."

"Tend my sheep," Jesus said. Then he said to him the third time, "Simon, son of John, do you love me?"

Peter was grieved because he asked this the third time, and he said, "Lord, you know everything; you know that I love you."

"Feed my sheep," Jesus said. "Truly, truly, I say to you, when you were young, you girded yourself and walked where you would; but when you are old, you will stretch out your hands, and another will gird you and carry you where you do not wish to go." (This he said to show by what death he was to glorify God.) Then he said, "Follow me." Peter turned and saw following them the disciple whom Jesus loved, who had lain close to his breast at the supper. "Lord," he asked, "what about this man?"

"If it is my will," Jesus answered, "that he remain until I come, what is that to you? Follow me!" The saying spread among the brethren that this disciple was not to die; yet Jesus did not say that he was not to die, but, "If it is my will that he remain until I come, what is that to you?" This is the disciple who is bearing witness to these things, and who has written these things; and we know that his testimony is true.

But there are also many other things which Jesus did; were every one of them to be written, I suppose that the world itself could not contain the books that would be written.

THE ACTS
OF THE APOSTLES

In its opening paragraph this book describes itself as a continuation of the Gospel according to Luke. It is the earliest account of the formation and spread of the Christian church after the resurrection of Jesus Christ. It tells of the first apostolic sermon, the first apostolic miracle, the first steps toward organization, the first persecution, the first Christian martyr, the first Gentile convert, the first European church. The book forms a natural transition between the four Gospel accounts and the twenty-one letters written by Paul and others.

Initially, the apostles Peter and John play the leading roles; then the narrative concentrates on the work of Paul, apostle to the Gentiles. In this section the author sometimes writes "we" instead of "they," suggesting that he has made verbatim use of a "travel diary." Nothing is said at the close of the book about Paul's fate in Rome. This is seen by some as indicating the date of composition, that is, about A.D. 68. Others prefer a date between 75 and 85.

A special feature is the emphasis on the work of the Holy Spirit in guiding the disciples and their converts. Luke also tries to reassure his readers that Christians are not a subversive political threat to the Roman Empire. The Christian faith, he explains, is the fulfillment of the Jewish religion, and membership is open to all who repent and believe the gospel.

IN THE FIRST book, O Theophilus, I have dealt with all that Jesus began to do and teach, until the day when he was taken up, after he had given commandment through the Holy Spirit to the apostles whom he had chosen. He presented himself alive after his passion by many proofs, appearing and speaking to them during forty days. And while staying with them he charged them not to depart from Jerusalem, but to wait for the promise of the Father. "John baptized with water," he said, "but before many days you shall be baptized with the Holy Spirit."

When the disciples had come together at Mount Olivet, they asked him, "Lord, will you at this time restore the kingdom to Israel?"

"It is not for you to know times or seasons," he said, "which the Father has fixed by his own authority. But you shall receive power when the Holy Spirit has come upon you; and you shall be my witnesses in Jerusalem and in all Judea and Samaria and to the end of the earth."

When he had said this he was lifted up, and a cloud took him out of their sight. And behold, two men stood by them in white robes and said, "Men of Galilee, why do you stand looking into heaven? This Jesus, who was taken up into heaven, will come in the same way as you saw him go." They returned to Jerusalem and went to the upper room, where they were staying. With one accord they devoted themselves to prayer, together with the women, and Mary the mother of Jesus, and his brothers.

In those days Peter stood up among the brethren (in all about a hundred and twenty). "The scripture had to be fulfilled," he said, "which the Holy Spirit spoke by the mouth of David, concerning Judas, who was one of our number and shared in this ministry. (This man bought a field with the reward of his wickedness; and falling headlong he burst open in the middle and all his bowels gushed out; that field is called Akeldama, Field of Blood.) Now it is written in the book of Psalms, 'His office let another take.' So one of the men who accompanied us during all the time that the Lord Jesus went in and out among us must become with us a witness to his resurrection." They put forward two men, and they prayed, "Lord, who knowest the hearts of all men, show which of these two thou hast chosen." Then they cast lots, and the lot fell on Matthias, and he was enrolled with the eleven apostles.

When the day of Pentecost had come,

they were all together in one place. Suddenly there was a sound from heaven like the rush of a mighty wind, filling the house. And there appeared tongues as of fire, distributed and resting on each one of them. All were filled with the Holy Spirit, and they left the house and began to speak in other tongues, as the Spirit gave them utterance.

Now there were dwelling in Jerusalem devout Jews from every nation under heaven. And the multitude was amazed because each one heard them speaking in his own language. "Are not all these Galileans?" they said. "How is it that each of us hears in his own tongue?"

"They are filled with new wine," others mocked.

But Peter addressed the crowd in a loud voice. "Men of Judea and all who dwell in Jerusalem," he said, "give ear to my words. These men are not drunk, as you suppose, since it is still early morning. But this is what was spoken by the prophet Joel: 'And in the last days it shall be, God declares, that I will pour out my Spirit upon all flesh, and your sons and your daughters shall prophesy, and your young men shall see visions, and your old men shall dream dreams. And I will show wonders in the heaven above and signs on the earth beneath; the sun shall be turned into darkness and the moon into blood, before the day of the Lord comes. And whoever calls on the name of the Lord shall be saved.' Men of Israel, hear these words: Jesus of Nazareth, a man attested to you by God with mighty works and signs, delivered up according to the definite plan and foreknowledge of God, you crucified and killed by the hands of lawless men. But God raised him up, having loosed the pangs of death, because it was not possible for him to be held by it. For David says concerning him, 'Thou wilt not abandon my soul to Hades, nor let thy Holy One see corruption.' Now David both died and was buried, and his tomb is with us to this day. Being therefore a prophet, he foresaw and spoke of the resurrection of the Christ, that he was not abandoned to Hades, nor did his flesh see corruption. This Jesus God raised up, and of that we all are witnesses. Being therefore exalted at the right hand of God, and having received from the Father the promise of the Holy Spirit, he has poured out this which you see and hear."

When the people heard this they were cut to the heart. "Brethren," they said, "what shall we do?"

"Repent," said Peter, "and be baptized in the name of Jesus Christ for the forgiveness of your sins; and you shall receive the gift of the Holy Spirit. For the promise is to you and to your children and to all that are far off, every one whom the Lord our God calls to him. Save yourselves from this crooked generation." Those who received his word were baptized, and there were added that day about three thousand souls.

All who believed were together and had all things in common. They sold their possessions and goods and distributed them to all, as any had need. Attending the temple together and breaking bread in their homes, they partook of food with glad and generous hearts, praising God and having favor with all the people. And day by day the Lord added to their number.

Now as Peter and John were going up to the temple at the hour of afternoon prayer, a man lame from birth asked for alms. Peter directed his gaze at him and said, "I have no silver and gold, but I give you what I have; in the name of Jesus Christ of Nazareth, walk." And he took him by the right hand and raised him up, and immediately his feet and ankles were made strong. Leaping up, he entered the temple with them, walking and leaping and praising God. The people recognized him as the one who always sat for alms at the temple, a man more than forty years old, and they were filled with amazement at what had happened.

While he clung to Peter and John, all the people ran to them in the portico called Solomon's. "Men of Israel, why do you stare at us," said Peter, "as though by our own power or piety we had made him walk? The God of Abraham, Isaac, and Jacob glorified his servant Jesus, whom you delivered up and denied in the presence of Pilate. You denied the Holy and Righteous One, and killed the Author of life, whom God raised from the dead. To this we are witnesses. And the faith which is through Jesus has given this man perfect health in the presence of you all. I know that you acted in ignorance, brethren, as did also your rulers. But what God foretold by the prophets, that his Christ should suffer, he thus fulfilled. Repent therefore, and turn again, that your sins may be blotted out, and that God may send the Christ appointed for you, Jesus, whom heaven must receive until the time for establishing all that God spoke by the mouth of his holy prophets from of old. You are the sons of the prophets and of the covenant which God gave to your fathers, saying to Abraham, 'In your posterity shall all the families of the earth be blessed.' God, having raised up his servant, sent him to you first, to bless you in turning every one of you from your wickedness."

As Peter and John were speaking, the priests and the captain of the temple and the Sadducees came up, annoyed because they were proclaiming in Jesus the resurrection from the dead. They arrested them and put them in custody until the morrow, for it was already evening. But many of those who heard the word believed; and the number of the men came to about five thousand.

The next day the rulers, elders, and scribes were gathered together, with Annas the high priest and Caiaphas and all who were of the high-priestly family, and with Peter and John set in their midst. "By what power or by what name did you do this?" they inquired.

"Rulers of the people and elders," said Peter, "if we are being examined today concerning a good deed done to a cripple, by what means this man has been healed, be it known that by the name of Jesus Christ of Nazareth, whom you crucified, whom God raised from the dead, by him this man is standing before you well. This is the stone which was rejected by you builders, but which has become the head of the corner. And there is salvation in no one else, for there is no other name under heaven given among men by which we must be saved."

When the rulers saw the boldness of Peter and John, and knowing that they were uneducated, common men, they won-

dered; and they recognized that they had
been with Jesus. But seeing the man that
had been healed standing beside them,
they had nothing to say in opposition.
Then they commanded Peter and John to
go aside out of the council, and they conferred with one another. "What shall we
do with these men?" they said. "For that a
notable sign has been performed through
them we cannot deny. In order that it may
spread no further among the people, let us
warn them to speak no more to any one in
this name." Calling the two back, they
charged them not to speak or teach at all
in the name of Jesus. But Peter and John
answered, "Whether it is right in the sight
of God to listen to you rather than to God,
you must judge. We cannot but speak of
what we have seen and heard." When the
rulers had further threatened them, they
let them go, finding no way to punish
them, because of the people; for all men
praised God for what had happened.

Afterward Peter and John reported to
their friends what the chief priests and the
elders had said, and they all lifted their
voices together to God. "Sovereign Lord,"

they prayed, "who didst make the heaven and the earth and the sea and everything in them, grant to thy servants to speak thy word with all boldness, while thou stretchest out thy hand to heal, and signs and wonders are performed through the name of thy holy servant Jesus." Then the place in which they were gathered together was shaken; and they were all filled with the Holy Spirit and spoke the word of God with boldness.

Now in the company of those who believed, no one said that any of the things which he possessed was his own. Those who had lands or houses sold them, and laid the proceeds at the apostles' feet. But a man named Ananias sold a piece of property, and with his wife's knowledge secretly kept back some of the proceeds. At this Peter said, "Ananias, why has Satan filled your heart to lie to the Holy Spirit? While the land remained unsold, was it not your own? And after it was sold, was it not at your disposal? You have not lied to men but to God." When Ananias heard these words, he fell down and died, and the young men wrapped him up and carried him out and buried him. About three hours later his wife, Sapphira, came in, not knowing what had happened. "Tell me," said Peter, "whether you sold the land for so much." She said, "Yes, for so much." Then Peter said to her, "How is it that you have agreed together to tempt the Spirit of the Lord? Hark, the feet of those that have buried your husband are at the door, and they will carry you out." Immediately she fell down and died. The young men carried her out and buried her beside her husband, and great fear came upon all who heard of these things.

Many signs and wonders were done by the hands of the apostles, and people even carried out the sick into the streets, and laid them on pallets, that as Peter came by at least his shadow might fall on them. From the towns around Jerusalem the sick were brought, and those afflicted with unclean spirits, and they were all healed. But at this the high priest and those with him, that is, the party of the Sadducees, were filled with jealousy. So they arrested the apostles and put them in the common prison. That night an angel of the Lord opened the prison doors and brought them out, saying, "Go and stand in the temple and speak to the people all the words of this Life." And at daybreak they entered the temple and taught.

Now the high priest called together the council and all the senate of Israel, and sent to the prison for the apostles. When the officers returned they reported, "We found the prison securely locked and the sentries standing at the doors, but when we opened it we found no one inside." At first the chief priests were much perplexed; then some one came and told them that the apostles were teaching in the temple. So the officers went and brought them, but without violence, for they were afraid of being stoned by the people.

Setting the apostles before the council, the high priest questioned them. "We strictly charged you," he said, "not to teach in this name, yet here you have filled Jerusalem with your teaching and you intend to bring this man's blood upon us."

"We must obey God rather than men," they answered. "The God of our fathers raised Jesus whom you killed by hanging him on a tree. God exalted him at his right hand as Leader and Savior, to give repentance to Israel and forgiveness of sins. And we are witnesses to these things, and so is the Holy Spirit whom God has given to those who obey him."

At this the council was enraged and wanted to kill them. But a Pharisee named Gamaliel, a teacher held in honor by all the people, stood up and ordered the apostles to be put outside. "Men of Israel," he said to the council, "take care what you do. For before these days Theudas arose, giving himself out to be somebody, and about four hundred men joined him; but he was slain and his movement came to nothing. After him Judas the Galilean drew some of the people after him, but he also perished. So in the present case I tell you, let these men alone. If this undertaking is of men, it will fail; but if it is of God, you will not be able to overthrow them. You might even be found opposing God!" They called in the apostles, beat them, charged them not to speak in the name of Jesus, then let them go. And every day in the temple and at home the apostles did not cease preaching Jesus as the Christ.

Now in these days when the disciples were increasing in number, the Hellenists murmured against the Hebrews because their widows were neglected in the daily distribution. So the twelve summoned the disciples and said, "It is not right that we should give up preaching the word of God to serve tables. Therefore, brethren, pick out from among you seven men of good repute, full of the Spirit and of wisdom, whom we may appoint to this duty. We will devote ourselves to prayer and to the ministry of the word." This pleased the whole multitude, so they chose the seven and set them before the apostles, who prayed and laid hands upon them.

One of the seven was a man named Stephen. Full of grace and power, he did great wonders and signs among the people, and also disputed with those who belonged to the synagogue of the Freedmen, and others. But none could withstand the wisdom and the Spirit with which he spoke, so they secretly instigated men who said, "We have heard him speak blasphemous words against Moses and God."

They also stirred up the people and the elders and the scribes. Finally they seized Stephen, brought him before the council, and set up false witnesses who said, "This man never ceases to speak words against this holy place and the law. We have heard him say that this Jesus of Nazareth will destroy this place, and will change the customs which Moses delivered to us."

"Is this so?" asked the high priest.

"Brethren, hear me," said Stephen. "The God of glory appeared to our father Abraham, and gave him the covenant of circumcision. And Abraham became the father of Isaac, and Isaac of Jacob, and Jacob of the twelve patriarchs. And the patriarchs, jealous of Joseph, sold him into Egypt; but God was with him, and rescued him out of all his afflictions. Then in Egypt God raised up Moses, and he led the people out, having performed wonders and signs in Egypt and at the Red Sea and in the wilderness. But our fathers refused to obey him. They thrust him aside, and they made a calf and offered a sacrifice to the idol and rejoiced in the works of their hands. Our fathers had the tent of witness in the wilderness, and so it was until Solomon built the temple, yet the Most High does not dwell in houses made with hands. As the prophet says, 'Heaven is my throne, and earth my footstool.'

"You stiff-necked people, uncircumcised in heart and ears! You always resist the Holy Spirit. As your fathers did, so do you. Which of the prophets did not your fathers persecute? They killed those who announced beforehand the coming of the Righteous One, whom you have now betrayed and murdered, you who received the law as delivered by angels and did not keep it."

When they heard these things they were enraged, and they ground their teeth against Stephen. But he, full of the Holy Spirit, gazed into heaven and saw the glory of God, and Jesus standing at his right hand. And Stephen's face was like the face of an angel. "Behold, I see the heavens opened," he said, "and the Son of man standing at the right hand of God." Then they cried out with a loud voice and stopped their ears and rushed together upon him. They cast him out of the city and stoned him, and as they were stoning him he prayed, "Lord Jesus, receive my spirit." Then he knelt down and cried with a loud voice, "Lord, do not hold this sin against them." And he fell asleep, and he was buried by devout men who made great lamentation over him.

Those who threw the stones had laid their garments at the feet of a man named Saul, who was consenting to Stephen's death. Now on that day a great persecution arose against the church in Jerusalem, and all except the apostles were scattered throughout the region of Judea and Samaria. Saul himself began ravaging the church, and entering house after house, he dragged off men and women and committed them to prison.

Those who were scattered went about preaching the word. Philip proclaimed the Christ in the city of Samaria, and the multitudes with one accord gave heed to what he said when they saw the signs he did; unclean spirits came out of many who were possessed, and many who were paralyzed or lame were healed. Also in Samaria there was a man named Simon, a magician, who amazed every one. All gave heed to him, from the least to the greatest, saying, "This man is that power of God which is called Great." But when Philip preached the good news about the kingdom of God and Jesus Christ, even Simon himself believed, and after being baptized he continued with Philip. But Simon's heart was not right before God.

When the apostles at Jerusalem heard that many Samaritans had received the word of God and been baptized, but that the Holy Spirit had not yet fallen on any of them, they sent Peter and John. The two laid their hands on them and they received the Holy Spirit. When Simon saw this, he offered them money. "Give me this power," he said, "that any one on whom I lay my hands may receive the Holy Spirit."

"Your silver perish with you," said Peter, "because you thought you could obtain the gift of God with money! Repent and pray to the Lord that, if possible, this may be forgiven you. For I see that you are in the gall of bitterness and the bond of iniquity."

"Pray for me to the Lord," Simon answered, "that nothing of what you have said may come upon me." Peter and John then returned to Jerusalem, preaching the gospel to many villages of the Samaritans.

Now an angel of the Lord said to Philip, "Rise and go toward the south to the road that goes down from Jerusalem to Gaza." Philip went, and behold, he saw an Ethiopian, a eunuch, a minister of the Candace, queen of Ethiopia. He had come to Jerusalem to worship and was returning; seated in his chariot, he was reading aloud the prophet Isaiah. To Philip the Spirit said, "Go up and join this chariot." Philip ran up, heard him reading Isaiah, and asked, "Do you understand what you are reading?"

"How can I, unless some one guides me?" the eunuch replied, inviting Philip to sit with him. Now the passage he was reading was this: "As a sheep led to the slaughter or a lamb before its shearer is dumb, so he opens not his mouth. In his humiliation justice was denied him. Who can describe his generation? For his life is taken up from the earth."

"About whom," the eunuch asked,

"does the prophet say this, about himself or about some one else?"

Then Philip, beginning with this scripture, told the good news of Jesus. As they went along the road they came to some water, and the eunuch said, "See, here is water! What is to prevent my being baptized?" He commanded the chariot to stop, and they both went down into the water, and the eunuch was baptized. And the Spirit of the Lord caught up Philip, and the eunuch saw him no more, and he went on his way rejoicing. But Philip was found at Azotus, and he preached the gospel to all the towns till he came to Caesarea.

About this time Saul, still breathing threats against the disciples, went to the high priest and asked for letters to the synagogues at Damascus, so that if he found any there belonging to the Way he might bring them bound to Jerusalem. Now as he approached Damascus on his journey, a light from heaven suddenly flashed about him. He fell to the ground and he heard a voice saying, "Saul, Saul, why do you persecute me?"

"Who are you, Lord?" Saul asked.

"I am Jesus, whom you are persecuting," said the voice. "But rise and enter the city, and you will be told what you are to do."

The men who were traveling with Saul stood speechless, hearing the voice but seeing no one. Saul arose, but he was without sight, so they led him by the hand into Damascus, and for three days he neither ate nor drank.

At Damascus there was a disciple named Ananias. To him the Lord said in a vision, "Rise and go to the street called Straight, and inquire in the house of Judas for a man of Tarsus named Saul; for behold, he is praying, and he has seen a man named Ananias come in and lay his hands on him so that he might regain his sight."

"Lord," Ananias answered, "I have heard from many about this man, how much evil he has done to thy saints at Jerusalem. He has authority from the chief priests to bind all who call upon thy name."

But the Lord said, "Go, for he is a chosen instrument of mine to carry my name before the Gentiles and kings and the sons of Israel; for I will show him how much he must suffer for the sake of my name."

Ananias departed, entered the house, and laid his hands on Saul. "Brother," he said, "the Lord Jesus, who appeared to you on the road by which you came, has sent me that you may regain your sight and be filled with the Holy Spirit." Immediately something like scales fell from Saul's eyes and he regained his sight. Then he rose and was baptized, and took food and was strengthened. Several days later, in the synagogues of Damascus, he proclaimed Jesus, saying, "He is the Son of God."

All who heard Saul were amazed. "Is not this the man who made havoc in Jerusalem of those who called on this name?" they said. "Has he not come here to bring them bound before the chief priests?" But Saul increased all the more in strength, and confounded the Jews who lived in Damascus by proving that Jesus was the Christ. At last the Jews plotted to kill him, and they were watching the gates night and day. The plot became known to Saul, so his disciples took him by night and let him down over the wall in a basket.

Going to Jerusalem, Saul attempted to join the disciples. But they were all afraid of him, for they did not believe that he had changed. Then Barnabas (a Levite and a native of Cyprus, whose name means Son of encouragement) brought him to the apostles, and told how, on the road to Damascus, Saul had seen and heard the Lord, and how he had afterward preached boldly in the name of Jesus. So Saul was accepted, and for a time he went in and out among them at Jerusalem. But when he spoke and disputed against the Hellenists, they were displeased and began seeking to kill him. When the brethren heard this, they brought Saul to Caesarea, then to Tarsus.

In those days, as Peter traveled here and there among the brethren, he visited the saints that lived at Lydda. A man was there named Aeneas, who had been bedridden for eight years and was paralyzed. Peter spoke to him, saying, "Aeneas, Jesus Christ heals you; rise and make your bed." Immediately he rose, and all the residents of Lydda saw him, and they turned to the

Lord. After this, at Joppa, which was near Lydda, a disciple named Tabitha, full of good works and charity, fell sick and died. Hearing that Peter was at Lydda, the disciples sent men to entreat him to come without delay. Peter went with them, and at Joppa they took him to an upper room where all the widows were gathered, weeping and showing tunics and other garments which Tabitha had made. Putting them all outside, Peter knelt down and prayed. Then, turning to the body, he said, "Tabitha, rise." She opened her eyes, and when she saw Peter she sat up. He gave her his hand and lifted her from the bed. Then, calling the saints and widows, he presented her alive. This became known throughout all Joppa, and many believed in the Lord.

At Caesarea there was a man named Cornelius, a centurion of the Italian Cohort, a devout man who feared God with all his household, who gave alms liberally and prayed constantly. One day he saw clearly in a vision an angel of God, and he stared at the angel in terror. "Cornelius," said the angel, "your prayers and your alms have ascended as a memorial before God. Now send men to Joppa, and bring one Simon who is called Peter; he is lodging with Simon, a tanner, whose house is by the seaside." Then Cornelius called two of his servants and a devout soldier and sent them off.

The next day, as the three men were nearing Joppa, Peter went up on the housetop to pray. He became hungry and asked for something to eat, but while food was being prepared, he fell into a trance. He saw the heaven opened, and something descending, like a great sheet, let down by its four corners upon the earth. In it were all kinds of animals and reptiles and birds of the air. And there came a voice: "Rise, Peter, kill and eat."

"No, Lord," said Peter, "for I have never eaten anything that is common or unclean." The voice came again: "What God has cleansed, you must not call common." This happened three times; then the thing was taken up at once to heaven.

While Peter was inwardly perplexed as to what the vision might mean, the men sent by Cornelius stood before the gate and called out to ask whether Peter was lodging there. To Peter the Spirit said, "Behold, three men are looking for you. Rise and go down, and accompany them without hesitation; for I have sent them." Peter went down and said, "I am the one you are looking for; what is the reason for your coming?"

"Cornelius, a centurion," they said, "an upright and God-fearing man, well spoken of by the whole Jewish nation, was directed by a holy angel to send for you, to hear what you have to say." Peter called them in to be his guests that night, and the next day he went off with them, accompanied by some of the brethren.

At Caesarea, Cornelius was expecting them, and he had called together his kinsmen and close friends. When Peter entered, Cornelius met him and, falling down at his feet, worshiped him. "Stand up," said Peter, lifting him, "I too am a man." Inside he found many persons gathered. "You yourselves know," Peter said to them, "how unlawful it is for a Jew to associate with or to visit any one of another nation. But God has shown me that I should not call any man common or unclean. So when I was sent for, I came without objection. I ask then why you sent for me."

Then Cornelius told Peter about his vision. "Now therefore," he said, "we are all here present in the sight of God, to hear all that you have been commanded by the Lord."

"Truly," answered Peter, "I perceive that God shows no partiality, but in every nation any one who fears him and does what is right is acceptable to him. You know the word which he sent to Israel, preaching good news of peace by Jesus Christ, the word which was proclaimed throughout all Judea: how God anointed Jesus of Nazareth with the Holy Spirit and with power, how he went about doing good and healing all that were oppressed by the devil, how they put him to death by hanging him on a tree, and how God raised him on the third day and made him manifest, not to all the people but to us who were chosen by God as witnesses, who ate and drank with him after he rose from the dead. And Jesus commanded us to preach to the people, and to testify that he is the one ordained by God to be judge of the living and the dead. To him all the prophets bear witness that every one who believes in him receives forgiveness of sins through his name."

While Peter was talking, the Holy Spirit fell on those listening, and they began speaking in tongues and extolling God. The brethren who came with Peter were amazed, because the gift of the Holy Spirit had been poured out even on the Gentiles. Then Peter declared, "Can any one forbid water for baptizing these people who have received the Holy Spirit just as we have?" And he commanded them to be baptized in the name of Jesus Christ.

Now the apostles and the brethren who were in Judea heard how the Gentiles at Caesarea had received the word of God. So when Peter went up to Jerusalem, the circumcision party criticized him. "Why did you go to uncircumcised men and eat with them?" they asked. Peter explained all that had happened at Joppa and at Caesarea. "The Holy Spirit fell on them," he said, "just as on us at the beginning. And I remembered the word of the Lord, how he said, 'John baptized with water, but you shall be baptized with the Holy Spirit.' If then God gave the same gift to them as he gave to us, who was I that I could withstand God?" When they heard this they glorified God, saying, "Then to the Gentiles also God has granted repentance unto life."

Those who scattered because of the persecution that arose over Stephen traveled as far as Phoenicia and Cyprus and Antioch, speaking the word to none except Jews. But in Antioch there were some who spoke to the Greeks also, preaching the Lord Jesus, and a great number believed. When news of this came to the church in Jerusalem, they sent Barnabas, a man full of the Holy Spirit, to Antioch. And he saw the grace of God and was glad, and he exhorted them all to remain faithful. Then he went to Tarsus to look for Saul, so that he might help in the work. When he had found him, he brought him to Antioch, and for a whole year they met with the church, teaching a large company of people. It was in Antioch that the disciples were for the first time called Christians.

In these days a prophet named Agabus came from Jerusalem to Antioch, and he foretold that there would be a great famine over all the world. This did take place in the days of Claudius, and the disciples at Antioch determined, every one according to his ability, to send relief to the brethren in Judea. They sent it by the hand of Barnabas and Saul, and when they had fulfilled their mission they returned, bringing with them John, whose other name was Mark.

About that time Herod the king laid violent hands upon some in the church. He killed James, the son of Zebedee, with the sword, and he arrested Peter, whom he put in prison. The night before Herod was to bring him out for trial, Peter was sleeping between two soldiers, bound with two chains, and there were sentries at the door. And behold, an angel of the Lord appeared, and a light shone in the cell. Striking Peter on the side, the angel said, "Get up quickly," and the chains fell off Peter's hands. "Put on your sandals," said the angel, "wrap your mantle around you and follow me." Peter thought he was seeing a vision, but he followed the angel. When they had passed the first and the second guard, they came to an iron gate. It opened to them of its own accord. They went out and passed on through one street; then the angel left him, and Peter came to himself. "Now I am sure," he said, "that the Lord has sent his angel and rescued me from the hand of Herod."

He went to the house of Mary, the mother of Mark, where many were gathered together and were praying for him. When he knocked at the door of the gateway, a maid named Rhoda came to answer. Recognizing Peter's voice, in her joy she did not open the gate but ran in and said that it was Peter.

"You are mad," they said. But she insisted that it was so. "It is his angel!" they said.

Peter continued knocking, and when they opened they saw him and were amazed. Motioning to them with his hand to be silent, he described how the Lord had brought him out of prison. "Tell this to all the brethren," he said. Then he departed and went to another place.

Next day there was no small stir among the guards over what had become of Peter. When Herod sought for him and could not find him, he examined the sentries and ordered that they be put to death. Then Herod went down from Judea to Caesarea, where an angel of the Lord smote him; and he was eaten by worms and died.

IN THE CHURCH at Antioch, among the prophets and teachers were Barnabas and Saul. Concerning these two the Holy Spirit said, "Set them apart for me, for the work to which I have called them." After fasting and praying, and the laying on of hands, they were sent off, with Mark to assist them.

The three sailed to Cyprus, and when they reached Salamis they proclaimed the word of God in the synagogues of the Jews. Going through the whole island as far as Paphos, they came upon a certain magician, a Jewish false prophet, named Elymas. He served the proconsul, Sergius Paulus, a man of intelligence, who summoned Barnabas and Saul and sought to hear the word of God. But Elymas withstood them, seeking to turn away the proconsul from the faith. Saul (who is also called Paul) was filled with the Holy Spirit, and he looked intently at Elymas. "You son of the devil," he said, "you enemy of all righteousness, full of all deceit and villainy, will you not stop making crooked the straight paths of the Lord? Behold, the hand of the Lord is upon you, and you shall be blind and unable to see the sun for a time." Immediately mist and darkness fell upon Elymas, and he went about seeking people to lead him by the hand. Then the proconsul, when he saw what had occurred, believed the teaching of the Lord.

Setting sail from Paphos, Paul and his company came to Perga in Pamphylia, where Mark left them to return to Jerusalem. They passed on to Antioch of Pisidia, and on the sabbath day they went into the synagogue and sat down. After the reading of the law and the prophets, the rulers of the synagogue said to them, "Brethren, if you have any word of exhortation for the people, say it." Paul stood up, and motioning with his hand, he spoke, reminding the people how God had given them their land as an inheritance, and then had raised up for them judges, and Samuel the prophet, and when the people asked for a king had given them Saul for forty years, and then had raised up David.

"Of this man's posterity," said Paul, "God has brought to Israel a Savior, Jesus, as he promised. Brethren, sons of the family of Abraham, and those among you that fear God, to us has been sent the message of this salvation. Those who live in Jerusalem and their rulers, because they did not recognize Jesus or understand the utterances of the prophets, fulfilled these by condemning him. Though they could charge him with nothing deserving death, yet they asked Pilate to have him killed. And when they had fulfilled all that was written of him, they took him down from the tree, and laid him in a tomb. But God raised him from the dead; and for many days he appeared to those who came up with him from Galilee to Jerusalem, who are now his witnesses to the people. And we bring you the good news that what God promised to the fathers, this he has fulfilled to us their children by raising Jesus. As it is written in the second psalm, 'Thou art my Son, today I have begotten thee.' And as for the fact that he raised him from the dead, he spoke in this way in another psalm, 'Thou wilt not let thy Holy One see corruption.' Let it be known to you therefore, brethren, that through this man forgiveness of sins is proclaimed to you. By him every one that believes is freed from everything from which you could not be freed by the law of Moses. Beware, therefore, lest there come upon you what is said in the prophets: 'Behold, you scoffers, and wonder, and perish; for I do a deed in your days, a deed you will never believe, if one declares it to you.' "

As they left the synagogue, the people begged that more about these things might be told them the next sabbath, and many followed Paul and Barnabas, who spoke to them and urged them to continue in the grace of God. The next sabbath almost the whole city gathered together to hear the word of God. But when certain Jews saw the multitudes, they were filled with jealousy, and contradicted what was spoken by Paul, and reviled him. Then Paul said boldly, "It was necessary that the word of God should be spoken first to you. Since you thrust it from you, and judge yourselves unworthy of eternal life, behold, we turn to the Gentiles. For so the Lord has commanded us, saying, 'I have set you to be a light for the Gentiles, that you may bring salvation to the uttermost parts of the earth.' "

But the Jews incited the devout women of high standing and the leading men of the city, and they stirred up persecution against Paul and Barnabas, and drove them out of their district. Filled with joy and with the Holy Spirit, they shook off the dust from their feet against them, and went to Iconium. Here they entered the Jewish synagogue, and so spoke that a great company believed. Speaking boldly for the Lord, who granted signs and wonders to be done by their hands, they remained for a long time in Iconium. But the unbelieving Jews stirred up the Gentiles and poisoned their minds against the brethren, and the people of the city were divided, some siding with the Jews, some with the apostles. When an attempt was made by both Gentiles and Jews to molest the two and to stone them, they learned of it and fled to Lystra and Derbe, cities of Lycaonia.

Now at Lystra there was a man who was a cripple from birth. As he listened to Paul speaking, Paul looked intently at him and saw that he had faith to be made well. "Stand upright on your feet," said Paul in a loud voice. And the man sprang up and walked. When the crowds saw what Paul had done, they lifted up their voices, saying, "The gods have come down to us in the likeness of men!" Barnabas they called Zeus, and Paul, because he was the chief speaker, they called Hermes. The priest of Zeus brought oxen and garlands and wanted to offer sacrifice to them with the people.

At this Barnabas and Paul tore their garments and rushed out among the multitude. "Men, why are you doing this?" they cried. "We also are men, of like nature with you, and bring you good news, that you should turn from these vain things to a living God who made the heaven and the earth and the sea and all that is in them. In past generations he allowed all the nations to walk in their own ways; yet he did not leave himself without witness, for he did good and gave you from heaven rains and fruitful seasons, satisfying your hearts with food and gladness." With these words they scarcely restrained the people from offering sacrifice to them.

Later, Jews came to Lystra from Antioch and Iconium, and they managed to persuade the people against the apostles. They stoned Paul and dragged him out of the city, supposing that he was dead. But when the disciples gathered about him, he rose up and entered the city. The next day he went on with Barnabas to Derbe, where they preached the gospel and made many disciples. Then they returned to Lystra and to Iconium and to Antioch, strengthening the souls of the disciples and saying that through many tribulations we must enter the kingdom of God. And in every church, after prayer and fasting, they appointed elders.

They passed through Pamphylia, and when they had spoken the word in Perga, they went down to Attalia, from where they sailed back to Antioch. Here they gathered the church together and declared all that God had done with them, and how he had opened a door of faith to the Gentiles.

Afterward some of the brethren came to Antioch from Judea and were teaching, "Unless you are circumcised according to the custom of Moses, you cannot be saved." Paul and Barnabas had no small dissension and debate with them about this question, and the two, with some of the others, were appointed to go up to Jerusalem to confer with the apostles and elders. At Jerusalem they were welcomed by the church and declared all that God had done with them. But some believers who belonged to the party of the Pharisees rose up and said, "It is necessary to circumcise the Gentiles, and to charge them to keep the law of Moses." To consider this matter, the apostles and elders gathered together, and after much debate, Peter arose.

"Brethren," he said, "you know that in the early days God made choice among you, that by my mouth the Gentiles should hear the word of the gospel and believe. And God who knows the heart bore witness to them, giving them the Holy Spirit just as he did to us; he made no distinction between us and them, but cleansed their hearts by faith. Now therefore why do you make trial of God by putting a yoke upon the neck of the disciples which neither our fathers nor we have been able to bear? But we believe that we shall be saved through the grace of the Lord Jesus, just as they will."

The assembly then listened to Barnabas and Paul as they related what signs and wonders God had done through them among the Gentiles. After they finished speaking, James, the brother of the Lord, arose. "Brethren, listen to me," he said. "Peter has related how God first visited the Gentiles, to take out of them a people for his name. And with this the words of the prophets agree, as it is written, 'After this I will return, and I will rebuild the dwelling of David, which has fallen; I will rebuild its ruins, and I will set it up, that the rest of men may seek the Lord, and all

the Gentiles who are called by my name,
says the Lord, who has made these things
known from of old.' Therefore my judgment is that we should not trouble those of
the Gentiles who turn to God, but should
write to them to abstain from the pollu-
tions of idols and from unchastity and
from what is strangled and from blood.
For from early generations Moses has had
in every city those who preach him, for he
is read every sabbath in the synagogues."

Then the apostles and the elders, with
the whole church, chose men to send to
Antioch with Paul and Barnabas. They
sent Judas, called Barsabbas, and Silas,
leading men among the brethren, with the
following letter:

The brethren, both the apostles and the
elders, to the brethren who are of the Gentiles in Antioch and Syria and Cilicia, greeting. Since we have heard that some persons
from us have troubled you with words, un-
settling your minds, although we gave them
no instructions, it has seemed good to us,
having come to one accord, to choose men
and send them to you with our beloved
Barnabas and Paul, men who have risked

their lives for the sake of our Lord Jesus
Christ. We have therefore sent Judas and
Silas, who themselves will tell you the same
things by word of mouth. For it has seemed
good to the Holy Spirit and to us to lay
upon you no greater burden than these necessary things: that you abstain from what
has been sacrificed to idols and from blood
and from what is strangled and from unchastity. If you keep yourselves from these,
you will do well. Farewell.

At Antioch, having gathered the congregation together, they read the letter, and
the brethren rejoiced. Judas and Silas, after
some time, were sent off in peace, but Paul
and Barnabas remained in Antioch, teaching and preaching the word of the Lord.

After some days Paul said to Barnabas,
"Come, let us return and visit the brethren
in every city where we proclaimed the
word of the Lord, and see how they are."
Barnabas wanted to take Mark with them,
but Paul thought best not to take one who
had withdrawn in Pamphylia, and had not
gone with them to the work. There arose a
sharp contention, so that they separated
from each other. Then Barnabas took

Mark with him and sailed away to Cyprus. Paul chose Silas and departed for Syria and Cilicia.

At Lystra there was a disciple named Timothy, the son of a Jewish woman, who was a believer, and a Greek father. He was well spoken of by the brethren. Paul wanted Timothy to accompany him, so he had him circumcised, because of the Jews that were in those places, for they all knew that his father was a Greek. As they went through the cities, they delivered the decisions which had been reached at Jerusalem. So the churches were strengthened in the faith, and they increased in numbers daily.

When they had come opposite Mysia, they attempted to go into Bithynia, but the Spirit of Jesus did not allow them, so they went down to Troas. Here a vision appeared to Paul in the night: a man of Macedonia was beseeching him, "Come over to Macedonia and help us." Immediately we set sail for Macedonia, concluding that God had called us to preach the gospel there.

We made a direct voyage to Samothrace, then to Neapolis, and from there to Philippi, the leading city of Macedonia and a Roman colony. We remained some days, and on the sabbath we went outside the gate to the riverside, where there was a place of prayer, and spoke to the women who had come there. One who heard was Lydia, a seller of purple goods, who was a worshiper of God. The Lord opened her heart to what was said by Paul, and when she was baptized, she said, "If you have judged me to be faithful to the Lord, come to my house and stay." And she prevailed upon us.

Another day, as we were going to the place of prayer, we were met by a slave girl who had a spirit of divination and brought her owners much gain by soothsaying. She followed us, crying, "These men are servants of the Most High God, who proclaim to you the way of salvation." She did this for many days, and at last Paul was annoyed. "In the name of Jesus Christ," he said to the spirit, "come out of her." And it came out that very hour.

But when the girl's owners saw that their hope of gain was gone, they seized

Paul and Silas and dragged them into the market place before the magistrates. "These men are Jews," they said, "and they are disturbing our city. They advocate customs which it is not lawful for us Romans to accept or practice." The crowd joined in attacking them, and the magistrates tore the garments off them and gave orders to beat them with rods. And when they had inflicted many blows upon them, they threw them into prison, and their feet were fastened in the stocks.

About midnight Paul and Silas were praying and singing hymns, and the prisoners were listening to them. Suddenly there was a great earthquake, so that the foundations of the prison were shaken. Immediately all the doors were opened and every one's fetters were unfastened. When the jailer woke and saw that the prison doors were open, he supposed that the prisoners had escaped. He drew his sword and was about to kill himself when Paul cried loudly, "Do not harm yourself, for we are all here." The jailer called for lights and rushed in, and trembling with fear he fell down before Paul and Silas. Then he brought them out and took them to his house and washed their wounds. "Men," he said, "what must I do to be saved?"

"Believe in the Lord Jesus," they said, "and you will be saved, you and your household." And they spoke the word of the Lord to him and to all that were in his house. He was baptized at once, with all his family; then he set food before them, and rejoiced that he had believed in God.

When it was day, the magistrates sent the police, saying, "Let those men go." The jailer told Paul, but Paul said, "They have beaten us publicly, uncondemned, men who are Roman citizens, and have thrown us into prison. Do they now cast us out secretly? No! Let them come themselves and take us out." The police reported these words to the magistrates, who were afraid when they heard that Paul and Silas were Roman citizens. They came and apologized to them, took them out, and asked them to leave the city. When the two had exhorted the brethren, they departed.

Next they came to Thessalonica, where there was a synagogue of the Jews. As was his custom, Paul went in, and for three weeks he argued with them from the scriptures, explaining and proving that it was necessary for the Christ to suffer and to rise from the dead. "This Jesus," he said, "whom I proclaim to you, is the Christ." Some were persuaded and joined Paul and Silas, as did a great many of the devout Greeks and the leading women. But others of the Jews were jealous, and taking some wicked fellows of the rabble, they gathered a crowd, set the city in an uproar, and attacked the house of Jason, where Paul and Silas were staying. When they could not find them they dragged Jason and some of the brethren before the city authorities. "These men who have turned the world upside down," they cried, "have come here also, and Jason has received them; and they are all acting against the decrees of Caesar, saying that there is another king, Jesus." But when the authorities had taken security from Jason and the rest, they let them go.

The brethren immediately sent Paul and Silas away by night to Beroea, where they went into the Jewish synagogue. Now these

Jews received the word with all eagerness, examining the scriptures to see if these things were so, and many believed. But when the Jews of Thessalonica learned of this, they came there too, stirring up and inciting the crowds. Then the brethren sent Paul off to Athens, with Silas and Timothy to follow as soon as possible.

At Athens, Paul saw that the city was full of idols, and his spirit was provoked. He argued in the synagogue with the Jews and the devout persons, and in the market place every day with those who chanced to be there. Some also of the Epicurean and Stoic philosophers met him. "He seems to be a preacher of foreign divinities," they said, because he preached Jesus and the resurrection. They brought him to the Areopagus, saying, "May we know what this new teaching is which you present? For you bring some strange things to our ears." Now all the Athenians and the foreigners who lived there spent their time in nothing except telling or hearing something new.

Paul stood in the middle of the Areopagus and spoke. "Men of Athens," he said,

"I perceive that in every way you are very religious. For as I passed along and observed the objects of your worship, I found an altar with this inscription, 'To an unknown god.' What therefore you worship as unknown, this I proclaim to you. The God who made the world and everything in it, being Lord of heaven and earth, does not live in shrines made by man, nor is he served by human hands, as though he needed anything, since he himself gives to all men life and breath and everything. And he made from one every nation of men to live on all the face of the earth, having determined allotted periods and the boundaries of their habitation, that they should seek God, in the hope that they might feel after him and find him. Yet he is not far from each one of us, for 'In him we live and move and have our being'; as even some of your poets have said, 'For we are indeed his offspring.' Being then God's offspring, we ought not to think that the Deity is like gold, or silver, or stone, a representation by the art and imagination of man. The times of ignorance God overlooked, but now he commands all men everywhere to repent, because he has fixed a day on which he will judge the world in righteousness by a man whom he has appointed, and of this he has given assurance to all men by raising him from the dead."

When the listeners heard Paul speak of the resurrection of the dead, some mocked; others said, "We will hear you again about this." But some joined Paul and believed, among them Dionysius the Areopagite and a woman named Damaris.

After this Paul went to Corinth. Here he found a Jew named Aquila, lately come from Italy with his wife, Priscilla, after all Jews had been commanded to leave Rome. Because he was of the same trade he stayed with them, and they worked, for they were tentmakers. When Silas and Timothy arrived, Paul was occupied with testifying to the Jews that the Christ was Jesus. But when they opposed him, he shook out his garments and said, "Your blood be upon your heads! I am innocent. From now on I will go to the Gentiles."

Next door to the synagogue was the house of a man named Titius Justus, a worshiper of God. Here Paul preached, and Crispus, the ruler of the synagogue, believed in the Lord, together with all his household; and many Corinthians believed and were baptized. Then one night in a vision the Lord said to Paul, "Do not be afraid, but speak and do not be silent; for I am with you, and no man shall attack you to harm you; for I have many people in this city." For a year and six months Paul stayed in Corinth, teaching the word of God.

After this Paul took leave of the brethren, and with Priscilla and Aquila he sailed for Syria. At Cenchreae he cut his hair, for he had taken a vow of thanksgiving. At Ephesus he went into the synagogue and argued with the Jews. When they asked him to stay longer, he declined. "I will return to you if God wills," he said, and he set sail from Ephesus, leaving Priscilla and Aquila behind. At Caesarea he greeted the church, and then went down to Antioch, where he spent some time. Then he departed and went from place to place through Galatia and Phrygia, strengthening all the disciples.

Now a Jew named Apollos, an eloquent man, well versed in the scriptures, came to

Ephesus. He knew the way of the Lord, and being fervent in spirit, he spoke and taught accurately the things concerning Jesus, though he knew only the baptism of John. But when Priscilla and Aquila heard him speaking in the synagogue, they expounded to him the way of God more accurately. When he wished to go to Corinth, the brethren wrote to the disciples to receive him, and he greatly helped those who through grace had believed. In public he powerfully confuted the Jews, showing by the scriptures that the Christ was Jesus.

While Apollos was at Corinth, Paul came back to Ephesus, where he found some disciples of Apollos, about twelve in all. "Did you receive the Holy Spirit when you believed?" he asked.

"No," they said, "we have never even heard that there is a Holy Spirit."

"Into what then," he said, "were you baptized?"

"Into John's baptism," they answered.

"John baptized with the baptism of repentance," Paul said, "telling the people to believe in the one who was to come after him, that is, Jesus."

On hearing this, they were baptized in the name of the Lord Jesus. And when Paul had laid his hands upon them, the Holy Spirit came on them; and they spoke with tongues and prophesied. Paul continued at Ephesus for two years, speaking in the hall of Tyrannus, so that all the residents of Asia heard the word of the Lord, both Jews and Greeks.

God did extraordinary miracles by the hands of Paul. When handkerchiefs or aprons were carried from his body to the sick, diseases and evil spirits left them. Seeing these things, some Jewish exorcists undertook to pronounce the name of the Lord Jesus over those who had evil spirits, saying, "I adjure you by the Jesus whom Paul preaches." Once the evil spirit answered them, "Jesus I know, and Paul I know; but who are you?" And the man who had the evil spirit leaped and overpowered them, so that they fled naked and wounded. This became known to the Jews and Greeks of Ephesus, and fear fell upon them all. Many who were believers came, confessing and divulging their practices; some who practiced magic arts brought their books together and burned them. So the word of the Lord grew and prevailed mightily.

About this time there arose no little stir concerning the Way. A silversmith named Demetrius, who made silver shrines of Artemis which brought no little business to the craftsmen, called together the workmen of like occupation. "Men, you know that from this business we have our wealth," he said. "And you see and hear that not only at Ephesus but almost throughout all Asia this Paul has persuaded and turned away a considerable company of people, saying that gods made with hands are not gods. There is danger not only that this trade of ours may come into disrepute but also that the temple of the great goddess Artemis may count for nothing. She may even be deposed from her magnificence, she whom all Asia and the world worship."

At this the workmen were enraged. "Great is Artemis of the Ephesians!" they cried. The city was filled with confusion, and they rushed together into the theater, dragging with them Gaius and Aristarchus,

Paul's companions. Paul wished to go in but the disciples would not let him. Now some cried one thing, some another, for the assembly was in confusion, and most did not know why they had come together. Some of the Jews put forward Alexander to make a defense, but when the people recognized that he was a Jew, for about two hours they cried out, "Great is Artemis of the Ephesians!"

Then the town clerk quieted the crowd. "Men of Ephesus," he said, "what man is there who does not know that the city of the Ephesians is temple keeper of the great Artemis, and of the sacred stone that fell from the sky? Since these things cannot be contradicted, you ought to be quiet and do nothing rash. You have brought these men here who are neither sacrilegious nor blasphemers of our goddess. If there is a complaint against any one, the courts are open. If you seek anything further, it shall be settled in the regular assembly. But we are in danger of being charged with rioting today, there being no cause that we can give to justify this commotion." He then dismissed the assembly.

After the uproar ceased, Paul sent for the disciples, and having exhorted them he departed for Macedonia and Achaia, intending to go to Jerusalem. "After I have been there," he said, "I must also see Rome." When he had gone through these parts and had given them much encouragement, he came to Troas, where he stayed for seven days.

At Troas, on the first day of the week, we gathered to break bread in an upper chamber where there were many lights. Paul talked, and he prolonged his speech until midnight. Sitting in the window was a young man named Eutychus, and he sank into a deep sleep as Paul talked. Being overcome, he fell out of the window from the third story and was taken up dead. But Paul went down and embraced him. "Do not be alarmed," he said, "for his life is in him." They took the lad away alive, and were comforted.

Paul was hastening to be at Jerusalem, if possible, on the day of Pentecost, so he had decided to sail past Ephesus. But when he reached Miletus he sent to Ephesus for the elders of the church. When they came, he spoke to them. "You yourselves know," he said, "how I lived among you all the time from the first day that I set foot in Asia, serving the Lord with all humility and with tears and with trials which befell me through the plots of the Jews. I did not shrink from declaring to you anything that was profitable, and teaching you in public and from house to house, testifying both to Jews and to Greeks of repentance to God and of faith in our Lord Jesus Christ. Now I am going to Jerusalem, bound in the Spirit, not knowing what shall befall me there, except that the Holy Spirit testifies to me that imprisonment and afflictions await me. But I do not account my life of any value nor as precious to myself, if only I may accomplish my course and the ministry which I received from the Lord Jesus, to testify to the gospel of the grace of God. You will see my face no more. Therefore I testify that I am innocent of the blood of all of you, for I did not shrink from declaring to you the whole counsel of God. Take heed to yourselves and to all the flock, in which the Holy Spirit has made you overseers, to care for the church of God which he obtained with the blood of his own Son. I know that after my departure fierce wolves will come in among you, and from among your own selves will arise men speaking perverse things, to draw away the disciples after them. Therefore be alert. Now I commend you to God and to the word of his grace, which is able to give you the inheritance among all those who are sanctified. I coveted no one's silver or gold or apparel. You yourselves know that these hands ministered to my necessities, and to those who were with me. In all things I have shown you that by so toiling one must help the weak, remembering the words of the Lord Jesus, how he said, 'It is more blessed to give than to receive.' "

When he had spoken, he knelt down and prayed, and they wept and embraced him and kissed him, sorrowing because he said they should see his face no more.

When we left Miletus, we sailed by a straight course to Cos, the next day to Rhodes, then to Patara, where we found a cargo ship crossing to Phoenicia. We passed Cyprus on the left and sailed to

Tyre, where the ship unloaded. Having sought out the disciples, we stayed at Tyre for seven days, and when we departed, all the disciples, with wives and children, accompanied us outside the city. Kneeling down, we prayed and bade one another farewell.

Sailing down the coast to Ptolemais, we greeted the brethren there and stayed one day. Next we came to Caesarea, where we stayed at the house of Philip the evangelist; he had four unmarried daughters who prophesied. While we were there, the prophet Agabus came to us from Judea. He took Paul's belt and bound his own feet and hands and said, "Thus says the Holy Spirit, 'So shall the Jews at Jerusalem bind the man who owns this belt and deliver him into the hands of the Gentiles.' " At this we and the people there begged Paul not to go up to Jerusalem.

"What are you doing," Paul answered, "weeping and breaking my heart? I am ready not only to be imprisoned but even to die at Jerusalem for the name of the Lord Jesus."

"The will of the Lord be done," we said.

After this we went up to Jerusalem, where the brethren received us gladly. To James and the elders Paul related one by one the things that God had done among the Gentiles through his ministry, and when they heard this, they glorified God. But then they cautioned him. "You see, brother," they said, "there are many thousands among the Jews of those who have believed, all zealous for the law. They have been told that you teach all the believing Jews who live among the Gentiles to forsake Moses, telling them not to circumcise their children or observe the customs. What then is to be done? They will certainly hear that you have come. Do therefore what we tell you. We have four men who are under a vow. Purify yourself along with them and pay their expenses. Thus all will know that you yourself live in observance of the law." The next day Paul purified himself with the four, and he gave notice at the temple that when the seven days of purification had been fulfilled, the offering would be presented for each of them.

When the seven days were almost completed, some Jews from Asia who had seen Paul in the temple stirred up the crowd and laid hands on him. "Men of Israel, help!" they cried. "This is the man who is teaching men everywhere against the people and the law and this place. He also brought Greeks into the temple, and he has defiled this holy place." (They had seen Trophimus the Ephesian with him in the city, and they supposed that Paul had brought him into the temple.) Then all the people ran together. They seized Paul, dragged him out of the temple, and tried to kill him.

Word of this came to the Roman tribune, and he at once took soldiers and ran down, and when the crowd saw the soldiers they stopped beating Paul. Then the tribune arrested Paul, ordered him to be bound with two chains, and inquired of the crowd who Paul was and what he had done. Some shouted one thing, some another; and since he could not learn the facts because of the uproar, the tribune ordered Paul to be brought into the barracks. The mob followed, crying, "Away with him!" and because of the violence of the crowd, Paul was actually carried up the steps by the soldiers.

As he was about to enter the barracks, Paul spoke to the tribune. "I am a Jew from Tarsus in Cilicia," he said, "a citizen of no mean city. I beg you, let me speak to the people." The tribune gave him leave, and when Paul, standing on the steps, motioned with his hand to the people, there was a great hush. "Brethren," he said in Hebrew, "hear the defense which I now make before you." When they heard that he addressed them in the Hebrew language, they were even more quiet.

"I am a Jew," Paul went on, "born at Tarsus but brought up in this city at the feet of Gamaliel, educated according to the strict law of our fathers, being zealous for God as you all are this day. At first I persecuted this Way to the death, as the high priest and the elders bear me witness. I even journeyed to Damascus to punish those also who were there. But near Damascus a great light from heaven suddenly blinded me, and I heard a voice saying, 'Saul, Saul, why do you persecute me? I am Jesus of Nazareth whom you are persecuting.' I asked what I should do, and the Lord said, 'Go into Damascus, and there you will be told.' I was led by the hand into Damascus, where a devout man came to me and said, 'Brother Saul, receive your sight.' I received my sight, and he said, 'The God of our fathers appointed you to know his will, to see the Just One and to hear a voice from his mouth; for you will be a witness for him to all men of what you have seen and heard. Rise and be baptized, and wash away your sins, calling on his name.' When I had returned to Jerusalem and was praying in the temple, I fell into a trance and saw the Lord saying to me, 'Make haste and get quickly out of Jerusalem, because they will not accept your testimony about me. Depart; for I will send you to the Gentiles.' "

Up to this the crowd had listened; now they lifted up their voices and cried, "Away with such a fellow from the earth! For he ought not to live." As they cried out and waved their garments and threw dust into the air, the tribune commanded Paul to be brought in and examined by scourging, to find out why they shouted against him. As they tied him with thongs, Paul said to the centurion standing by, "Is it lawful for you to scourge a man who is a Roman citizen, and uncondemned?" The centurion went to the tribune and said, "What are you about to do? This man is a Roman citizen." The tribune came and asked Paul, "Are you a Roman citizen?" And he said, "Yes, I was born a citizen." Instantly those who were about to scourge him withdrew.

The tribune, desiring to know the real reason why the Jews accused Paul, the next day commanded the chief priests and all the council to meet, and he set Paul before them. Looking intently at the council, Paul said, "Brethren, I have lived before God in all good conscience up to this day." At this the high priest Ananias commanded those nearby to strike him on the mouth.

"God shall strike you," Paul said, "you whitewashed wall! Are you sitting to judge me according to the law, and yet contrary to the law you order me to be struck?"

"Would you revile God's high priest?" asked those who stood by.

"I did not know, brethren," Paul answered, "that he was the high priest; for it is written, 'You shall not speak evil of a ruler of your people.' "

When Paul perceived that one part of the council were Sadducees and the other Pharisees, he cried, "Brethren, I am a Pharisee, a son of Pharisees; with respect to the resurrection of the dead I am on trial." With this a dissension arose between the two parties, for the Sadducees say that there is no resurrection, nor angel, nor spirit; but the Pharisees acknowledge them all. A great clamor arose, and some of the Pharisees stood up and contended, "We find nothing wrong in this man. What if it was a spirit or an angel that spoke to him?" When the dissension became violent, the tribune sent the soldiers to get Paul and bring him into the barracks. That night the Lord stood by Paul and said, "Take courage, for as you have testified about me at Jerusalem, so you must bear witness also at Rome."

When it was day, more than forty of the Jews made a plot to kill Paul, and they bound themselves by an oath neither to eat nor drink till they had done it. To the chief priests and elders they said, "We have bound ourselves by an oath to kill Paul. Give notice now to the tribune to bring him down to you, as though you were going to determine his case more exactly. We are ready to kill him before he comes near."

But the son of Paul's sister heard of the conspiracy, so he entered the barracks and told Paul. Calling one of the centurions, Paul said, "Take this young man to the tribune; for he has something to tell him." The centurion did so, and when the young man had told the tribune of the conspiracy, the tribune dismissed him, saying, "Tell no one that you have informed me of this." Then he called two centurions. "Tonight," he said, "get ready two hundred soldiers with seventy horsemen and two hundred spearmen to go as far as Caesarea. Provide a mount for Paul, and bring him safely to Felix the governor." Then he wrote the following letter:

Claudius Lysias to his Excellency the governor Felix, greeting. This man was seized by the Jews, and was about to be killed by them, when I came upon them with the soldiers and rescued him, having learned that he was a Roman citizen. And desiring to know the charge on which they accused him, I brought him down to their council. I found that he was accused about questions of their law, but charged with nothing deserving death or imprisonment. And when it was disclosed to me that there would be a plot against the man, I sent him to you at once, ordering his accusers also to state before you what they have against him.

The soldiers, according to their instructions, took Paul away at night and by the next day had delivered him to the governor at Caesarea. On reading the tribune's letter, Felix said, "I will hear you when your accusers arrive." After five days the high priest Ananias came down with some elders and a spokesman, one Tertullus. They laid their case before the governor, and when Paul was called, Tertullus spoke. "Through you, most excellent Felix, we enjoy much peace," he said, "and we accept this with all gratitude. But, to detain you no further, I beg you in your kindness to hear us briefly. We have found this man a pestilent fellow, an agitator among all the Jews throughout the world, and a ringleader of the sect of the Nazarenes. He even tried to profane the temple, but we seized him. By examining him yourself you will be able to learn about everything of which we accuse him."

Then the governor motioned Paul to speak, and he replied:

"Realizing that for many years you have been judge over this nation, I cheerfully make my defense. As you may ascertain, it is not more than twelve days since I went up to worship at Jerusalem; and they did not find me disputing with any one or stirring up a crowd. But this I admit, that according to the Way, which they call a sect, I worship the God of our fathers, believing everything laid down by the law or written in the prophets, having a hope in God which these themselves accept, that there will be a resurrection of both the just and the unjust. So I always take pains to have a clear conscience toward God and toward men. Now after some years I came to bring to my nation alms and offerings.

As I was doing this, some Jews from Asia found me purified in the temple, without any crowd or tumult. They ought to be here before you and to make an accusation, if they have anything against me. Or else let these men themselves say what wrongdoing they found when I stood before the council—except this one thing which I cried out, 'With respect to the resurrection of the dead I am on trial before you this day.' "

Now Felix, having a rather accurate knowledge of the Way, put the matter off. "When Lysias the tribune comes down," he said, "I will decide the case." Then he gave orders that Paul should be kept in custody but should have some liberty, and that his friends could attend to his needs.

Some days later Felix and his wife, Drusilla, who was a Jewess, visited Paul and heard him speak upon faith in Christ Jesus. As Paul argued about justice and self-control and future judgment, Felix was alarmed. "Go away for the present," he said; "when I have an opportunity I will summon you." At the same time Felix hoped that money would be given him by

Paul, so he often sent for him and conversed with him. But when two years had elapsed, Felix was succeeded by Porcius Festus. Desiring to do the Jews a favor, Felix left Paul in prison.

When Festus came into the province, he visited Jerusalem where the chief priests informed him against Paul. They asked, as a favor, to have Paul sent to Jerusalem, planning an ambush to kill him on the way. Festus replied that Paul was being kept at Caesarea. "So let the men of authority among you go down with me," he said, "and if there is anything wrong about the man, let them accuse him."

At Caesarea, Festus took his seat on the tribunal and ordered Paul to be brought. The Jews who had come from Jerusalem stood about him, bringing many serious charges which they could not prove. Festus, wishing to do the Jews a favor, said to Paul, "Do you wish to go up to Jerusalem, and there be tried on these charges before me?"

"I am standing before Caesar's tribunal," Paul answered, "where I ought to be tried. To the Jews I have done no wrong, as you know very well. If then I am a wrongdoer, and have committed anything for which I deserve to die, I do not seek to escape death. But if there is nothing in their charges against me, no one can give me up to them. I appeal to Caesar."

Festus, when he had conferred with his council, answered, "You have appealed to Caesar; to Caesar you shall go."

When some days had passed, Agrippa the king arrived at Caesarea to welcome Festus. He stayed many days, and Festus laid Paul's case before him, explaining that he was to be sent to Caesar. "I should like to hear the man myself," said Agrippa.

So the next day Agrippa entered the audience hall with the military tribunes and the prominent men of the city. Paul was brought in, and Festus said, "King Agrippa, you see this man about whom the whole Jewish people petitioned me, shouting that he ought not to live. But I found that he had done nothing deserving death; and as he himself appealed to the emperor, I decided to send him. But I have nothing definite to write about him. Therefore I have brought him before you, King Agrippa, that, after we have examined him, I may have something to write."

Agrippa said to Paul, "You have permission to speak for yourself." Then Paul, stretching out his hand, made his defense:

"I think myself fortunate that it is before you, King Agrippa, I am to make my defense. You are familiar with all customs and controversies of the Jews; therefore I beg you to listen to me patiently. My manner of life from my youth is known by all the Jews. They know that according to the strictest party of our religion I have lived as a Pharisee. And now I stand here on trial for hope in the promise made by God to our fathers. And for this hope I am accused by Jews, O king! Why is it thought incredible by any of you that God raises the dead? I myself was convinced that I ought to do many things in opposing the name of Jesus of Nazareth. I shut up many of the saints in prison, and when they were put to death I cast my vote against them. I punished them, tried to make them blaspheme, and in raging fury I persecuted them even to foreign cities. Then one day near Damascus I suddenly saw a light from heaven, brighter than the sun, and I heard a voice saying in Hebrew, 'Saul, Saul, why do you persecute me? It hurts you to kick against the goads. I am Jesus, whom you are persecuting. I will appoint you to serve and bear witness to the things in which you have seen me and to those in which I will appear to you, delivering you from the people and from the Gentiles—to whom I send you to open their eyes, that they may turn from darkness to light and from the power of Satan to God, that they may receive forgiveness of sins and a place among those who are sanctified by faith in me.'

"O King Agrippa, I was not disobedient to the heavenly vision, but declared to those at Damascus, at Jerusalem and throughout Judea, and also to the Gentiles, that they should repent and turn to God and perform deeds worthy of their repentance. For this reason the Jews seized me in the temple and tried to kill me. To this day I have had the help that comes from God, and so I stand here testifying both to small and great, saying nothing but what the prophets and Moses said would come to pass: that the Christ must suffer, and that, by being the first to rise from the dead, he would proclaim light both to the Jews and to the Gentiles."

"Paul, you are mad," said Festus in a loud voice; "your great learning is turning you mad."

"I am not mad, most excellent Festus," Paul replied, "but I am speaking the sober truth. For the king knows about these things, and to him I speak freely. I am persuaded that none of these things has escaped his notice, for this was not done in a corner. King Agrippa, do you believe the prophets? I know that you believe."

"In a short time," Agrippa said, "you think to make me a Christian!"

"Whether short or long," said Paul, "I would to God that not only you but also all who hear me this day might become such as I am—except for these chains."

Then the king and the governor rose, and those who were sitting with them; and when they had withdrawn, they said to one another, "This man is doing nothing to deserve death or imprisonment. He could have been set free if he had not appealed to Caesar."

When it was time for us to sail for Italy, they delivered Paul and some other prisoners to a centurion named Julius, who treated Paul kindly. Embarking in a ship bound for ports along the coast of Asia, we sailed east of Cyprus, and came to Myra in Lycia. There the centurion found a grain ship of Alexandria sailing for Italy, and put us on board (there were in all two hundred and seventy-six persons in the ship). We sailed slowly for a number of days, and arrived with difficulty off Cnidus, then sailed south to Crete. Coasting along with difficulty, we came to a harbor called Fair Havens. Because the season was late, the voyage was becoming dangerous, and since Fair Havens was not suitable to winter in, we sailed for Phoenix, a safer harbor of Crete. We were sailing close inshore when a tempestuous wind struck down from the land. The ship was caught and was driven seaward, violently storm-tossed. Next day the storm continued and they began to throw the cargo overboard. The third day they cast out the ship's tackle. When neither sun nor stars appeared for many days, and no small tempest lay on us, all hope of being saved was at last abandoned.

After they had been long without food, Paul came forward. "Men, I bid you take heart," he said, "for there will be no loss of life among you, but only of the ship. This very night there stood by me an angel of the God whom I worship, and he said, 'Do not be afraid, Paul; you must stand before Caesar; and lo, God has granted you all those who sail with you.' So take heart, men, for I have faith in God that it will be exactly as I have been told. But we shall have to run on some island."

When the fourteenth night had come, as we were drifting across the open sea, the sailors suspected that they were nearing land. They sounded and found twenty fathoms, and a little farther on they sounded again and found fifteen fathoms. Fearing that we might run on the rocks, they let out four sea anchors from the stern, and prayed for day to come. At dawn Paul urged all to take some food. "Today is the fourteenth day," he said, "that you have continued in suspense and without food. Therefore I urge you to eat; it will give you strength, since not a hair is to perish from

the head of any of you." Then he took
bread, and giving thanks to God in the
presence of all, he broke it and began to
eat. They were all encouraged and when
they had eaten enough, they lightened the
ship, throwing the grain into the sea.

When it was light, they saw land but did
not recognize it. Then they noticed a bay
with a beach, and here they planned if
possible to bring the ship ashore. Casting
off the anchors and hoisting the foresail to
the wind, they made for the beach. But the
vessel struck a shoal and ran aground. The
bow stuck and remained immovable, while
the stern was being broken up by the surf.
Lest any of the prisoners should swim
away and escape, the soldiers decided to
kill them, but the centurion, wishing to
save Paul, forbade it. He ordered those
who could swim to throw themselves overboard and make for the land, and the rest
to use planks or pieces of the ship. And so
it was that all escaped.

On land we learned that the island was
called Malta. The natives showed us un-
usual kindness, and because it had begun
to rain and was cold, they kindled a fire.

Paul had gathered a bundle of sticks, and as he put them on the fire a viper came out because of the heat and fastened on his hand. When the natives saw this they said, "No doubt this man is a murderer. Though he has escaped from the sea, justice has not allowed him to live." When Paul shook off the creature, they waited, expecting him to swell up or suddenly fall down dead. After a long time, when they saw no misfortune came to him, they changed their minds and said that he was a god.

The chief man of the island, Publius, received us and entertained us hospitably for three days. Now it happened that the father of Publius lay sick with fever and dysentery, so Paul visited him and prayed, and putting his hands on him healed him. After this, during the three months that we stayed on the island, the rest of the people who had diseases also came and were cured. They presented many gifts to us, and when we sailed, in another ship of Alexandria, they put on board whatever was needed.

At Syracuse we stayed three days, and at Rhegium one day. At Puteoli we found brethren and stayed with them for seven days. And so we came to Rome, and the brethren there, when they heard, came out of the city to meet us. In Rome, Paul was allowed to stay by himself, in his own hired dwelling, with the soldier that guarded him.

Soon Paul called together the local leaders of the Jews, and when they had gathered, he said, "Brethren, though I had done nothing against the people or the customs of our fathers, yet I was delivered prisoner from Jerusalem into the hands of the Romans. For this reason I have asked to see you and speak with you, since it is because of the hope of Israel that I am bound with this chain." The Jews answered that they had received no letters from Judea about Paul, nor had any of the brethren coming to Rome reported any evil against him. "But we desire to hear what your views are," they said, "for with regard to this sect we know that everywhere it is spoken against."

They appointed a day and they came to his lodging in great numbers. Paul expounded the matter to them from morning till evening, testifying to the kingdom of God and trying to convince them about Jesus both from the law of Moses and from the prophets. Some were convinced, while others disbelieved, and they disagreed among themselves. At this Paul made a statement: "The Holy Spirit was right in saying to your fathers through Isaiah the prophet: 'Go to this people, and say, You shall indeed hear but never understand, and you shall indeed see but never perceive. For this people's heart has grown dull.' Let it be known to you then that this salvation of God has been sent to the Gentiles; they will listen."

Paul lived in Rome two whole years at his own expense, and welcomed all who came to him, preaching the kingdom of God and teaching about the Lord Jesus Christ quite openly and unhindered.

LETTER OF PAUL
ROMANS

After years of spreading the gospel and founding churches through Asia Minor, Macedonia, and Greece, the apostle Paul at last decided to visit Rome, where there already existed a thriving Christian community. It was to introduce himself to the Roman Christians, apparently, that he wrote this letter from Corinth, about A.D. 58. Fully and systematically he sets forth his message, producing what amounts to a theological treatise rather than an ordinary letter. Since the Roman Christians were already converted, however, Paul does not attempt to lay bare the Christian way of life in its entirety. Instead, he concentrates on certain fundamental truths he feels require mentioning. After the usual salutation and thanksgiving, he discusses the need of the world for redemption. Next he takes up God's saving act in the earthly ministry of Jesus Christ, describing both its nature and the new life that it has made available. After a section on the role of the Jewish nation in God's plan, Paul closes with an exhortation to maintain Christian behavior and unity.

———

PAUL, A SERVANT of Jesus Christ, called to be an apostle, set apart for the gospel of God which he promised beforehand through his prophets in the holy scriptures, the gospel concerning his Son, who was descended from David according to the flesh and designated Son of God in power according to the Spirit of holiness by his resurrection from the dead, Jesus Christ our Lord.

To all God's beloved in Rome, who are called to be saints: grace to you and peace from God our Father and the Lord Jesus Christ.

First, I thank my God through Jesus Christ for all of you, because your faith is proclaimed in all the world. For God is my witness that without ceasing I mention you always in my prayers, asking that somehow by God's will I may succeed in coming to you. For I long to see you, that I may impart to you some spiritual gift to strengthen you, that is, that we may be mutually encouraged by each other's faith, both yours and mine.

For I am not ashamed of the gospel: it is the power of God for salvation to every one who has faith. In it the righteousness of God is revealed through faith for faith; as it is written, "He who through faith is righteous shall live."

The wrath of God is revealed against all ungodliness of men who by their wickedness suppress the truth. For what can be known about God is plain to them, because God has shown it to them. Ever since the creation of the world his invisible nature, namely, his eternal power and deity, has been clearly perceived in the things that have been made. So they are without excuse; for although they knew God they did not honor him as God, or give thanks to him, but they became futile in their thinking and their senseless minds were darkened. Claiming to be wise, they became fools, and exchanged the glory of the immortal God for images resembling mortal man or birds or animals or reptiles.

Therefore God gave them up in the lusts of their hearts to impurity, to the dishonoring of their bodies among themselves, because they exchanged the truth about God for a lie and worshiped and served the creature rather than the Creator, who is blessed for ever! Amen.

For this reason God gave them up to dishonorable passions. Their women exchanged natural relations for unnatural, and the men gave up natural relations with women and were consumed with passion for one another, men committing shameless acts with men and receiving in their own persons the due penalty for their error. Since they did not see fit to acknowledge God, God gave them up to a base mind and to improper conduct. They were filled with all manner of wickedness, evil, covetousness, malice. Full of envy, murder, strife, deceit, malignity, they are gossips, slanderers, haters of God, insolent, haughty, boastful, inventors of evil, disobedient to

parents, foolish, faithless, heartless, ruth-
less. Though they know God's decree that
those who do such things deserve to die,
they not only do them but approve those
who practice them.

Therefore you have no excuse, O man,
whoever you are, when you judge another;
for in passing judgment upon him you condemn yourself, because you, the judge, are
doing the very same things. Do you suppose, O man, you will escape the judgment
of God? Or do you presume upon the
riches of his forbearance and patience? Do
you not know that God's kindness is
meant to lead you to repentance? But by
your impenitent heart you are storing up
wrath for yourself on the day when God's
judgment will be revealed. For he will render to every man according to his works:
to those who by patience in well-doing
seek for glory and honor and immortality,
he will give eternal life; but for those who
do not obey the truth there will be wrath
and fury. For God shows no partiality.

All who have sinned without the law
will perish without the law, and all who
have sinned under the law will be judged

by the law. For it is not the hearers of the law who are righteous before God, but the doers of the law. When Gentiles who have not the law do by nature what the law requires, they are a law to themselves. They show that the law is written on their hearts. Their conscience also bears witness and their conflicting thoughts accuse or perhaps excuse them on that day when God judges the secrets of men by Christ Jesus.

But if you call yourself a Jew and rely upon the law, and if you are sure that you are a light to those who are in darkness, a corrector of the foolish, a teacher of children, having in the law the embodiment of knowledge and truth—you then who teach others, will you not teach yourself? While you preach against stealing, do you steal? You who say that one must not commit adultery, do you commit adultery? You who abhor idols, do you rob temples? You who boast in the law, do you dishonor God by breaking the law?

Circumcision indeed is of value if you obey the law; but if you break the law, your circumcision becomes uncircumcision. For he is not a real Jew who is one outwardly, nor is true circumcision something external and physical. He is a Jew who is one inwardly, and real circumcision is a matter of the heart, spiritual and not literal. Then what is the value of circumcision? Much in every way. To begin with, the Jews are entrusted with the oracles of God. What if some were unfaithful? Does their faithlessness nullify the faithfulness of God? By no means! Let God be true though every man be false.

What then? Are we Jews any better off? No, not at all; for all men are under the power of sin, as it is written: "None is righteous, no, not one; no one understands, no one seeks for God. All have turned aside, together they have gone wrong; no one does good, not even one."

Now we know that whatever the law says it speaks to those who are under the law, so that every mouth may be stopped, and the whole world may be held accountable to God. For no human being will be justified in his sight by works of the law, since through the law comes knowledge of sin.

But now the righteousness of God has been manifested apart from law, although the law and the prophets bear witness to it, through faith in Jesus Christ for all who believe. For there is no distinction; since all have sinned and fall short of the glory of God, they are justified by his grace as a gift, through the redemption which is in Christ Jesus. This was to show God's righteousness, because in his divine forbearance he had passed over former sins; it was to prove at the present time that he himself is righteous and that he justifies him who has faith in Jesus.

Then what becomes of our boasting? It is excluded. On what principle? On the principle of works? No, but on the principle of faith. For we hold that a man is justified by faith apart from works of law. Or is God the God of Jews only? Is he not the God of Gentiles also? Yes, of Gentiles also, since God is one; and he will justify the circumcised on the ground of their faith and the uncircumcised through their faith. Do we then overthrow the law by this faith? By no means! On the contrary, we uphold the law.

What then shall we say about Abraham, our forefather according to the flesh? For if Abraham was justified by works, he has something to boast about, but not before God. For what does the scripture say? "Abraham believed God, and it was reckoned to him as righteousness." Now to one who works, his wages are not reckoned as a gift but as his due. And to one who does not work but trusts him who justifies the ungodly, his faith is reckoned as righteousness. We say that faith was reckoned to Abraham as righteousness. How was it reckoned to him? Was it before or after he had been circumcised? It was not after, but before. He received circumcision as a sign or seal of the righteousness which he had by faith while he was still uncircumcised. The purpose was to make him the father of all who believe without being circumcised and who thus have righteousness reckoned to them, and likewise the father of the circumcised who also follow the example of the faith Abraham had before he was circumcised.

The promise to Abraham and his descendants, that they should inherit the world, did not come through the law but through the righteousness of faith. If it is the adherents of the law who are to be the heirs, faith is null and the promise is void. For the law brings wrath, but where there is no law there is no transgression. That is why it depends on faith, in order that the promise may rest on grace and be guaranteed to all his descendants—not only to the adherents of the law but also to those who share the faith of Abraham, for he is the father of us all, as it is written, "I have made you the father of many nations"—in the presence of the God in whom he believed, who gives life to the dead and calls into existence the things that do not exist. In hope he believed against hope, that he should become the father of many nations; as he had been told, "So shall your descendants be."

He did not weaken in faith when he considered his own body, which was as good as dead because he was about a hundred years old, or when he considered the barrenness of Sarah's womb. No distrust made him waver concerning the promise of God, but he grew strong in his faith as he gave glory to God, fully convinced that God was able to do what he had promised. That is why his faith was "reckoned to him as righteousness." But the words, "it was reckoned to him," were written not for his sake alone, but for ours also. It will be reckoned to us who believe in him that raised from the dead Jesus our Lord, who was put to death for our trespasses and raised for our justification.

Therefore, since we are justified by faith, we have peace with God through our Lord Jesus Christ. Through him we have obtained access to this grace in which we stand, and we rejoice in our hope of sharing the glory of God. More than that, we rejoice in our sufferings, knowing that suffering produces endurance, and endurance produces character, and character produces hope, and hope does not disappoint us, because God's love has been poured into our hearts through the Holy Spirit.

God shows his love for us in that while we were yet sinners Christ died for us. Since we are now justified by his blood, much more shall we be saved by him from the wrath of God. For if while we were enemies we were reconciled to God by the death of his Son, much more, now that we are reconciled, shall we be saved by his life.

Therefore as sin came into the world through one man and death through sin, and so death spread to all men because all men sinned—sin indeed was in the world before the law was given, but sin is not counted where there· is no law. Yet death reigned from Adam to Moses, even over those whose sins were not like the transgression of Adam, who was a type of the one who was to come.

But the free gift is not like the trespass. For if many died through one man's trespass, much more have the grace of God and the free gift in the grace of that one man Jesus Christ abounded for many. And the free gift is not like the effect of that one man's sin. For the judgment following one trespass brought condemnation, but the free gift following many trespasses brings justification. If, because of one man's trespass, death reigned through that one man, much more will those who receive the abundance of grace and the free gift of righteousness reign in life through the one man Jesus Christ.

Then as one man's trespass led to condemnation for all men, so one man's act of righteousness leads to acquittal and life for all men. For as by one man's disobedience many were made sinners, so by one man's obedience many will be made righteous. Law came in, to increase the trespass; but where sin increased, grace abounded all the more, so that, as sin reigned in death, grace also might reign through righteousness to eternal life through Jesus Christ our Lord.

What shall we say then? Are we to continue in sin, that grace may abound? By no means! How can we who died to sin still live in it? Do you not know that all of us who have been baptized into Christ Jesus were baptized into his death? We were buried therefore with him by baptism into death, so that as Christ was raised from the dead by the glory of the Father, we too might walk in newness of life.

For if we have been united with him in a death like his, we shall certainly be united with him in a resurrection like his. We know that our old self was crucified with him so that the sinful body might be destroyed, and we might no longer be enslaved to sin. For he who has died is freed from sin. But if we have died with Christ, we believe that we shall also live with him. For we know that Christ being raised from the dead will never die again; death no longer has dominion over him. The death he died he died to sin, once for all, but the life he lives he lives to God. So you also must consider yourselves dead to sin and alive to God in Christ Jesus. Let not sin therefore reign in your mortal bodies, to make you obey their passions. For sin will have no dominion over you, since you are not under law but under grace.

Do you not know that if you yield yourselves as slaves, you are slaves of the one whom you obey, either of sin, which leads to death, or of obedience, which leads to righteousness? But thanks be to God, that you who were once slaves of sin have become obedient from the heart to the standard of teaching to which you were committed, and, having been set free from sin, have become slaves of righteousness. I am speaking in human terms, because of your natural limitations. For just as you once yielded your members to impurity and to greater and greater iniquity, so now yield your members to righteousness for sanctification.

When you were slaves of sin, you were free in regard to righteousness. But then what return did you get from the things of which you are now ashamed? The end of those things is death. But now that you have been set free from sin and have become slaves of God, the return you get is sanctification and its end, eternal life. For the wages of sin is death, but the free gift of God is eternal life in Christ Jesus our Lord.

Do you not know, brethren—for I am speaking to those who know the law—that the law is binding on a person only during his life? Thus a married woman is bound by law to her husband as long as he lives; but if her husband dies she is discharged from the law concerning the husband. Accordingly, she will be called an adulteress if she lives with another man while her husband is alive. But if her husband dies she is free from that law, and if she marries another man she is not an adulteress.

Likewise, my brethren, you have died to the law through the body of Christ, so that you may belong to another, to him who has been raised from the dead in order that we may bear fruit for God. While we were living in the flesh, our sinful passions, aroused by the law, were at work in our members to bear fruit for death. But now we are discharged from the law, dead to that which held us captive, so that we serve not under the old written code but in the new life of the Spirit.

What then shall we say? That the law is sin? By no means! Yet, if it had not been for the law, I should not have known sin. I should not have known what it is to covet if the law had not said, "You shall not covet." But sin, finding opportunity in the commandment, wrought in me all kinds of covetousness. Apart from the law sin lies dead. I was once alive apart from the law, but when the commandment came, sin revived and I died; the very commandment which promised life proved to be death to me. For sin, finding opportunity in the commandment, deceived me and by it killed me. So the law is holy, and the commandment is holy and just and good.

Did that which is good, then, bring death to me? By no means! It was sin, working death in me through what is good, in order that sin might be shown to be sin, and through the commandment might become sinful beyond measure. We know that the law is spiritual; but I am carnal, sold under sin. I do not understand my own actions. For I do not do what I want, but I do the very thing I hate. Now if I do what I do not want, I agree that the law is good. So then it is no longer I that do it, but sin which dwells within me. For I know that nothing good dwells within me, that is, in my flesh. I can will what is right, but I cannot do it. For I do not do the good I want, but the evil I do not want is what I do. Now if I do what I do not want, it is no longer I that do it, but sin which dwells within me.

So I find it to be a law that when I want to do right, evil lies close at hand. For I delight in the law of God, in my inmost self, but I see in my members another law at war with the law of my mind and making me captive to the law of sin which dwells in my members. Wretched man that I am! Who will deliver me from this body of death? Thanks be to God through Jesus Christ our Lord! So then, I of myself serve the law of God with my mind, but with my flesh I serve the law of sin.

There is therefore now no condemnation for those who are in Christ Jesus. For the law of the Spirit of life in Christ Jesus has set me free from the law of sin and death. For God has done what the law, weakened by the flesh, could not do: sending his own Son in the likeness of sinful flesh and for sin, he condemned sin in the flesh, in order that the just requirement of the law might be fulfilled in us. Those who live according to the flesh set their minds on the things of the flesh, but those who live according to the Spirit set their minds on the things of the Spirit. The mind that is set on the flesh is hostile to God; it does not submit to God's law, indeed it cannot.

Any one who does not have the Spirit of Christ does not belong to him. But if Christ is in you, although your bodies are dead because of sin, your spirits are alive because of righteousness. If the Spirit of him who raised Jesus from the dead dwells in you, he who raised Christ Jesus from the dead will give life to your mortal bodies also, through his Spirit which dwells in you.

All who are led by the Spirit of God are sons of God. For you did not receive the spirit of slavery, but you have received the spirit of sonship. When we cry, "Abba! Father!" it is the Spirit himself bearing witness with our spirit that we are children of God, and if children, then heirs, heirs of God and fellow heirs with Christ, provided we suffer with him in order that we may also be glorified with him.

I consider that the sufferings of this present time are not worth comparing with the glory that is to be revealed to us. For the creation waits with eager longing for the revealing of the sons of God; because the creation itself will be set free from its bondage to decay and obtain the glorious liberty of the children of God. We know that the whole creation has been groaning in travail together until now; and not only the creation, but we ourselves, who have the first fruits of the Spirit, groan inwardly as we wait for adoption as sons, the redemption of our bodies. For in this hope we were saved. Now hope that is seen is not hope. Who hopes for what he sees? But if we hope for what we do not see, we wait for it with patience.

Likewise the Spirit helps us in our weakness; for we do not know how to pray as we ought, but the Spirit himself intercedes for us with sighs too deep for words. And he who searches the hearts of men knows what is the mind of the Spirit, because the Spirit intercedes for the saints according to the will of God.

We know that in everything God works for good with those who love him. Those whom he foreknew he also predestined to be conformed to the image of his Son. And those whom he predestined he also called; and those whom he called he also justified; and those whom he justified he also glorified.

What then shall we say to this? If God is for us, who is against us? He who did not spare his own Son but gave him up for us all, will he not also give us all things with him? It is God who justifies; who is to condemn? Is it Christ Jesus, who was raised from the dead and who is at the right hand of God, who indeed intercedes for us? Who shall separate us from the love of Christ? Shall tribulation, or distress, or persecution, or famine, or nakedness, or peril, or sword? No, in all these things we are more than conquerors through him who loved us. For I am sure that neither death, nor life, nor angels, nor principalities, nor things present, nor things to come, nor powers, nor height, nor depth, nor anything else in all creation, will be able to separate us from the love of God in Christ Jesus our Lord.

I am speaking the truth in Christ, I am not lying; my conscience bears me witness in the Holy Spirit that I have unceasing anguish in my heart. For I could wish that I myself were accursed and cut off from Christ for the sake of my kinsmen by race. They are Israelites, and to them belong the sonship, the glory, the covenants, the giving of the law, the worship, and the promises; to them belong the patriarchs, and of their race, according to the flesh, is the Christ. God, who is over all, be blessed for ever. Amen.

But it is not as though the word of God had failed. For not all who are descended from Israel belong to Israel, and not all are children of Abraham because they are his descendants; but "Through Isaac shall your descendants be named." This means that it is not the children of the flesh who are the children of God, but the children of the promise are reckoned as descendants. What shall we say then? Is there injustice on God's part? By no means! For he says to Moses, "I will have mercy on whom I have mercy, and I will have compassion on whom I have compassion." So it depends not upon man's will or exertion, but upon God's mercy. He has mercy upon whomever he wills, and he hardens the heart of whomever he wills.

You will say to me then, "Why does he still find fault? For who can resist his will?" But who are you, a man, to answer back to God? Will what is molded say to its molder, "Why have you made me thus?" Has the potter no right over the clay, to make out of the same lump one vessel for beauty and another for menial use? As indeed he says in Hosea, "Those who were not my people I will call 'my people,' and her who was not beloved I will call 'my beloved.' "

And Isaiah cries out concerning Israel: "Though the number of the sons of Israel be as the sand of the sea, only a remnant of them will be saved; for the Lord will execute his sentence upon the earth with rigor and dispatch."

What shall we say then? That Gentiles who did not pursue righteousness have attained it, that is, righteousness through faith; but that Israel who pursued the righteousness which is based on law did not succeed in fulfilling that law. Why? Because they did not pursue it through faith, but as if it were based on works. They have stumbled over the stumbling stone, as it is written, "Behold, I am laying in Zion a stone that will make men stumble, a rock that will make them fall; and he who believes in him will not be put to shame."

Brethren, my heart's desire and prayer to God for them is that they may be saved.

I bear them witness that they have a zeal for God, but it is not enlightened. Being ignorant of the righteousness that comes from God, and seeking to establish their own, they did not submit to God's righteousness.

Moses writes that the man who practices the righteousness which is based on the law shall live by it. But the righteousness based on faith says, Do not say in your heart, "Who will ascend into heaven?" (that is, to bring Christ down) or "Who will descend into the abyss?" (that is, to bring Christ up from the dead). But what does it say? The word is near you, on your lips and in your heart (that is, the word of faith which we preach). If you confess with your lips that Jesus is Lord and believe in your heart that God raised him from the dead, you will be saved. For man believes with his heart and so is justified, and he confesses with his lips and so is saved. The same Lord is Lord of all and the scripture says, "every one who calls upon the name of the Lord will be saved."

But how are men to call upon him in whom they have not believed? And how are they to believe in him of whom they have never heard? And how are they to hear without a preacher? And how can men preach unless they are sent? So faith comes from what is heard, and what is heard comes by the preaching of Christ.

But I ask, have they not heard? Indeed they have; for "Their voice has gone out to all the earth, and their words to the ends of the world." Again I ask, did Israel not understand? First Moses says, "I will make you jealous of those who are not a nation; with a foolish nation I will make you angry." Then Isaiah is so bold as to say, "I have been found by those who did not seek me; I have shown myself to those who did not ask for me." But of Israel he says, "All day long I have held out my hands to a disobedient people."

I ask, then, has God rejected his people? By no means! I myself am an Israelite, a member of the tribe of Benjamin. Do you not know what the scripture says of Elijah, how he pleads with God against Israel? "Lord, they have killed thy prophets, they have demolished thy altars, and I alone am left, and they seek my life." But what is

God's reply to him? "I have kept for my-self seven thousand men who have not bowed the knee to Baal." So too at the present time there is a remnant, chosen by grace. But if it is by grace, it is no longer on the basis of works; otherwise grace would no longer be grace.

What then? Israel failed to obtain what it sought. The elect obtained it, but the rest were hardened. So I ask, have they stum-bled so as to fall? By no means! But through their trespass salvation has come to the Gentiles, so as to make Israel jeal-ous. Now if their trespass means riches for the world, and if their failure means riches for the Gentiles, how much more will their full inclusion mean!

Now I am speaking to you Gentiles. In-asmuch then as I am an apostle to the Gentiles, I magnify my ministry in order to make my fellow Jews jealous, and thus save some of them. For if their rejection means the reconciliation of the world, what will their acceptance mean but life from the dead? If the dough offered as first fruits is holy, so is the whole lump; and if the root is holy, so are the branches.

But if some of the branches were broken off, and you, a wild olive shoot, were grafted in their place to share the richness of the olive tree, do not boast over the branches. Remember, it is not you that support the root, but the root that supports you. They were broken off because of their unbelief, but you stand fast only through faith. So do not become proud, but stand in awe. For if God did not spare the natural branches, neither will he spare you. Note then the kindness and the severity of God: severity toward those who have fallen, but kindness to you. And even the others, if they do not persist in their unbelief, will be grafted in again.

Lest you be wise in your own conceits, I want you to understand this mystery, brethren: a hardening has come upon part of Israel, until the full number of the Gentiles come in, and so all Israel will be saved. As regards the gospel, they are enemies of God, for your sake; but as regards election, they are beloved for the sake of their forefathers. For the gifts and the call of God are irrevocable. Just as you were once disobedient to God but now have received mercy because of their disobedience, so they have now been disobedient in order that by the mercy shown to you they also may receive mercy. For God has consigned all men to disobedience, that he may have mercy upon all.

O the depth of the riches and wisdom and knowledge of God! How unsearchable are his judgments and how inscrutable his ways! For from him and through him and to him are all things. To him be glory for ever. Amen.

I appeal to you therefore, brethren, to present your bodies as a living sacrifice, holy and acceptable to God, which is your spiritual worship. Do not be conformed to this world but be transformed by the renewal of your mind, that you may prove what is the will of God, what is good and acceptable and perfect.

For by the grace given to me I bid every one among you not to think of himself more highly than he ought to think, but to think with sober judgment, each according to the measure of faith which God has assigned him. For as in one body we have many members, and all the members do not have the same function, so we, though many, are one body in Christ, and individually members one of another. Having gifts that differ according to the grace given to us, let us use them: if prophecy, in proportion to our faith; if service, in our serving; he who teaches, in his teaching; he who exhorts, in his exhortation; he who contributes, in liberality; he who gives aid, with zeal; he who does acts of mercy, with cheerfulness.

Let love be genuine; hate what is evil, hold fast to what is good; love one another with brotherly affection; outdo one another in showing honor. Never flag in zeal, be aglow with the Spirit, serve the Lord. Rejoice in your hope, be patient in tribulation, be constant in prayer. Contribute to the needs of the saints, practice hospitality.

Bless those who persecute you; bless and do not curse them. Rejoice with those who rejoice, weep with those who weep. Live in harmony with one another; do not be haughty, but associate with the lowly; never be conceited. Repay no one evil for evil, but take thought for what is noble in the sight of all. If possible, so far as it depends upon you, live peaceably with all. Beloved, never avenge yourselves, but leave it to the wrath of God; for it is written, "Vengeance is mine, I will repay, says the Lord." No, "if your enemy is hungry, feed him; if he is thirsty, give him drink; for by so doing you will heap burning coals upon his head." Do not be overcome by evil, but overcome evil with good.

Let every person be subject to the governing authorities. For there is no authority except from God, and those that exist have been instituted by God. Therefore he who resists the authorities resists what God has appointed, and those who resist will incur judgment. For rulers are not a terror to good conduct, but to bad. Would you have no fear of him who is in authority? Then do what is good, and you will receive his approval, for he is God's servant for your good. But if you do wrong, be afraid, for he does not bear the sword in vain. Therefore one must be subject, not only to avoid God's wrath but also for the sake of conscience. For the same reason you also pay taxes, for the authorities are ministers of God, attending to this very thing. Pay all of them their dues, taxes to whom taxes are due, revenue to whom revenue is due, respect to whom respect is due, honor to whom honor is due.

Owe no one anything, except to love one another; for he who loves his neighbor has fulfilled the law. The commandments, "You shall not commit adultery, You shall not kill, You shall not steal, You shall not covet," and any other commandment, are summed up in this sentence, "You shall love your neighbor as yourself." Love does no wrong to a neighbor; therefore love is the fulfilling of the law.

The night is far gone, the day is at hand. Let us then cast off the works of darkness and put on the armor of light; let us conduct ourselves becomingly as in the day, not in reveling and drunkenness, not in debauchery and licentiousness, not in quarreling and jealousy. But put on the Lord Jesus Christ, and make no provision for the flesh, to gratify its desires.

Let us no more pass judgment on one another, but rather decide never to put a stumbling block or hindrance in the way of a brother. I know and am persuaded in the

Lord Jesus that nothing is unclean in itself; but it is unclean for any one who thinks it unclean. If your brother is being injured by what you eat, you are no longer walking in love. Do not let what you eat cause the ruin of one for whom Christ died. So do not let your good be spoken of as evil. For the kingdom of God is not food and drink but righteousness and peace and joy in the Holy Spirit. Do not, for the sake of food, destroy the work of God. Everything is indeed clean, but it is wrong for any one to make others fall by what he eats; it is right not to eat meat or drink wine or do anything that makes your brother stumble. The faith that you have, keep between yourself and God.

We who are strong ought to bear with the failings of the weak, and not to please ourselves; let each of us please his neighbor for his good, to edify him. Welcome one another, therefore, as Christ has welcomed you, for the glory of God. For I tell you that Christ became a servant to the circumcised to show God's truthfulness, in order to confirm the promises given to the patriarchs, and in order that the Gentiles might glorify God for his mercy. May the God of hope fill you with all joy and peace in believing, so that by the power of the Holy Spirit you may abound in hope.

I myself am satisfied about you, my brethren, that you yourselves are full of goodness, filled with all knowledge, and able to instruct one another. But on some points I have written to you very boldly by way of reminder, because of the grace given me by God to be a minister of Christ Jesus to the Gentiles. In Christ Jesus, then, I have reason to be proud of my work for God. For I will not venture to speak of anything except what Christ has wrought through me to win obedience from the Gentiles, so that from Jerusalem as far round as Illyricum I have fully preached the gospel, thus making it my ambition to preach not where Christ has already been named, lest I build on another man's foundation, but as it is written, "They shall see who have never been told of him, and they shall understand who have never heard of him."

This is the reason why I have so often been hindered from coming to you. But now, since I no longer have any room for work in these regions, and since I have longed for many years to come to you, I hope to see you in passing as I go to Spain. At present, however, I am going to Jerusalem with aid for the saints. Macedonia and Achaia have been pleased to make some contribution for the poor among the saints at Jerusalem; they were pleased to do it, for if the Gentiles have come to share in their spiritual blessings, they ought to be of service to them in material blessings. When I have completed this, I shall go on by way of you to Spain; and I know that when I come to you I shall come in the fulness of the blessing of Christ.

I commend to you our sister Phoebe, a deaconess of the church at Cenchreae, that you may help her in whatever she may require from you, for she has been a helper of many and of myself as well. Greet Prisca and Aquila, who risked their necks for my life, to whom not only I but also all the churches of the Gentiles give thanks; greet also the church in their house.

Now to him who is able to strengthen you according to my gospel and the preach-

ing of Jesus Christ, according to the revelation of the mystery which was kept secret
for long ages but is now disclosed and
through the prophetic writings is made
known to all nations, according to the
command of the eternal God, to bring
about the obedience of faith—to the only
wise God be glory for evermore through
Jesus Christ! Amen.

1 CORINTHIANS

Corinth was one of the most important cities of Greece. Not long after Paul had planted the Christian faith there and left the city, news reached him in Ephesus of problems beginning to trouble the young church. Factions had split the community, and there was a growing tendency to be overly impressed by a certain kind of human "wisdom." Also, some of the faithful were taking undue pride in their ability to speak with tongues. Paul deals forthrightly with these and other problems, and in his effort to guide this local church he has bequeathed to the universal church some of the most exalted passages in his correspondence. Especially notable are the hymn on Christian love and the teaching on the meaning of Christ's resurrection.

Paul, called by the will of God to be an apostle of Christ Jesus, and our brother Sosthenes, to the church of God which is at Corinth, to those sanctified in Christ Jesus, called to be saints together with all those who in every place call on the name of our Lord Jesus Christ, both their Lord and ours: Grace to you and peace from God our Father and the Lord Jesus Christ.

I give thanks to God always for you because of the grace of God which was given you in Christ Jesus, that in every way you were enriched in him, so that you are not lacking in any spiritual gift, as you wait for the revealing of our Lord Jesus Christ, who will sustain you to the end. God is faithful, by whom you were called into the fellowship of his Son.

I appeal to you, brethren, that there be no dissensions among you. For it has been reported to me by Chloe's people that there is quarreling. Each one of you says, "I belong to Paul," or "I belong to Apollos," or "I belong to Cephas," or "I belong to Christ." Is Christ divided? Was Paul crucified for you? Or were you baptized in the name of Paul? I am thankful that I baptized none of you except Crispus and Gaius; lest any one should say that you were baptized in my name. (I did baptize also the household of Stephanas. Beyond that, I do not know whether I baptized any one else.) For Christ did not send me to baptize but to preach the gospel, and not with eloquent wisdom, lest the cross of Christ be emptied of its power. For the word of the cross is folly to those who are perishing, but to us who are being saved it is the power of God. For it is written, "I will destroy the wisdom of the wise, and the cleverness of the clever I will thwart."

Has not God made foolish the wisdom of the world? For since, in the wisdom of God, the world did not know God through wisdom, it pleased God through the folly of what we preach to save those who believe. Jews demand signs and Greeks seek wisdom, but we preach Christ crucified, a stumbling block to Jews and folly to Gentiles, but to those who are called, both Jews and Greeks, Christ the power of God and the wisdom of God. For the foolishness of God is wiser than men, and the weakness of God is stronger than men.

Consider your call, brethren; not many of you were wise according to worldly standards, not many were powerful, not many were of noble birth; but God chose what is foolish in the world to shame the wise, what is weak in the world to shame the strong, what is low and despised, even things that are not, to bring to nothing things that are, so that no human being might boast in the presence of God. He is the source of your life in Christ Jesus, whom God made our wisdom, our righteousness and sanctification and redemption; therefore, as it is written, "Let him who boasts, boast of the Lord."

When I came to you, brethren, I did not proclaim the testimony of God in lofty words or wisdom. For I decided to know nothing among you except Jesus Christ and him crucified. I was with you in weakness and in much fear and trembling; and my speech and my message were not in plausible words of wisdom, but in demonstration of the Spirit and of power, that your faith might not rest in the wisdom of men but in the power of God.

Yet among the mature we do impart

wisdom, although it is not a wisdom of this age or of the rulers of this age, who are doomed to pass away. But we impart a secret and hidden wisdom of God, decreed before the ages for our glorification. None of the rulers of this age understood this; for if they had, they would not have crucified the Lord of glory. But, as it is written, "What no eye has seen, nor ear heard, nor the heart of man conceived, what God has prepared for those who love him," God has revealed to us through the Spirit.

For the Spirit searches everything, even the depths of God. For what person knows a man's thoughts except the spirit of the man which is in him? So also no one comprehends the thoughts of God except the Spirit of God. Now we have received the Spirit which is from God, that we might understand the gifts bestowed on us by God. And we impart this in words not taught by human wisdom but taught by the Spirit, interpreting spiritual truths to those who possess the Spirit.

The unspiritual man does not receive the gifts of the Spirit of God, for they are folly to him, and he is not able to understand them because they are spiritually discerned. The spiritual man judges all things, but is himself to be judged by no one. "For who has known the mind of the Lord so as to instruct him?" But we have the mind of Christ.

But I, brethren, could not address you as spiritual men, but as men of the flesh, as babes in Christ. I fed you with milk, not solid food; for you were not ready for it; and even yet you are not ready, for you are still of the flesh. While there is jealousy and strife among you, are you not of the flesh, and behaving like ordinary men?

What then is Apollos? What is Paul? Servants through whom you believed, as the Lord assigned to each. I planted, Apollos watered, but God gave the growth. So neither he who plants nor he who waters is anything, but only God who gives the growth. He who plants and he who waters are equal, and each shall receive his wages according to his labor. For we are God's fellow workers; you are God's field, God's building.

Let no one deceive himself. If any one among you thinks he is wise in this age, let him become a fool, that he may become wise. For the wisdom of this world is folly with God. So let no one boast of men. For all things are yours, whether Paul or Apollos or Cephas or the world or life or death or the present or the future, all are yours; and you are Christ's; and Christ is God's.

This is how one should regard us, as servants of Christ and stewards of the mysteries of God. Moreover it is required of stewards that they be found trustworthy. But with me it is a very small thing that I should be judged by you or by any human court. I do not even judge myself. I am not aware of anything against myself, but I am not thereby acquitted. It is the Lord who judges me. Therefore do not pronounce judgment before the time, before the Lord comes, who will bring to light the things now hidden in darkness and will disclose the purposes of the heart. Then every man will receive his commendation from God.

I have applied all this to myself and Apollos for your benefit, brethren, that you may learn by us not to go beyond what is written, that none of you may be puffed up in favor of one against another. For who sees anything different in you? What have you that you did not receive? If then you received it, why do you boast as if it were not a gift?

I think that God has exhibited us apostles as last of all, like men sentenced to death; because we have become a spectacle to the world. We are fools for Christ's sake, but you are wise in Christ. We are weak, but you are strong. You are held in honor, but we in disrepute. To the present hour we hunger and thirst, we are ill-clad and buffeted and homeless, and we labor, working with our own hands. When reviled, we bless; when persecuted, we endure; when slandered, we try to conciliate; we have become, and are now, as the refuse of the world, the offscouring of all things.

I do not write this to make you ashamed, but to admonish you as my beloved children. For though you have countless guides in Christ, you do not have many fathers. I became your father in Christ Jesus through the gospel. I urge you, then, be imitators of me. I will come to you soon, if the Lord wills, and I will find out not the talk of these arrogant people but their power. For the kingdom of God does not consist in talk but in power. What do you wish? Shall I come to you with a rod, or with love in a spirit of gentleness?

IT IS ACTUALLY reported that there is immorality among you, and of a kind that is not found even among pagans; for a man is living with his father's wife. Let him who has done this be removed from among you. For though absent in body I am present in spirit, and I have already pronounced judgment in the name of the Lord Jesus on the man who has done such a thing. When you are assembled, you are to deliver this man to Satan for the destruction of the flesh, that his spirit may be saved.

I wrote to you in my letter not to associate with immoral men; not meaning the immoral of this world, since then you would need to go out of the world. Rather I wrote to you not to associate with any one who bears the name of brother if he is guilty of immorality, not even to eat with such a one. "Drive out the wicked person from among you." Do not be deceived; neither the immoral, nor idolaters, nor adulterers, nor sexual perverts, nor thieves, nor the greedy, nor drunkards, nor revilers, nor robbers will inherit the kingdom of God. And such were some of you. But you were washed, you were sanctified, you were justified in the name of the Lord Jesus Christ and in the Spirit of our God.

"All things are lawful for me," you say, but not all things are helpful. "All things are lawful for me," but I will not be enslaved by anything. "Food is meant for the stomach and the stomach for food"—and God will destroy both one and the other. The body is not meant for immorality, but for the Lord, and the Lord for the body. And God raised the Lord and will also raise us up by his power. Do you not know that your bodies are members of Christ? Shall I therefore take the members of Christ and make them members of a prostitute? Never! Shun immorality. Every other sin which a man commits is outside the body; but the immoral man sins against his own body. Do you not know that your body is a temple of the Holy Spirit within you, which you have from God? You are not your own; you were bought with a price. So glorify God in your body.

Now concerning the matters about which you wrote. It is well for a man not to touch a woman. But because of the temptation to immorality, each man should have his own wife and each woman her own husband. The husband should give to his wife her conjugal rights, and likewise the wife to her husband. For the wife does not rule over her own body, but the husband does; likewise the husband does not rule over his own body, but the wife does. Do not refuse one another except perhaps by agreement for a season, that you may devote yourselves to prayer; but then come together again, lest Satan tempt you through lack of self-control. I say this by way of concession, not of command. I wish that all were as I myself am. But each has his own special gift from God, one of one kind and one of another.

To the unmarried and the widows I say that it is well for them to remain single as I do. But if they cannot exercise self-control, they should marry. For it is better to marry than to be aflame with passion.

To the married I give charge, not I but the Lord, that the wife should not separate from her husband (but if she does, let her remain single or else be reconciled to her husband)—and that the husband should not divorce his wife.

To the rest I say, not the Lord, that if any brother has a wife who is an unbeliever, and she consents to live with him, he should not divorce her. If any woman has a husband who is an unbeliever, and he consents to live with her, she should not divorce him. For the unbelieving husband is consecrated through his wife, and the unbelieving wife is consecrated through her husband. Otherwise, your children would be unclean, but as it is they are holy. But if the unbelieving partner desires to separate, let it be so; in such a case the brother or sister is not bound. For God has called us to peace. Wife, how do you know whether you will save your husband? Husband, how do you know whether you will save your wife?

Only, let every one lead the life which

the Lord has assigned to him, and in which God has called him. This is my rule in all the churches. In whatever state each was called, there let him remain with God.

Now concerning the unmarried, I have no command of the Lord, but I give my opinion as one who by the Lord's mercy is trustworthy. I think that in view of the present distress it is well for a person to remain as he is. Are you bound to a wife? Do not seek to be free. Are you free from a wife? Do not seek marriage. But if you marry, you do not sin, and if a girl marries, she does not sin. Yet those who marry will have worldly troubles, and I would spare you that. I mean, brethren, the appointed time has grown very short; from now on, let those who have wives live as though they had none, and those who mourn as though they were not mourning, and those who rejoice as though they were not rejoicing, and those who buy as though they had no goods, and those who deal with the world as though they had no dealings with it. For the form of this world is passing away.

I want you to be free from anxieties. The

unmarried man is anxious about the affairs
of the Lord, how to please the Lord; but
the married man is anxious about worldly
affairs, how to please his wife, and his
interests are divided. And the unmarried
woman or girl is anxious about the affairs
of the Lord, how to be holy in body and
spirit; but the married woman is anxious
about worldly affairs, how to please her
husband. I say this for your own benefit,
not to lay any restraint upon you, but to
promote good order and to secure your
undivided devotion to the Lord.

If any one thinks that he is not behaving
properly toward his betrothed, if his passions are strong, and it has to be, let him
do as he wishes: let them marry—it is no
sin. But whoever is firmly established in
his heart, being under no necessity but
having his desire under control, and has
determined this in his heart, to keep her as
his betrothed, he will do well. So that he
who marries his betrothed does well; and
he who refrains from marriage will do
better.

A wife is bound to her husband as long
as he lives. If the husband dies, she is free

to be married to whom she wishes, only in the Lord. But in my judgment she is happier if she remains as she is. And I think that I have the Spirit of God.

AM I NOT free? Am I not an apostle? Have I not seen Jesus our Lord? Are not you my workmanship in the Lord? If to others I am not an apostle, at least I am to you; for you are the seal of my apostleship in the Lord. This is my defense to those who would examine me. Do we not have the right to our food and drink? Do we not have the right to be accompanied by a wife, as the other apostles and the brothers of the Lord and Cephas? Or is it only Barnabas and I who have no right to refrain from working for a living? Who serves as a soldier at his own expense? Who plants a vineyard without eating any of its fruit?

Do I say this on human authority? Does not the law say the same? For it is written in the law of Moses, "You shall not muzzle an ox when it is treading out the grain." Is it for oxen that God is concerned? Does he not speak entirely for our sake? If we have sown spiritual good among you, is it too much if we reap your material benefits? Do you not know that those who are employed in the temple service get their food from the temple? In the same way, the Lord commanded that those who proclaim the gospel should get their living by the gospel.

But I have made no use of any of these rights, nor am I writing this to secure any such provision. For I would rather die than have any one deprive me of my ground for boasting. For if I preach the gospel, that gives me no ground for boasting; necessity is laid upon me. Woe to me if I do not preach the gospel! If I do this of my own will, I have a reward; but if not of my own will, I am entrusted with a commission. What then is my reward? Just this: that in my preaching I may make the gospel free of charge, not making full use of my right in the gospel.

For though I am free from all men, I have made myself a slave to all, that I might win the more. To the Jews I became as a Jew, in order to win Jews; to those under the law I became as one under the law—though not being myself under the law—that I might win those under the law. To those outside the law I became as one outside the law—not being without law toward God but under the law of Christ—that I might win those outside the law. To the weak I became weak, that I might win the weak. I have become all things to all men, that I might by all means save some. I do it all for the sake of the gospel, that I may share in its blessings.

Do you not know that in a race all the runners compete, but only one receives the prize? So run that you may obtain it. Every athlete exercises self-control in all things. They do it to receive a perishable wreath, but we an imperishable. Well, I do not run aimlessly, I do not box as one beating the air; but I pommel my body and subdue it, lest after preaching to others I myself should be disqualified.

I want you to know, brethren, that our fathers were all under the cloud, and all passed through the sea, and all were baptized into Moses in the cloud and in the sea, and all ate the same supernatural food and all drank the same supernatural drink.

For they drank from the supernatural Rock which followed them, and the Rock was Christ. Nevertheless, with most of them God was not pleased; for they were overthrown in the wilderness. Now these things are warnings for us. We must not indulge in immorality, must not put the Lord to the test, nor grumble. No temptation has overtaken you that is not common to man. God is faithful, and he will not let you be tempted beyond your strength, but with the temptation will also provide the way of escape.

Therefore, my beloved, shun the worship of idols. I speak as to sensible men; judge for yourselves what I say. The cup of blessing which we bless, is it not a participation in the blood of Christ? The bread which we break, is it not a participation in the body of Christ? Because there is one bread, we who are many are one body, for we all partake of the one bread. What pagans sacrifice they offer to demons and not to God. You cannot drink the cup of the Lord and the cup of demons. You cannot partake of the table of the Lord and the table of demons.

I commend you because you remember me in everything and maintain the traditions even as I have delivered them to you. But I want you to understand that the head of every man is Christ, the head of a woman is her husband, and the head of Christ is God. Any man who prays or prophesies with his head covered dishonors his head, but any woman who prays or prophesies with her head unveiled dishonors her head—it is the same as if her head were shaven. For if a woman will not veil herself, then she should cut off her hair; but if it is disgraceful for a woman to be shorn or shaven, let her wear a veil. For a man ought not to cover his head, since he is the image and glory of God; but woman is the glory of man. (For man was not made from woman, but woman from man. Neither was man created for woman, but woman for man.) That is why a woman ought to have a veil on her head, because of the angels. (Nevertheless, in the Lord woman is not independent of man nor man of woman; for as woman was made from man, so man is now born of woman. And all things are from God.)

In the following I do not commend you, because when you assemble as a church, I hear that there are divisions among you; and I partly believe it. When you meet together, it is not the Lord's supper that you eat. For in eating, each one goes ahead with his own meal, and one is hungry and another is drunk. What! Do you not have houses to eat and drink in? Or do you despise the church of God and humiliate those who have nothing? Shall I commend you in this? No, I will not.

For I received from the Lord what I also delivered to you, that the Lord Jesus on the night when he was betrayed took bread, and when he had given thanks, he broke it, and said, "This is my body which is for you. Do this in remembrance of me." In the same way also the cup, after supper, saying, "This cup is the new covenant in my blood. Do this, as often as you drink it, in remembrance of me." For as often as you eat this bread and drink the cup, you proclaim the Lord's death until he comes.

Whoever, therefore, eats the bread or drinks the cup of the Lord in an unworthy manner will be guilty of profaning the body and blood of the Lord. Let a man examine himself, and so eat of the bread and drink of the cup. For any one who eats and drinks without discerning the body eats and drinks judgment upon himself. That is why many of you are weak and ill, and some have died. But if we judged ourselves truly, we should not be judged. But when we are judged by the Lord, we are chastened so that we may not be condemned along with the world. My brethren, when you come together to eat, wait for one another—if any one is hungry, let him eat at home—lest you come together to be condemned.

Now concerning spiritual gifts, brethren, I do not want you to be uninformed. You know that when you were heathen, you were led astray to dumb idols, however you may have been moved. Therefore I want you to understand that no one speaking by the Spirit of God ever says "Jesus be cursed!" and no one can say "Jesus is Lord" except by the Holy Spirit.

Now there are varieties of gifts, but the same Spirit; and there are varieties of service, but the same Lord; and there are varieties of working, but it is the same God who inspires them all in every one. To each is given the manifestation of the Spirit for the common good. To one is given through the Spirit the utterance of wisdom, and to another the utterance of knowledge according to the same Spirit, to another faith by the same Spirit, to another gifts of healing by the one Spirit, to another the working of miracles, to another prophecy, to another the ability to distinguish between spirits, to another various kinds of tongues, to another the interpretation of tongues. All these are inspired by one and the same Spirit, who apportions to each one individually as he wills. For just as the body is one and has many members, and all the members of the body, though many, are one body, so it is with Christ. For by one Spirit we were all baptized into one body—Jews or Greeks, slaves or free—and all were made to drink of one Spirit.

The body does not consist of one member but of many. If all were a single organ, where would the body be? As it is, there are many parts, yet one body. The eye cannot say to the hand, "I have no need of you," nor again the head to the feet, "I have no need of you." On the contrary, the parts of the body which seem to be weaker are indispensable, and those parts of the body which we think less honorable we invest with the greater honor, and our unpresentable parts are treated with greater modesty, which our more presentable parts do not require. But God has so composed the body, giving the greater honor to the inferior part, that there may be no discord in the body, but that the members may have the same care for one another. If one member suffers, all suffer together; if one member is honored, all rejoice together.

Now you are the body of Christ and individually members of it. And God has appointed in the church first apostles, second prophets, third teachers, then workers of miracles, then healers, helpers, administrators, speakers in various kinds of tongues. Are all apostles? Are all prophets? Are all teachers? Do all work miracles? Do all possess gifts of healing? Do all speak with tongues? Do all interpret?

But earnestly desire the higher gifts.

And I will show you a still more excellent way.

If I speak in the tongues of men and of angels, but have not love, I am a noisy gong or a clanging cymbal. And if I have prophetic powers, and understand all mysteries and all knowledge, and if I have all faith, so as to remove mountains, but have not love, I am nothing. If I give away all I have, and if I deliver my body to be burned, but have not love, I gain nothing.

Love is patient and kind; love is not jealous or boastful; it is not arrogant or rude. Love does not insist on its own way; it is not irritable or resentful; it does not rejoice at wrong, but rejoices in the right. Love bears all things, believes all things, hopes all things, endures all things.

Love never ends; as for prophecies, they will pass away; as for tongues, they will cease; as for knowledge, it will pass away. For our knowledge is imperfect and our prophecy is imperfect; but when the perfect comes, the imperfect will pass away. When I was a child, I spoke like a child, I thought like a child, I reasoned like a child; when I became a man, I gave up childish ways. For now we see in a mirror dimly, but then face to face. Now I know in part; then I shall understand fully, even as I have been fully understood. So faith, hope, love abide, these three; but the greatest of these is love.

Make love your aim, and earnestly desire the spiritual gifts, especially that you may prophesy. For one who speaks in a tongue speaks not to men but to God; for no one understands him, but he utters mysteries in the Spirit. On the other hand, he who prophesies speaks to men for their up-building and encouragement and consolation. He who speaks in a tongue edifies himself, but he who prophesies edifies the church. Now I want you all to speak in tongues, but even more to prophesy. He who prophesies is greater than he who speaks in tongues, unless some one interprets, so that the church may be edified. I thank God that I speak in tongues more than you all; nevertheless, in church I would rather speak five words with my mind, in order to instruct others, than ten thousand words in a tongue.

Brethren, do not be children in your thinking; be babes in evil, but in thinking be mature. Tongues are a sign not for believers but for unbelievers, while prophecy is not for unbelievers but for believers. If, therefore, the whole church assembles and all speak in tongues, and outsiders or unbelievers enter, will they not say that you are mad? But if all prophesy, and an unbeliever or outsider enters, he is convicted by all, he is called to account by all, the secrets of his heart are disclosed; and so, falling on his face, he will worship God and declare that God is really among you.

When you come together, each one has a hymn, a lesson, a revelation, a tongue, or an interpretation. If any speak in a tongue, let there be only two or at most three, and each in turn; and let one interpret. But if there is no one to interpret, let each of them keep silence in church and speak to himself and to God. Let two or three prophets speak, and let the others weigh what is said. If a revelation is made to another sitting by, let the first be silent. For you can all prophesy one by one, so that all may learn and all be encouraged;

and the spirits of prophets are subject to prophets. For God is not a God of confusion but of peace.

As in all the churches of the saints, the women should keep silence. For they are not permitted to speak, but should be subordinate, as even the law says. If there is anything they desire to know, let them ask their husbands at home. For it is shameful for a woman to speak in church.

Now I WOULD remind you, brethren, in what terms I preached to you the gospel, by which you are saved if you hold it fast. I delivered to you as of first importance that Christ died for our sins in accordance with the scriptures, that he was buried, that he was raised on the third day in accordance with the scriptures, and that he appeared to Cephas, then to the twelve. Then he appeared to more than five hundred brethren at one time, most of whom are still alive, though some have fallen asleep. Then he appeared to James, then to all the apostles. Last of all, as to one untimely born, he appeared also to me. For I am the least of the apostles, unfit to be called an apostle, because I persecuted the church of God. But by the grace of God I am what I am, and his grace toward me was not in vain. On the contrary, I worked harder than any of them, though it was not I, but the grace of God which is with me.

Now if Christ is preached as raised from the dead, how can some of you say that there is no resurrection of the dead? But if there is no resurrection of the dead, then Christ has not been raised; if Christ has not been raised, then our preaching is in vain and your faith is in vain. We are even found to be misrepresenting God, because we testified of God that he raised Christ, whom he did not raise if it is true that the dead are not raised. Then those also who have fallen asleep in Christ have perished. If for this life only we have hoped in Christ, we are of all men most to be pitied.

But in fact Christ has been raised from the dead, the first fruits of those who have fallen asleep. For as by a man came death, by a man has come also the resurrection of the dead. For as in Adam all die, so also in Christ shall all be made alive. But each in his own order: Christ the first fruits, then at his coming those who belong to Christ. Then comes the end, when he delivers the kingdom to God the Father after destroying every rule and every authority and power. For he must reign until he has put all his enemies under his feet. The last enemy to be destroyed is death. "For God has put all things in subjection under his feet." But when it says, "All things are put in subjection under him," it is plain that he is excepted who put all things under him. When all things are subjected to him, then the Son himself will also be subjected to him who put all things under him, that God may be everything to every one.

Otherwise, what do people mean by being baptized on behalf of the dead? If the dead are not raised at all, why are people baptized on their behalf? If the dead are not raised, "Let us eat and drink, for tomorrow we die." Do not be deceived: "Bad company ruins good morals." Come to your right mind, and sin no more. For some have no knowledge of God. I say this to your shame.

But some one will ask, "How are the dead raised? With what kind of body do they come?" You foolish man! What you sow does not come to life unless it dies. And what you sow is not the body which is to be, but a bare kernel, perhaps of wheat or of some other grain. But God gives it a body as he has chosen, and to each kind of seed its own body. For not all flesh is alike, but there is one kind for men, another for animals, another for birds, and another for fish. There are celestial bodies and there are terrestrial bodies; but the glory of the celestial is one, and the glory of the terrestrial is another. There is one glory of the sun, and another glory of the moon, and another glory of the stars; for star differs from star in glory.

So is it with the resurrection of the dead. What is sown is perishable, what is raised is imperishable. It is sown in dishonor, it is raised in glory. It is sown in weakness, it is raised in power. It is sown a physical body, it is raised a spiritual body. If there is a physical body, there is also a spiritual body. Thus it is written, "The first man Adam became a living being"; the last Adam became a life-giving spirit. But it is not the spiritual which is first but the physical, and then the spiritual. The first man was from the earth, a man of dust; the second man is from heaven. As was the man of dust, so are those who are of the dust; and as is the man of heaven, so are those who are of heaven. Just as we have borne the image of the man of dust, we shall also bear the image of the man of heaven. I tell you this, brethren: flesh and blood cannot inherit the kingdom of God, nor does the perishable inherit the imperishable.

Lo! I tell you a mystery. We shall not all sleep, but we shall all be changed, in a moment, in the twinkling of an eye, at the last trumpet. For the trumpet will sound, and the dead will be raised imperishable, and we shall be changed. For this perishable nature must put on the imperishable, and this mortal nature must put on immortality. When the perishable puts on the imperishable, and the mortal puts on immortality, then shall come to pass the saying that is written: "Death is swallowed up in victory." "O death, where is thy victory? O death, where is thy sting?" The sting of death is sin, and the power of sin is the law. But thanks be to God, who gives us the victory through our Lord Jesus Christ.

Therefore, my brethren, be steadfast, immovable, always abounding in the work of the Lord, knowing that in the Lord your labor is not in vain.

Now concerning the contribution for the saints: as I directed the churches of Galatia, so you also are to do. On the first day of every week, each of you is to put something aside and store it up, as he may prosper, so that contributions need not be made when I come. And when I arrive, I will send those whom you accredit by letter to carry your gift to Jerusalem. If it seems advisable that I should go also, they will accompany me.

I will visit you after passing through Macedonia, and perhaps I will stay with you or even spend the winter. But I will stay in Ephesus until Pentecost, for a wide door for effective work has opened to me, and there are many adversaries.

When Timothy comes, see that you put him at ease among you, for he is doing the work of the Lord, as I am. Speed him on his way in peace, that he may return to me. As for our brother Apollos, I strongly urged him to visit you with the other brethren, but it was not at all his will to come. He will come when he has opportunity.

The churches of Asia send greetings. Aquila and Prisca, together with the church in their house, send you hearty greetings in the Lord. All the brethren send greetings. Greet one another with a holy kiss.

I, Paul, write this greeting with my own hand. If any one has no love for the Lord, let him be accursed. Our Lord, come! The grace of the Lord Jesus be with you. My love be with you all in Christ Jesus. Amen.

2 CORINTHIANS

This letter was written about a year after 1 Corinthians. Its principal topic is Paul's personal relationship to the church at Corinth, which had taken a turn for the worse. Grieved by the wavering attitude of some of the Corinthians toward his authority and motives, Paul wrote them a severe letter (not known to us), *"out of much affliction and anguish of heart and with many tears."* Anxious to hear how they had reacted to this reprimand, he was overjoyed at the news brought by Titus of their change of heart. In relief and gratitude, Paul wrote the present letter to explain his actions and give news of his work. Because so much of 2 Corinthians is a response to the words and feelings of others, unrecorded here, it is sometimes hard to follow. Its pages preserve a good deal, however, that illuminates Paul's own life and ministry.

————

Pᴀᴜʟ, ᴀɴ ᴀᴘᴏꜱᴛʟᴇ of Christ Jesus by the will of God, and Timothy our brother. To the church of God which is at Corinth, with all the saints who are in the whole of Achaia: Grace to you and peace from God our Father and the Lord Jesus Christ.

Blessed be the God and Father of our Lord Jesus Christ, the Father of mercies, who comforts us in all our affliction, so that we may be able to comfort others. For as we share abundantly in Christ's sufferings, so through Christ we share abundantly in comfort too. If we are afflicted, it is for your comfort and salvation; and if we are comforted, it is for your comfort, when you patiently endure the same sufferings that we suffer.

For we do not want you to be ignorant, brethren, of the affliction we experienced in Asia; we were so utterly, unbearably crushed that we despaired of life itself.

Why, we felt that we had received the sentence of death; but that was to make us rely not on ourselves but on God, who raises the dead; he delivered us from so deadly a peril, and he will deliver us; on him we have set our hope that he will deliver us again.

For our boast is this, the testimony of our conscience that we have behaved in the world, and still more toward you, with holiness and godly sincerity, not by earthly wisdom but by the grace of God. I hope you will understand that you can be proud of us as we can be of you, on the day of the Lord Jesus.

Because I was sure of this, I wanted to come to you first, so that you might have a double pleasure; I wanted to visit you on my way to Macedonia, and to come back to you from Macedonia and have you send me on my way to Judea. But I call God to witness, it was to spare you that I refrained from coming to Corinth. I made up my mind not to make you another painful visit. For if I cause you pain, who is there to make me glad but the one whom I have pained? And I wrote as I did, so that when

I came I might not suffer pain from those who should have made me rejoice. I wrote you out of much affliction and anguish of heart and with many tears, not to cause you pain but to let you know the abundant love that I have for you.

But if any one has caused pain, he has caused it not to me, but in some measure—not to put it too severely—to you all. For such a one this punishment by the majority is enough; so you should rather turn to forgive and comfort him, or he may be overwhelmed by excessive sorrow. So I beg you to reaffirm your love for him. Any one whom you forgive, I also forgive. What I have forgiven, if I have forgiven anything, has been for your sake in the presence of Christ, to keep Satan from gaining the advantage over us; for we are not ignorant of his designs.

When I came to Troas to preach the gospel of Christ, a door was opened for me in the Lord; but my mind could not rest because I did not find my brother Titus there. So I took leave of them and went on to Macedonia. But thanks be to God, who in Christ always leads us in triumph, and through us spreads the fragrance of the knowledge of him everywhere. For we are the aroma of Christ to God among those who are being saved and among those who are perishing, to one a fragrance from death to death, to the other a fragrance from life to life.

Are we beginning to commend ourselves again? Or do we need letters of recommendation to you, or from you? You yourselves are our letter of recommendation, written on your hearts, to be read by all men; you are a letter from Christ delivered by us, written not with ink but with the Spirit of the living God, not on tablets of stone but on tablets of human hearts. Not that we claim anything as coming from us; our competence is from God, who has made us ministers of a new covenant, not in a written code but in the Spirit; for the written code kills, but the Spirit gives life.

Now if the dispensation of death, carved in letters on stone, came with such splendor that the Israelites could not look at Moses' face because of its brightness, will not the dispensation of the Spirit be attended with greater splendor? Since we have such a hope, we are very bold, not like Moses, who put a veil over his face. But their minds were hardened; for to this day, when they read the old covenant, that same veil remains unlifted, because only through Christ is it taken away. Yes, to this day, whenever Moses is read, a veil lies over their minds; but when a man turns to the Lord the veil is removed. And we all, with unveiled face, beholding the glory of the Lord, are being changed into his likeness from one degree of glory to another.

Therefore, having this ministry by the mercy of God, we do not lose heart. We have renounced disgraceful, underhanded ways; we refuse to practice cunning or to tamper with God's word, but by the open statement of the truth we would commend ourselves to every man's conscience in the sight of God. What we preach is not ourselves, but Jesus Christ as Lord, with ourselves as your servants for Jesus' sake. For it is the God who said, "Let light shine out of darkness," who has shone in our hearts to give the light of the knowledge of the glory of God in the face of Christ.

But we have this treasure in earthen vessels, to show that the transcendent power belongs to God and not to us. We are afflicted in every way, but not crushed; perplexed, but not driven to despair; persecuted, but not forsaken; struck down, but not destroyed; always carrying in the body the death of Jesus, so that the life of Jesus may also be manifested in our bodies. For while we live we are always being given up to death for Jesus' sake. Death is at work in us, but life in you. So we speak, knowing that he who raised the Lord Jesus will raise us also with Jesus and bring us with you into his presence. This slight momentary affliction is preparing for us an eternal weight of glory beyond all comparison, because we look not to the things that are seen but to the things that are unseen; for the things that are seen are transient, but the things that are unseen are eternal. For we know that if the earthly tent we live in is destroyed, we have a building from God, a house not made with hands, eternal in the heavens.

So we are always of good courage; we know that while we are at home in the body we are away from the Lord, for we walk by faith, not by sight. We would rather be away from the body and at home with the Lord. So we make it our aim to please him. For we must all appear before the judgment seat of Christ, so that each may receive good or evil, according to what he has done in the body.

Therefore, knowing the fear of the Lord, we persuade men; but what we are is known to God, and I hope it is known also to your conscience. We are not commending ourselves to you again but giving you cause to be proud of us, so that you may be able to answer those who pride themselves on a man's position and not on his heart. For if we are beside ourselves, it is for God; if we are in our right mind, it is for you. The love of Christ controls us, because we are convinced that one has died for all; therefore all have died. And he died for all, that those who live might live no longer for themselves but for him who for their sake died and was raised.

Therefore, if any one is in Christ, he is a new creation; the old has passed away, behold, the new has come. All this is from

God, who through Christ reconciled us to himself and gave us the ministry of reconciliation; that is, in Christ God was reconciling the world to himself, not counting their trespasses against them, and entrusting to us the message of reconciliation. So we are ambassadors for Christ, God making his appeal through us. We beseech you on behalf of Christ, be reconciled to God.

Working together with him, then, we entreat you not to accept the grace of God in vain. For he says, "At the acceptable time I have listened to you, and helped you on the day of salvation." Behold, now is the acceptable time; now is the day of salvation. We put no obstacle in any one's way, so that no fault may be found with our ministry, but as servants of God we commend ourselves in every way: through great endurance, in afflictions, hardships, calamities, beatings, imprisonments, tumults, labors, watching, hunger; by purity, knowledge, forbearance, kindness, the Holy Spirit, genuine love, truthful speech, and the power of God; with the weapons of righteousness for the right hand and for the left; in honor and dishonor, in ill repute and good repute. We are treated as impostors, and yet are true; as unknown, and yet well known; as dying, and behold, we live; as punished, and yet not killed; as sorrowful, yet always rejoicing; as poor, yet making many rich; as having nothing, and yet possessing everything.

Do NOT BE mismated with unbelievers. For what partnership have righteousness and iniquity? Or what fellowship has light with darkness? What accord has Christ with Belial? Or what has a believer in common with an unbeliever? What agreement has the temple of God with idols? For we are the temple of the living God.

Open your hearts to us; we have wronged no one, we have corrupted no one, we have taken advantage of no one. If I made you sorry with my letter, I do not regret it (though I did regret it), for I see that that letter grieved you. I rejoice, not because you were grieved, but because you were grieved into repenting; for you felt a godly grief, so that you suffered no loss through us. For godly grief produces a repentance that leads to salvation and brings no regret, but worldly grief produces death. See what earnestness this godly grief has produced in you, what eagerness to clear yourselves, what indignation, what alarm, what longing, what zeal, what punishment! At every point you have proved yourselves guiltless in the matter.

We want you to know, brethren, about the grace of God which has been shown in the churches of Macedonia, for in a severe test of affliction, their abundance of joy and their extreme poverty have overflowed in a wealth of liberality on their part. For they gave according to their means, as I can testify, and beyond their means, of their own free will, begging us earnestly for the favor of taking part in the relief of the saints. Accordingly, we have urged Titus that he should complete among you this gracious work. Now as you excel in everything, see that you excel in this also. I say this not as a command, but to prove by the earnestness of others that your love also is genuine.

But thanks be to God, who puts the same earnest care for you into the heart of

Titus. With him we are sending the brother who is famous among all the churches for his preaching of the gospel; he has been appointed by the churches to travel with us in this gracious work which we are carrying on, for the glory of the Lord and to show our good will.

We intend that no one should blame us about this liberal gift which we are administering, for we aim at what is honorable not only in the Lord's sight but also in the sight of men. I am sending the brethren so that you may be ready, as I said you would be; lest if some Macedonians come with me and find that you are not ready, we be humiliated—to say nothing of you—for being so confident. So I thought it necessary to urge the brethren to go on before me, and arrange in advance for this gift you have promised.

The point is this: he who sows sparingly will also reap sparingly, and he who sows bountifully will also reap bountifully. Each one must do as he has made up his mind, not reluctantly or under compulsion, for God loves a cheerful giver. And God is able to provide you with every blessing in abundance. The rendering of this service not only supplies the wants of the saints but also overflows in many thanksgivings to God. Under the test of this service, you will glorify God by your obedience in acknowledging the gospel of Christ, and by the generosity of your contribution for them and for all others.

I entreat you, by the meekness and gentleness of Christ—I who am humble when face to face with you, but bold to you when I am away!—that when I am present I may not have to show boldness with such confidence as I count on showing against some who suspect us of acting in worldly fashion. For though we live in the world we are not carrying on a worldly war, for the weapons of our warfare are not worldly but have divine power to destroy strongholds. We destroy arguments and every proud obstacle to the knowledge of God, and take every thought captive to obey Christ, being ready to punish every disobedience, when your obedience is complete.

Look at what is before your eyes. If any one is confident that he is Christ's, let him remind himself that as he is Christ's, so are we. For even if I boast a little too much of our authority, which the Lord gave for building you up and not for destroying you, I shall not be put to shame. I would not seem to be frightening you with letters. For they say, "His letters are weighty and strong, but his bodily presence is weak, and his speech of no account." Let such people understand that what we say by letter when absent, we do when present.

But we will not boast beyond limit, but will keep to the limits God has apportioned us, to reach even to you. We were the first to come all the way to you with the gospel of Christ. We do not boast beyond limit, in other men's labors; but our hope is that as your faith increases, our field among you may be greatly enlarged, so that we may preach the gospel in lands beyond you, without boasting of work already done in another's field. "Let him who boasts, boast of the Lord." For it is not the man who commends himself that is accepted, but the man whom the Lord commends.

I wish you would bear with me in a little

foolishness. Do bear with me! I feel a divine jealousy for you, for I betrothed you to Christ to present you as a pure bride to her one husband. But I am afraid that as the serpent deceived Eve by his cunning, your thoughts will be led astray from a sincere and pure devotion to Christ. For if some one comes and preaches another Jesus than the one we preached, or if you receive a different spirit from the one you received, or if you accept a different gospel from the one you accepted, you submit to it readily enough. I think that I am not in the least inferior to these superlative apostles. Even if I am unskilled in speaking, I am not in knowledge; in every way we have made this plain to you in all things.

Let no one think me foolish; but even if you do, accept me as a fool, so that I too may boast a little. (What I am saying I say not with the Lord's authority but as a fool, in this boastful confidence; since many boast of worldly things, I too will boast.) For you gladly bear with fools, being wise yourselves!

Whatever any one dares to boast of—I

am speaking as a fool—I also dare to boast
of that. Are they Hebrews? So am I. Are
they Israelites? So am I. Are they descendants of Abraham? So am I. Are they servants of Christ? I am a better one—I am
talking like a madman—with far greater
labors, far more imprisonments, with
countless beatings, and often near death.
Five times I have received at the hands of
the Jews the forty lashes less one. Three
times I have been beaten with rods; once I
was stoned. Three times I have been
shipwrecked; a night and a day I have
been adrift at sea; on frequent journeys, in
danger from rivers, danger from robbers,
danger from my own people, danger from
Gentiles, danger in the city, danger in the
wilderness, danger at sea, danger from
false brethren; in toil and hardship,
through many a sleepless night, in hunger
and thirst, often without food, in cold and
exposure. And, apart from other things,
there is the daily pressure upon me of my
anxiety for all the churches. Who is weak,
and I am not weak? Who is made to fall,
and I am not indignant?

If I must boast, I will boast of the things

that show my weakness. The God and Father of the Lord Jesus, he who is blessed for ever, knows that I do not lie. At Damascus, the governor under King Aretas guarded the city in order to seize me, but I was let down in a basket through a window in the wall and escaped his hands.

I must boast; there is nothing to be gained by it, but I will go on to visions and revelations of the Lord. I know a man in Christ who fourteen years ago was caught up to the third heaven—whether in the body or out of the body I do not know, God knows. And I know that this man was caught up into Paradise—whether in the body or out of the body I do not know, God knows—and he heard things that cannot be told, which man may not utter. On behalf of this man I will boast, but on my own behalf I will not boast, except of my weaknesses. And to keep me from being too elated by the abundance of revelations, a thorn was given me in the flesh, a messenger of Satan, to harass me. Three times I besought the Lord about this, that it should leave me; but he said to me, "My grace is sufficient for you, for my power is made perfect in weakness." For the sake of Christ, then, I am content with weaknesses, insults, hardships, persecutions, and calamities; for when I am weak, then I am strong.

Here for the third time I am ready to come to you. And I will not be a burden, for I seek not what is yours but you; for children ought not to lay up for their parents, but parents for their children. I will most gladly spend and be spent for your souls. If I love you the more, am I to be loved the less?

Have you been thinking all along that we have been defending ourselves before you? It is in the sight of God that we have been speaking in Christ, and all for your upbuilding, beloved. For I fear that perhaps I may come and find you not what I wish, and that you may find me not what you wish; that perhaps there may be quarreling, jealousy, anger, selfishness, slander, gossip, conceit, and disorder. I fear that when I come again my God may humble me before you, and I may have to mourn over many of those who sinned before and have not repented of the impurity, immorality, and licentiousness which they have practiced.

Any charge must be sustained by the evidence of two or three witnesses. I warned those who sinned before and all the others, and I warn them now while absent, that if I come again I will not spare them—since you desire proof that Christ is speaking in me. He is not weak in dealing with you, but is powerful in you. For he was crucified in weakness, but lives by the power of God. For we are weak in him, but in dealing with you we shall live with him by the power of God.

Examine yourselves, to see whether you are holding to your faith. Test yourselves. Do you not realize that Jesus Christ is in you?—unless indeed you fail to meet the test! I hope you will find out that we have not failed. For we cannot do anything against the truth, but only for the truth. We are glad when we are weak and you are strong. What we pray for is your improvement. I write this in order that when I come I may not have to be severe in my use of the authority which the Lord has given me.

Finally, brethren, farewell. Mend your ways, heed my appeal, agree with one another, live in peace, and the God of love and peace will be with you. Greet one another with a holy kiss. All the saints greet you.

The grace of the Lord Jesus Christ and the love of God and the fellowship of the Holy Spirit be with you all.

LETTER OF PAUL
GALATIANS

Paul's reason for writing to the churches of Galatia, founded by him, is quite clear: he has just received news about other Christian preachers from Jerusalem who are telling Galatia's converts that they must obey the Mosaic law of circumcision, eat only kosher food, and honor all other Jewish religious observances. This was contrary to the gospel, and Paul writes at once to remind his readers that salvation is God's free gift to all who have faith in Christ, not something earned by the keeping of certain rules. Those who are "in Christ," he insists, are free from the law, and are to be guided by the Spirit. Then, lest anyone should use the doctrine as a reason for indifference to the moral code, he concludes with some practical applications of his teaching.

PAUL AN APOSTLE—not from men nor through man, but through Jesus Christ and God the Father, who raised him from the dead—and all the brethren who are with me, to the churches of Galatia: Grace to you and peace from God the Father and our Lord Jesus Christ, who gave himself for our sins to deliver us from the present evil age.

I am astonished that you are so quickly turning to a different gospel—not that there is another gospel, but there are some who want to pervert the gospel of Christ. But even if an angel from heaven should preach to you a gospel contrary to that which we preached to you, let him be accursed.

I would have you know, brethren, that the gospel which was preached by me is not man's gospel. For I did not receive it from man, but it came through a revelation of Jesus Christ. You have heard of my former life in Judaism, how I persecuted the church of God, so extremely zealous was I for the traditions of my fathers. But when he who had set me apart before I was born was pleased to reveal his Son to me, in order that I might preach him among the Gentiles, I did not go up to Jerusalem to those who were apostles before me, but I went away into Arabia; and again I returned to Damascus. Then after three years I went up to Jerusalem to visit Cephas, and remained with him fifteen days. But I saw none of the other apostles except James the Lord's brother. (In what I am writing to you, before God, I do not lie!) Then I went into the regions of Syria and Cilicia. And I was still not known by sight to the churches of Christ in Judea; they only heard it said, "He who once persecuted us is now preaching the faith he once tried to destroy." And they glorified God because of me.

After fourteen years I went up again to Jerusalem with Barnabas and Titus. I laid before those who were of repute the gospel which I preach, lest somehow I should be running in vain. But even Titus was not compelled to be circumcised, though he was a Greek. False brethren tried to bring us into bondage, but we did not yield submission, even for a moment, that the truth of the gospel might be preserved for you. Those who were reputed to be something (what they were makes no difference to me; God shows no partiality) added nothing to me. On the contrary, when they saw that I had been entrusted with the gospel to the uncircumcised, just as Peter had been entrusted with the gospel to the circumcised, James and Cephas and John gave to me and Barnabas the right hand of fellowship.

But when Cephas came to Antioch I opposed him to his face, because he stood condemned. For before certain men came from James, he ate with the Gentiles; when they came he separated himself, fearing the circumcision party. And with him the rest of the Jews acted insincerely, so that even Barnabas was carried away by their insincerity. But when I saw this, I said to Cephas before them all, "If you, though a Jew, live like a Gentile, how can you compel the Gentiles to live like Jews?" We ourselves, who are Jews by birth, know that a man is not justified by works of the law but through faith in Jesus Christ, because by works of the law shall no one be justified. But if, in our endeavor to be justified in Christ, we ourselves were found to be sinners, is Christ then an agent of sin? Certainly not! But if I build up again those things which I tore down, then I prove myself a transgressor. For I through the law died to the law, that I might live to God. I have been crucified with Christ; it is no longer I who live, but Christ who lives in me; and the life I now live in the flesh I live by faith in the Son of God, who loved me and gave himself for me. I do not nullify the grace of God; for if justification were through the law, then Christ died to no purpose.

O foolish Galatians! Who has bewitched you, before whose eyes Jesus Christ was publicly portrayed as crucified? Did you receive the Spirit by works of the law, or by hearing with faith? Having begun with the Spirit, are you now ending with the flesh? Does he who supplies the Spirit to you and works miracles among you do so by works of the law, or by hearing with faith? Thus Abraham "believed God, and it was reckoned to him as righteousness." So you see that it is men of faith who are the sons of Abraham. And the scripture, foreseeing that God would justify the Gentiles by faith, preached the gospel beforehand to Abraham, saying, "In you shall all the nations be blessed." So then, those who are men of faith are blessed with Abraham who had faith.

To give a human example, brethren: no one annuls even a man's will, or adds to it, once it has been ratified. Now the promises were made to Abraham and to his offspring. It does not say, "And to offsprings," referring to many; but, referring to one, "And to your offspring," which is Christ. This is what I mean: the law, which came afterward, does not annul a covenant previously ratified by God. For if the inheritance is by the law, it is no longer by promise; but God gave it to Abraham by a promise. Why then the law? It was added because of transgressions, till the offspring should come to whom the promise had been made.

Before faith came we were confined under the law, so that the law was our custodian until Christ came. Now we are no longer under a custodian; for in Christ Jesus you are all sons of God, through faith. For as many of you as were baptized into

Christ have put on Christ. There is neither
Jew nor Greek, slave nor free, male nor
female; for you are all one in Christ Jesus.
And if you are Christ's, then you are Abraham's offspring, heirs according to promise.

The heir, as long as he is a child, is no
better than a slave, but is under guardians
and trustees. So with us; when we were
children, we were slaves to the elemental
spirits of the universe. But when the time
had fully come, God sent forth his Son,
born of woman, born under the law, to
redeem those who were under the law, so
that we might receive adoption as sons.
And because you are sons, God has sent
the Spirit of his Son into our hearts, crying, "Abba! Father!" So through God you
are no longer a slave but a son, and if a
son then an heir. Now that you have come
to know God, or rather to be known by
God, how can you turn back again to the
weak and beggarly elemental spirits? You
observe days, and months, and seasons,
and years! I am afraid I have labored over
you in vain.

Brethren, I beseech you, become as I
am, for I also have become as you are. You

received me as an angel of God, as Christ Jesus. What has become of the satisfaction you felt? For I bear you witness that, if possible, you would have plucked out your eyes and given them to me. Have I then become your enemy by telling you the truth? My little children, with whom I am again in travail until Christ be formed in you! I could wish to be present with you now and to change my tone, for I am perplexed about you.

Tell me, you who desire to be under law, do you not hear the law? For it is written that Abraham had two sons, one by a slave and one by a free woman. But the son of the slave was born according to the flesh, the son of the free woman through promise. Now this is an allegory: these women are two covenants. One is from Mount Sinai, bearing children for slavery; she is Hagar and corresponds to the present Jerusalem, for she is in slavery with her children. But the Jerusalem above is free, and she is our mother. For it is written, "Rejoice, O barren one who does not bear; break forth and shout, you who are not in travail; for the children of the desolate one are many more than the children of her that is married." Now we, brethren, like Isaac, are children of promise. But as at that time he who was born according to the flesh persecuted him who was born according to the Spirit, so it is now. But what does the scripture say? "Cast out the slave and her son; for the son of the slave shall not inherit with the son of the free woman." So, brethren, we are not children of the slave but of the free woman. Christ has set us free; stand fast therefore, and do not submit again to a yoke of slavery.

Now I, Paul, say to you that if you receive circumcision, Christ will be of no advantage to you. I testify again to every man who receives circumcision that he is bound to keep the whole law. You are severed from Christ, you who would be justified by the law; you have fallen away from grace. For in Christ Jesus neither circumcision nor uncircumcision is of any avail, but faith working through love. You were running well; who hindered you from obeying the truth? I have confidence in the Lord that you will take no other view than mine; and he who is troubling you will bear his judgment, whoever he is. But if I, brethren, still preach circumcision, why am I still persecuted? In that case the stumbling block of the cross has been removed. I wish those who unsettle you would mutilate themselves!

Brethren, do not use your freedom as an opportunity for the flesh, but through love be servants of one another. For the whole law is fulfilled in one word, "You shall love your neighbor as yourself." But if you bite and devour one another, take heed that you are not consumed by one another. Walk by the Spirit, and do not gratify the desires of the flesh. For the desires of the flesh are against the Spirit, and the desires of the Spirit are against the flesh. Now the works of the flesh are plain: fornication, impurity, licentiousness, idolatry, sorcery, enmity, strife, jealousy, anger, selfishness, dissension, party spirit, envy, drunkenness, carousing, and the like. I warn you, as I warned you before, that those who do such things shall not inherit the kingdom of God. But the fruit of the Spirit is love, joy, peace, patience, kindness, goodness, faithfulness, gentleness, self-control. And those who belong to Christ Jesus have crucified the flesh with its passions and desires.

Brethren, if a man is overtaken in any trespass, you who are spiritual should restore him in a spirit of gentleness. Look to yourself, lest you too be tempted. Bear one another's burdens, and so fulfil the law of Christ. For if any one thinks he is something, when he is nothing, he deceives himself. But let each one test his own work, and then his reason to boast will be in himself alone and not in his neighbor. For each man will have to bear his own load.

Do not be deceived; God is not mocked, for whatever a man sows, that he will also reap. For he who sows to his own flesh will from the flesh reap corruption; but he who sows to the Spirit will from the Spirit reap eternal life. And let us not grow weary in well-doing, for in due season we shall reap, if we do not lose heart. As we have opportunity, let us do good to all men, and especially to those who are of the household of faith.

The grace of our Lord Jesus Christ be with your spirit, brethren. Amen.

LETTER OF PAUL
EPHESIANS

More like a sermon or meditation than Paul's other letters, Ephesians does not deal with the needs of one particular church, and it contains no personal messages. It may in fact have been an encyclical or "circular letter." Opening with an exposition of God's eternal purpose to redeem Jews and Gentiles alike, the whole letter is pervaded with the doctrine of the mystical body of Christ, the apostle's analogy of the perfect union of Christian believers. This provides, too, the best example for the ideal harmony of husbands and wives. Unlike the Old Testament, the New Testament has no book that is purely poetry. But Ephesians comes near to it.

Paul, an apostle of Christ Jesus by the will of God, to the saints who are also faithful in Christ Jesus: Grace to you and peace from God our Father and the Lord Jesus Christ.

Blessed be the God and Father of our Lord Jesus Christ, who has blessed us in Christ with every spiritual blessing in the heavenly places, even as he chose us in him before the foundation of the world, that we should be holy and blameless before him. He destined us in love to be his sons through Jesus Christ, according to the purpose of his will. In him we have redemption through his blood, the forgiveness of our trespasses, according to the riches of his grace. For he has made known to us the mystery of his will, according to his purpose which he set forth in Christ as a plan for the fulness of time, to unite in him all things in heaven and on earth.

In him we who first hoped in Christ have been appointed to live for the praise of his glory. In him you also, who have heard the gospel and have believed, were sealed with the Holy Spirit, which is the guarantee of our inheritance. For this reason, because I have heard of your faith in the Lord Jesus and your love toward all the saints, I do not cease to give thanks for you, remembering you in my prayers, that God may give you a spirit of wisdom, so that you may know what is the hope to which he has called you, and what is the immeasurable greatness of his power in us who believe, according to the working of his great might which he accomplished in Christ when he raised him from the dead. He made him sit at his right hand, far above all rule and authority and power and dominion, and above every name that is named, not only in this age but also in that which is to come. He has put all things under his feet and has made him the head over all things for the church, which is his body, the fulness of him who fills all in all.

And you he made alive, when you were dead through sins. We all once lived in the passions of our flesh, following the desires of body and mind, and so we were by nature children of wrath, like the rest of mankind. But God, even when we were dead through our trespasses, made us alive together with Christ, and raised us up with him. For by grace you have been saved through faith; and this is not your own doing, it is the gift of God—not because of works, lest any man should boast. For we are his workmanship, created in Christ Jesus for good works, which God prepared beforehand, that we should walk in them.

Remember that at one time you Gentiles were separated from Christ, alienated from Israel and the covenants of promise, having no hope and without God in the world. But now you who once were far off have been brought near in the blood of Christ. For he has broken down the dividing wall of hostility, by abolishing in his flesh the law of commandments and ordinances, that he might create in himself one new man in place of the two, and might reconcile us both to God in one body through the cross. He came and preached peace to those both far off and near; for through him we both have access in one Spirit to the Father. So you are no longer strangers, but are members of the household of God, built upon the foundation of the apostles and prophets, Christ Jesus himself being the cornerstone.

For this reason I, Paul, am a prisoner for Christ Jesus on behalf of you Gentiles— assuming that you have heard how the mystery was made known to me by revelation. When you read this you can perceive my insight into the mystery of Christ, which was not made known to other generations as it has now been revealed to his holy apostles and prophets by the Spirit; that is, how the Gentiles are fellow heirs of the promise in Christ Jesus through the gospel. To me, though I am the very least of all the saints, this grace was given, to preach to the Gentiles the unsearchable riches of Christ, and to make all men see what is the plan of the mystery; that through the church the manifold wisdom of God might now be made known to the principalities and powers in the heavenly places. So I ask you not to lose heart over what I am suffering for you, which is your glory.

I bow my knees before the Father, that he may grant you to be strengthened through his Spirit in the inner man, and

that Christ may dwell in your hearts
through faith; that you, being rooted and
grounded in love, may comprehend with
all the saints what is the breadth and
length and height and depth, and know the
love of Christ which surpasses knowledge,
that you may be filled with all the fulness
of God.

Now to him who by the power at work
within us is able to do far more abundantly
than all that we ask or think, to him be
glory in the church and in Christ Jesus to
all generations. Amen.

I therefore, a prisoner for the Lord, beg
you to lead a life worthy of the calling to
which you have been called, with all lowli-
ness and meekness, with patience, forbearing one another in love, eager to maintain
the unity of the Spirit in the bond of peace.
There is one body and one Spirit, just as
you were called to the one hope that belongs to your call, one Lord, one faith, one
baptism, one God and Father of us all,
who is above all and through all and in all.
But grace was given to each of us according to the measure of Christ's gift. His gifts
were that some should be apostles, some

prophets, some evangelists, some pastors and teachers, to equip the saints for the work of ministry, for building up the body of Christ, until we all attain to the unity of the faith and of the knowledge of the Son of God, to mature manhood, to the stature of the fulness of Christ; so that we may no longer be children, tossed to and fro with every wind of doctrine, by the cunning of men. Rather, speaking the truth in love, we are to grow up in every way into him who is the head, into Christ, from whom the whole body, joined together, when each part is working properly, upbuilds itself in love.

Now this I testify in the Lord, that you must no longer live as the Gentiles do, darkened in their understanding, alienated from the life of God because of ignorance, callous, given up to licentiousness. You did not so learn Christ! Put off your old nature and be renewed in the spirit of your minds; put on the new nature, created after the likeness of God in true righteousness and holiness. Let every one speak the truth with his neighbor, for we are members one of another. Be angry but do not sin; do not let the sun go down on your anger, and give no opportunity to the devil. Let the thief no longer steal, but rather let him do honest work with his hands, to be able to give to those in need. Let no evil talk come out of your mouths, but only such as is edifying, as fits the occasion. And do not grieve the Holy Spirit of God, in whom you were sealed for the day of redemption. Let all bitterness and clamor and slander be put away, with all malice, and be kind to one another, tenderhearted, forgiving, as God in Christ forgave you.

Therefore be imitators of God, as beloved children. And walk in love, as Christ loved us and gave himself up for us, a sacrifice to God.

But fornication and all impurity or covetousness must not even be named among you. No impure man, or one who is covetous (that is, an idolater), has any inheritance in the kingdom of Christ and of God. Once you were darkness, but now you are light in the Lord; walk as children of light (for the fruit of light is found in all that is good and right and true), and try to learn what is pleasing to the Lord. Take no part in the unfruitful works of darkness, but instead expose them.

Look carefully then how you walk, not as unwise men but as wise, making the most of the time, because the days are evil. Do not get drunk with wine, for that is debauchery; but be filled with the Spirit, addressing one another in psalms, singing to the Lord with all your heart, always giving thanks in the name of our Lord Jesus Christ to God the Father.

Be subject to one another out of reverence for Christ. Wives, be subject to your husbands, as to the Lord. For the husband is the head of the wife as Christ is the head of the church, his body, and is its Savior. Husbands, love your wives, as Christ loved the church and gave himself up for her, that he might sanctify her, having cleansed her by water with the word, that he might present the church in splendor, holy and without blemish. Even so husbands should love their wives as their own bodies. He who loves his wife loves himself. For no man ever hates his own flesh, but nourishes and cherishes it, as Christ does the church. "A man shall leave his father and mother and be joined to his wife, and the two shall become one flesh." This mystery is a profound one, and I am saying that it refers to Christ and the church.

Children, obey your parents in the Lord, for this is right. "Honor your father and mother" (this is the first commandment with a promise), "that it may be well with you and that you may live long on the earth." Fathers, do not provoke your children to anger, but bring them up in the discipline and instruction of the Lord.

Slaves, be obedient to your earthly masters, with fear and trembling, in singleness of heart, not as men-pleasers, but as servants of Christ, doing the will of God from the heart, rendering service with a good will. Know that whatever good any one does, he will receive the same again from the Lord, whether he is a slave or free. Masters, do the same to them, and forbear threatening, knowing that he who is both their Master and yours is in heaven, and that there is no partiality with him.

Finally, be strong in the Lord and in the strength of his might. Put on the whole armor of God, that you may be able to stand against the wiles of the devil. For we are not contending against flesh and blood, but against the spiritual hosts of wickedness in the heavenly places. Stand therefore, having girded your loins with truth, and having put on the breastplate of righteousness, and having shod your feet with the equipment of the gospel of peace; taking the shield of faith, with which you can quench all the flaming darts of the evil one. And take the helmet of salvation, and the sword of the Spirit, which is the word of God. Pray at all times in the Spirit. To that end keep alert with all perseverance, making supplication for all the saints, and also for me, that utterance may be given me to proclaim boldly the mystery of the gospel, for which I am an ambassador in chains.

Peace be to the brethren, and love with faith, from God the Father and the Lord Jesus Christ. Grace be with all who love our Lord Jesus Christ with love undying.

LETTER OF PAUL
PHILIPPIANS

One of Paul's most cordial and affection-
ate letters, Philippians was addressed to a
Christian community in Macedonia, at Philippi, the first of the churches he founded
in Europe. Writing from prison, probably
in Rome, the apostle thanks the Philippians for having sent him, through Epaphroditus, some things he needed. When, after
some time, Epaphroditus wanted to return
home, Paul sent him back with this letter
to express his warm regard for his friends
there and to give them news and encouragement. The entire letter shows Paul's ra-
diant joy and serene happiness in Christ,
even while in prison and in danger of
death.

———

PAUL AND TIMOTHY, servants of Christ Jesus, to all the saints in Christ Jesus who are at Philippi, with the bishops and deacons: Grace to you and peace from God our Father and the Lord Jesus Christ.

I thank my God, always in every prayer, for your partnership in the gospel from the first day until now. I am sure that he who began a good work in you will bring it to completion at the day of Jesus Christ. You are all partakers with me of grace, both in my imprisonment and in the defense and confirmation of the gospel. For God is my witness, how I yearn for you all with the affection of Christ Jesus. It is my prayer that your love may abound, with knowledge and all discernment, so that you may be pure and blameless for the day of Christ, filled with the fruits of righteousness which come through Jesus Christ, to the glory and praise of God.

I want you to know, brethren, that what has happened to me has really served to advance the gospel, so that it has become known throughout the whole praetorian guard and to all the rest that my imprisonment is for Christ; and most of the brethren have been made confident in the Lord because of my imprisonment, and are much more bold to speak the word of God without fear.

I rejoice, for I know that through your prayers and the help of the Spirit of Jesus Christ this will turn out for my deliverance, as it is my eager expectation and hope that with full courage now as always Christ will be honored in my body, whether by life or by death. For to me to live is Christ, and to die is gain. If it is to be life in the flesh, that means fruitful labor for me. Yet I am hard pressed between the two. My desire is to depart and be with Christ. But to remain in the flesh is more necessary on your account. Convinced of this, I know that I shall remain and continue with you all, for your progress and joy in the faith.

Only let your manner of life be worthy of the gospel of Christ, so that whether I come and see you or am absent, I may hear of you that you stand firm in one spirit, striving side by side for the faith of the gospel, and not frightened in anything by your opponents.

So if there is any encouragement in Christ, any incentive of love, any participation in the Spirit, complete my joy by being in full accord and of one mind. Do nothing from selfishness or conceit, but in humility count others better than yourselves. Let each of you look not only to his own interests, but also to the interests of others. Have this mind among yourselves, which is yours in Christ Jesus, who, though he was in the form of God, did not count equality with God a thing to be grasped, but emptied himself, taking the form of a servant, being born in the likeness of men. And being found in human form he humbled himself and became obedient unto death, even death on a cross. Therefore God has highly exalted him and bestowed on him the name which is above every name, that at the name of Jesus every knee should bow, in heaven and on earth and under the earth, and every tongue confess that Jesus Christ is Lord, to the glory of God the Father.

Therefore, my beloved, as you have always obeyed, not only in my presence but much more in my absence, work out your own salvation with fear and trembling; for God is at work in you.

Do all things without grumbling or questioning, that you may be children of God without blemish in the midst of a crooked and perverse generation, among whom you shine as lights in the world, holding fast the word of life, so that in the day of Christ I may be proud that I did not run in vain or labor in vain. Even if I am to be poured as a libation upon the sacrificial offering of your faith, I am glad and rejoice with you all. Likewise you also should be glad and rejoice with me.

I hope in the Lord Jesus to send Timothy to you soon, so that I may be cheered by news of you. I have no one like him, who will be genuinely anxious for your welfare. Timothy's worth you know, how as a son with a father he has served with me in the gospel. I hope therefore to send him just as soon as I see how it will go with me; and I trust in the Lord that shortly I myself shall come also.

I have thought it necessary to send you Epaphroditus, your messenger and minister to my need. He has been longing for you all, and has been distressed because you heard that he was ill. Indeed he was ill, near to death, but God had mercy on him. So receive him in the Lord with all joy; and honor such men, for he nearly died for the work of Christ, risking his life to complete your service to me.

Finally, my brethren, look out for the dogs, look out for the evil-workers, look out for those who mutilate the flesh. For we are the true circumcision, who worship God in spirit, and glory in Christ Jesus, and put no confidence in the flesh. If any man thinks he has reason for confidence in the flesh, I have more: circumcised on the eighth day, of the people of Israel, of the tribe of Benjamin, a Hebrew born of Hebrews; as to the law a Pharisee, as to zeal a persecutor of the church, as to righteousness under the law blameless. But whatever gain I had, I counted as loss for the sake of Christ. Indeed I count everything as loss because of the surpassing worth of knowing Christ Jesus my Lord. For his sake I have suffered the loss of all things, and count them as refuse, in order that I may gain Christ and be found in him, not having a righteousness of my own, based on law, but that which is through faith in Christ, the righteousness from God that depends on faith; that I may know him and the power of his resurrection, and may share his sufferings, becoming like him in his death, that if possible I may attain the resurrection from the dead.

Not that I have already obtained this or am already perfect; but I press on to make it my own, because Christ Jesus has made me his own. Forgetting what lies behind and straining forward to what lies ahead, I press on toward the goal for the prize of the upward call of God in Christ Jesus. Let those of us who are mature be thus minded; and if in anything you are otherwise minded, God will reveal that also to you. Only let us hold true to what we have attained.

Brethren, join in imitating me, and mark those who so live as you have an example in us. For many, of whom I have often told you and now tell you even with tears, live as enemies of the cross of Christ. Their end is destruction, their god is the belly, and they glory in their shame, with minds set on earthly things. But our common-wealth is in heaven, and from it we await a Savior, the Lord Jesus Christ, who will change our lowly body to be like his glorious body, by the power which enables him even to subject all things to himself.

Therefore, my brethren, whom I love and long for, my joy and crown, stand firm thus in the Lord, my beloved.

I entreat Euodia and Syntyche to agree in the Lord. And I ask you also, true yoke-fellow, help these women, for they have labored side by side with me in the gospel together with Clement and the rest of my fellow workers, whose names are in the book of life.

Rejoice in the Lord always; again I will say, Rejoice. Let all men know your for-bearance. The Lord is at hand. Have no anxiety about anything, but in everything by prayer and supplication with thanksgiving let your requests be made known to God. And the peace of God, which passes all understanding, will keep your hearts and your minds in Christ Jesus.

Finally, brethren, whatever is true, what-ever is honorable, whatever is just, whatever is pure, whatever is lovely, whatever is gracious, if there is any excellence, if there is anything worthy of praise, think about these things.

I rejoice in the Lord greatly that you have revived your concern for me; you were indeed concerned for me, but you had no opportunity. Not that I complain of want; for I have learned, in whatever state I am, to be content. I know how to be abased, and I know how to abound; in any and all circumstances I have learned the secret of facing plenty and hunger, abundance and want. I can do all things in him who strengthens me. Yet it was kind of you to share my trouble. Not that I seek the gift; but I seek the fruit which increases to your credit. And my God will supply every need of yours according to his riches in glory in Christ Jesus. To our God and Father be glory for ever and ever. Amen.

Greet every saint in Christ Jesus. The brethren who are with me greet you. All the saints greet you, especially those of Caesar's household.

The grace of the Lord Jesus Christ be with your spirit.

LETTER OF PAUL
COLOSSIANS

The Christian church at Colossae, a city not far from Ephesus in Asia Minor, had been founded by Epaphras, whom Paul had sent to preach there. The apostle wrote this letter, probably from a prison in Rome, in order to correct some serious errors that were being taught at Colossae, and to instruct the recipients in the Christian life. The letter resembles Ephesians in tone, especially in the emphasis on the doctrine of the mystical body of Christ. At the same time Paul does not forget to give instructions for the Christian's daily life in the world.

———

PAUL, AN APOSTLE of Christ Jesus by the will of God, and Timothy our brother, to the saints and faithful brethren in Christ at

Colossae: Grace to you and peace from God our Father.

We always thank God, the Father of our Lord Jesus Christ, when we pray for you, because we have heard of your faith in Christ Jesus and of the love which you have for all the saints, because of the hope laid up for you in heaven. Of this you have heard before in the gospel which has come to you, as indeed in the whole world it is bearing fruit and growing—so among yourselves, from the day you heard and understood the grace of God in truth, as you learned it from Epaphras our beloved fellow servant. He is a faithful minister of Christ on our behalf and has made known to us your love in the Spirit.

And so, from the day we heard of it, we have not ceased to pray for you, asking that you may be filled with the knowledge of his will in all spiritual wisdom and understanding, to lead a life worthy of the Lord, fully pleasing to him, bearing fruit in every good work. May you be strengthened with all power, for all endurance with joy, giving thanks to the Father, who has qualified us to share in the inheritance of the saints in light. He has delivered us from the dominion of darkness and transferred us to the kingdom of his beloved Son, in whom we have redemption, the forgiveness of sins.

He is the image of the invisible God, the first-born of all creation; for in him all things were created, in heaven and on earth, visible and invisible, whether thrones or dominions or principalities or authorities—all things were created through him and for him. He is before all things, and in him all things hold together. He is the head of the body, the church; he is the beginning, the first-born from the dead, that in everything he might be preeminent. For in him all the fulness of God was pleased to dwell, and through him to reconcile to himself all things, whether on earth or in heaven, making peace by the blood of his cross.

And you, who once were estranged and hostile in mind, doing evil deeds, he has now reconciled in his body of flesh by his death, in order to present you holy and irreproachable before him, provided that

you continue in the faith, stable and steadfast, not shifting from the hope of the gospel, which has been preached to every
creature under heaven, and of which I,
Paul, became a minister.

Now I rejoice in my sufferings for your
sake, and in my flesh I complete what is
lacking in Christ's afflictions for the sake
of his body, that is, the church, of which I
became a minister according to the divine
office given to me for you, to make the
word of God fully known, the mystery hidden for ages and generations but now
made manifest to his saints. To them
God chose to make known how great
among the Gentiles are the riches of the
glory of this mystery, which is Christ in
you, the hope of glory. Him we proclaim,
warning and teaching every man in all
wisdom, that we may present every man
mature in Christ. For this I toil, striving
with all the energy which he mightily inspires within me.

For I want you to know how greatly I
strive for you, and for those at Laodicea,
and for all who have not seen my face, that
their hearts may be encouraged as they are

knit together in love, to have all the riches of assured understanding and the knowledge of God's mystery, of Christ, in whom are hid all the treasures of wisdom and knowledge. I say this in order that no one may delude you with beguiling speech. Though I am absent in body, yet I am with you in spirit, rejoicing to see your good order and the firmness of your faith in Christ. Live in him, rooted and built up in him and established in the faith, just as you were taught, abounding in thanksgiving.

See to it that no one makes a prey of you by philosophy and empty deceit, according to human tradition, according to the elemental spirits of the universe, and not according to Christ. For in him the whole fulness of deity dwells bodily, and you have come to fulness of life in him, who is the head of all rule and authority. You were buried with him in baptism, in which you were also raised with him through faith in the working of God. And you, who were dead in trespasses, God made alive together with him, having forgiven us all our trespasses, having canceled the bond which stood against us with its legal demands; this he set aside, nailing it to the cross. He disarmed the principalities and powers and made a public example of them, triumphing over them in him.

Therefore let no one pass judgment on you in questions of food and drink or a festival or a sabbath. These are only a shadow of what is to come; but the substance belongs to Christ. Let no one disqualify you, insisting on self-abasement and worship of angels, taking his stand on visions, puffed up without reason by his sensuous mind, and not holding fast to the Head, from whom the whole body, nourished and knit together through its joints and ligaments, grows with a growth that is from God.

If then you have been raised with Christ, seek the things that are above, where Christ is, seated at the right hand of God. For you have died, and your life is hid with Christ in God. When Christ, who is our life, appears, then you also will appear with him in glory.

Put to death therefore what is earthly in

you: fornication, impurity, passion, evil desire, and covetousness, which is idolatry.
On account of these the wrath of God is
coming. Put away anger, wrath, malice,
slander, and foul talk. Do not lie to one
another, seeing that you have put on the
new nature, which is being renewed in
knowledge after the image of its creator.
Here there cannot be Greek and Jew, circumcised and uncircumcised, barbarian,
Scythian, slave, free man, but Christ is all,
and in all.

Put on then, as God's chosen ones, holy
and beloved, compassion, kindness, lowli-
ness, meekness, and patience, forbearing
one another and, if one has a complaint
against another, forgiving each other; as
the Lord has forgiven you, so you also
must forgive. And above all these put on
love, which binds everything together in
perfect harmony. And let the peace of
Christ rule in your hearts, to which indeed
you were called in the one body. Let the
word of Christ dwell in you richly, teach
and admonish one another in all wisdom,
and sing psalms and hymns with thankful-
ness in your hearts to God. And whatever

you do, in word or deed, do everything in the name of the Lord Jesus.

Wives, be subject to your husbands, as is fitting in the Lord. Husbands, love your wives, and do not be harsh with them. Children, obey your parents in everything, for this pleases the Lord. Fathers, do not provoke your children, lest they become discouraged. Slaves, obey in everything your earthly masters. Whatever your task, work heartily, as serving the Lord and not men, knowing that from the Lord you will receive the inheritance as your reward. For the wrongdoer will be paid back for the wrong he has done, and there is no partiality. Masters, treat your slaves justly and fairly, knowing that you also have a Master in heaven.

Continue steadfastly in prayer with thanksgiving; and pray for us also, that God may open to us a door for the word, to declare the mystery of Christ, on account of which I am in prison, that I may make it clear, as I ought to speak.

Conduct yourselves wisely toward outsiders, making the most of the time. Let your speech always be gracious, seasoned with salt, so that you may know how you ought to answer every one.

Tychicus will tell you all about my affairs; he is a beloved brother and faithful minister and fellow servant in the Lord. I have sent him to you for this very purpose, and that he may encourage your hearts, and with him Onesimus, the faithful and beloved brother, who is one of yourselves.

Aristarchus my fellow prisoner greets you, and Mark the cousin of Barnabas, and Jesus who is called Justus. These are the only men of the circumcision among my fellow workers for the kingdom of God, and they have been a comfort to me. Epaphras, who is one of yourselves, a servant of Christ Jesus, greets you, always remembering you earnestly in his prayers, that you may stand mature and fully assured in all the will of God. He has worked hard for you and for those in Laodicea and in Hierapolis. Luke the beloved physician and Demas greet you. Give my greetings to the brethren at Laodicea, and to Nympha and the church in her house. And when this letter has been read among you, have it read also in the church of the Laodiceans; and see that you read also the letter from Laodicea.

I, Paul, write this greeting with my own hand. Remember my fetters. Grace be with you.

you have it read also in the church of the
Laodiceans; and see that you read also the
letter from Laodicea.
hand. Remember my fetters. Grace be
with you.

LETTER OF PAUL
1 THESSALONIANS

During his second missionary journey,
about A.D. 51, Paul visited Thessalonica,
the capital of Macedonia. Here he
preached for several weeks, then was
forced by enemies to leave the city. Arriv-
ing in Corinth, he remained anxious about
the immature congregation he had left behind, now deprived of its leadership and
persecuted by the opposition. Soon afterward he wrote this letter of encouragement
and instruction, warning his readers
against unchastity, dishonest conduct, and
idleness. He also deals with questions that
had begun to perplex the Thessalonians
concerning the Second Coming of Christ.
Christians who die before that hoped-for
event, Paul says, will not be deprived of
the blessings of the kingdom, but will rise
first and then, together with the living, be

united with Christ. He declines to make pronouncements on the time of these events, but bids his readers watch and be sober.

Paul, Silvanus, and Timothy, to the church of the Thessalonians in God the Father and the Lord Jesus Christ: Grace to you and peace.

We give thanks to God always for you all, constantly mentioning you in our prayers. For we know, brethren beloved by God, that he has chosen you; for our gospel came to you in power and in the Holy Spirit and with full conviction, so that you became an example to all the believers in Macedonia and in Achaia. They themselves report how you turned to God from idols, to serve a living and true God, and to wait for his Son from heaven, whom he raised from the dead, Jesus who delivers us from the wrath to come.

You know, brethren, that our visit to you was not in vain. We had courage in our God to declare to you the gospel in the

face of great opposition. But just as we
have been entrusted with the gospel, so we
speak, not to please men, but to please
God, who tests our hearts. We never used
words of flattery, or a cloak for greed, nor
did we seek glory from men, though we
might have made demands as apostles of
Christ. We worked night and day, that we
might not burden any of you, while we
preached to you the gospel of God. Like a
father with his children, we exhorted each
one of you and encouraged you to lead a
life worthy of God, who calls you into his
own kingdom and glory.

But since we were bereft of you, brethren, for a short time, in person not in
heart, we endeavored the more eagerly to
see you face to face, but Satan hindered
us. For what is our hope or joy or crown
of boasting before our Lord Jesus at his
coming? Is it not you? For you are our
glory and joy. When we could bear it no
longer, we sent Timothy to establish you in
your faith and to exhort you, that no one
be moved by these afflictions. You know
that this is to be our lot, for when we were
with you, we told you that we were to

suffer affliction, just as it has come to pass. So I sent that I might know your faith, for fear that somehow the tempter had tempted you and that our labor would be in vain.

Now that Timothy has brought us the good news and reported that you always remember us kindly and long to see us, as we long to see you, we have been comforted; for now we live, if you stand fast in the Lord. What thanksgiving can we render to God for you, praying earnestly night and day that we may see you face to face and supply what is lacking in your faith?

Brethren, we exhort you in the Lord Jesus, that as you learned from us how you ought to live and to please God, you do so more and more. For this is the will of God, your sanctification: that you abstain from unchastity; that each one of you know how to take a wife for himself in holiness and honor, not in the passion of lust like heathen who do not know God; that no man transgress, and wrong his brother in this matter, because the Lord is an avenger in all these things, as we solemnly forewarned you. For God has not called us for uncleanness, but in holiness. Therefore whoever disregards this, disregards not man but God, who gives his Holy Spirit to you.

Concerning love of the brethren you have no need to have any one write to you, for you yourselves have been taught by God to love one another. But we exhort you to do so more and more, to aspire to live quietly, to mind your own affairs, and to work with your hands, as we charged you; so that you may command the respect of outsiders, and be dependent on nobody.

But we would not have you ignorant, brethren, concerning those who are asleep, that you may not grieve as others do who have no hope. For since we believe that Jesus died and rose again, even so, through Jesus, God will bring with him those who have fallen asleep. For this we declare to you by the word of the Lord, that we who are alive, who are left until the coming of the Lord, shall not precede those who have fallen asleep. For the Lord himself will descend from heaven with a cry of command, with the archangel's call, and with the sound of the trumpet of God. And the dead in Christ will rise first; then we who are alive, who are left, shall be caught up together with them in the clouds to meet the Lord in the air; and so we shall always be with the Lord. Therefore comfort one another with these words.

As to times and seasons, you know well that the day of the Lord will come like a thief in the night. When people say, "There is peace and security," then sudden destruction will come upon them as travail comes upon a woman with child. But you are not in darkness, brethren, for that day to surprise you like a thief. For you are all sons of light and sons of the day. So let us not sleep, as others do, but keep awake and be sober. For those who sleep sleep at night, and those who get drunk are drunk at night. Since we belong to the day, let us be sober, and put on the breastplate of faith and love, and for a helmet the hope of salvation. For God has not destined us for wrath, but to obtain salvation through our Lord Jesus Christ, who died for us so that whether we wake or sleep we might live with him.

We beseech you, brethren, to respect

those who labor among you and are over you in the Lord. Admonish the idlers, encourage the faint-hearted, help the weak, be patient with them all. See that none of you repays evil for evil, but always seek to do good to one another and to all. Rejoice always, pray constantly, give thanks in all circumstances; for this is the will of God in Christ Jesus for you. Do not quench the Spirit, do not despise prophesying, but test everything; hold fast what is good, abstain from every form of evil.

May the God of peace himself sanctify you wholly; and may your spirit and soul and body be kept sound and blameless at the coming of our Lord Jesus Christ. He who calls you is faithful, and he will do it.

Brethren, pray for us. Greet all the brethren with a holy kiss. I adjure you by the Lord that this letter be read to all the brethren. The grace of our Lord Jesus Christ be with you.

2 THESSALONIANS

Not long after Paul sent his first letter to the Christians of Thessalonica he wrote again, probably because he had heard further disturbing news about them. They were suffering persecution in some way, it seems, and certain persons were still causing trouble by their mistaken ideas on the Second Coming of Christ. Reminding them of the apostolic tradition concerning the day of the Lord, Paul declares that the Second Coming might not be quite so near as some of them thought. Certain definite signs, he says, will precede that day, and he rebukes those who in their excitement over the Second Coming neglect their ordinary duties and live in idleness. The letter closes with a concluding note in Paul's own handwriting as a guarantee of genuineness.

PAUL, SILVANUS, AND Timothy, to the church of the Thessalonians in God our Father and the Lord Jesus Christ: Grace to you and peace from God the Father and the Lord Jesus Christ.

We are bound to give thanks to God always for you, brethren, because your faith is growing abundantly, and the love of one for another is increasing. We ourselves boast of you in the churches of God for your steadfastness in the afflictions which you are enduring.

This is evidence of the righteous judgment of God, that you may be made worthy—since indeed God deems it just to repay with affliction those who afflict you, and to grant rest to you when the Lord Jesus is revealed from heaven with his mighty angels in flaming fire, inflicting vengeance upon those who do not know God and upon those who do not obey the gospel. They shall suffer eternal destruction and exclusion from the presence of the Lord, when he comes on that day to be glorified and marveled at in all who have believed.

Now concerning the coming of our Lord

Jesus Christ and our assembling to meet him, we beg you, brethren, not to be quickly shaken in mind or excited, by spirit, by word, or by letter purporting to be from us, to the effect that the day of the Lord has come. For that day will not come, unless the rebellion comes first, and the man of lawlessness is revealed, the son of perdition, who exalts himself, proclaiming himself God. Do you not remember that when I was still with you I told you this? The mystery of lawlessness is already at work; only he who now restrains it will do so until he is out of the way. And then the lawless one will be revealed, and the Lord Jesus will slay him with the breath of his mouth and destroy him by his coming. The coming of the lawless one by the activity of Satan will be with all power and with wicked deception for those who are to perish, because they refused to love the truth. Therefore God sends upon them a strong delusion, so that all may be condemned who had pleasure in unrighteousness.

Now we command you, brethren, in the name of our Lord Jesus Christ, that you keep away from any brother who is living in idleness. For you know how you ought to imitate us; we were not idle when we were with you, we did not eat any one's bread without paying, but with toil and labor we worked night and day, that we might not burden any of you. It was not because we have not that right, but to give you in our conduct an example to imitate. If any one will not work, let him not eat. For we hear that some of you are living in idleness, mere busybodies. Now such persons we command in the Lord Jesus Christ to do their work in quietness and to earn their own living. Brethren, do not be weary in well-doing.

If any one refuses to obey what we say in this letter, note that man, and have nothing to do with him, that he may be ashamed. Do not look on him as an enemy, but warn him as a brother.

Now may the Lord of peace himself give you peace at all times in all ways. I, Paul, write this greeting with my own hand. This is the mark in every letter of mine; it is the way I write. The grace of our Lord Jesus Christ be with you all.

1 TIMOTHY

The two letters to Timothy, along with the one to Titus, are called the Pastoral Letters because they are concerned with the work of the two men as pastors of churches. Judging by differences in style and vocabulary from Paul's other letters, many modern scholars think that the Pastorals were not written by Paul. A loyal disciple, it is thought, expanded several previously unpublished messages of the apostle, perhaps a generation after Paul's death. In any case, the letters are especially valuable for the light they shed on early church organization and the discipline of the time. In this first letter the author offers Timothy suggestions for the regulation of public worship, defines the position of men and women in the community, lays down the qualifications of bishops and deacons, warns against false teachers, and concludes with various moral exhortations.

———

PAUL, AN APOSTLE of Christ Jesus by command of God our Savior and of Christ Jesus our hope, to Timothy, my true child in the faith: Grace, mercy, and peace from God the Father and Christ Jesus our Lord.

As I urged you when I was going to Macedonia, remain at Ephesus that you may charge certain persons not to teach any different doctrine, nor to occupy themselves with myths which promote speculations rather than the divine training that is in faith. The aim of our charge is love that issues from a pure heart, a good conscience and sincere faith. Certain persons by swerving from these have wandered into vain discussion, desiring to be teachers of the law, without understanding what they are saying.

Now we know that the law is good, if any one uses it lawfully. The law is not laid down for the just but for the disobedient, for the ungodly, for murderers, immoral persons, sodomites, kidnapers, liars, and whatever else is contrary to sound doctrine, in accordance with the glorious gospel.

I thank Christ Jesus our Lord because he judged me faithful by appointing me to his service, though I formerly persecuted him; but I had acted ignorantly, and the grace of our Lord overflowed for me. The saying is sure, that Christ Jesus came into the world to save sinners. And I am the foremost of sinners; but I received mercy, that in me Jesus Christ might display his perfect patience for an example to those who were to believe in him for eternal life.

This charge I commit to you, Timothy, my son, in accordance with the prophetic utterances which pointed to you, so that inspired by them you may wage the good warfare, holding faith and a good conscience. By rejecting conscience, certain persons have made shipwreck of their faith, among them Hymenaeus and Alexander, whom I have delivered to Satan, that they may learn not to blaspheme.

First of all I urge that prayers and

thanksgivings be made for all men, for kings and all who are in high positions. This is good in the sight of God our Savior, who desires all men to be saved and to come to the knowledge of the truth. For there is one God, and there is one mediator between God and men, the man Christ Jesus, who gave himself as a ransom for all, the testimony to which was borne at the proper time.

I desire that in every place the men should pray, lifting holy hands without quarreling; also that women should adorn themselves modestly and sensibly, not with braided hair or gold or pearls or costly attire but by good deeds, as befits women who profess religion. Let a woman learn in silence with all submissiveness. I permit no woman to teach or to have authority over men; she is to keep silent. For Adam was formed first, then Eve; and Adam was not deceived, but the woman was deceived and became a transgressor. Yet woman will be saved through bearing children, if she continues in faith and love and holiness, with modesty.

If any one aspires to the office of bishop,

he desires a noble task. A bishop must be above reproach, the husband of one wife, temperate, dignified, hospitable, an apt teacher, no drunkard, not violent, not quarrelsome, and no lover of money. He must manage his own household well, keeping his children submissive and respectful; for if a man does not know how to manage his own household, how can he care for God's church?

Deacons likewise must be serious, not double-tongued, not addicted to much wine, not greedy. Let them be tested first; then if they prove themselves blameless let them serve as deacons. The women likewise must be serious, no slanderers, but temperate, faithful in all things. Let deacons be the husband of one wife, and let them manage their children and their households well.

Now the Spirit expressly says that in later times some will depart from the faith by giving heed to deceitful spirits, through the pretensions of liars who forbid marriage and enjoin abstinence from foods which God created to be received with thanksgiving. Everything created by God is good, and nothing is to be rejected if it is received with thanksgiving; for then it is consecrated by the word of God and prayer.

Have nothing to do with godless and silly myths. Train yourself in godliness; for while bodily training is of some value, godliness is of value in every way, as it holds promise for the present life and also for the life to come. To this end we strive, because we have our hope set on the living God, who is the Savior of all men, especially of those who believe.

Command and teach these things. Let no one despise your youth, but set an example in speech and conduct. Attend to the public reading of scripture, to preaching, to teaching. Do not neglect the gift you have, which was given you by prophetic utterance when the council of elders laid their hands upon you. Practice these duties, devote yourself to them, for by so doing you will save both yourself and your hearers. Do not rebuke an older man but exhort him as you would a father; treat younger men like brothers, older women like mothers, younger women like sisters, in all purity.

If a widow has children or grandchildren, let them first learn their religious duty to their own family and make some return to their parents. She who is a widow, and is left all alone, has set her hope on God and continues in supplications and prayers night and day; whereas she who is self-indulgent is dead even while she lives. If any one does not provide for his relatives, and especially for his own family, he has disowned the faith and is worse than an unbeliever.

Let a widow be enrolled if she is not less than sixty years of age, having been the wife of one husband; and she must be well attested for her good deeds, as one who has brought up children, shown hospitality, washed the feet of the saints, relieved the afflicted, and devoted herself to doing good in every way. But refuse to enrol younger widows; for when they grow wanton against Christ they desire to marry, and so they incur condemnation for having violated their first pledge. Besides that, they learn to be idlers, gadding about from house to house, gossips and busybodies.

So I would have younger widows marry, bear children, rule their households, and give the enemy no occasion to revile us.

Let the elders who rule well be considered worthy of double honor, especially those who labor in preaching and teaching; for the scripture says, "You shall not muzzle an ox when it is treading out the grain," and, "The laborer deserves his wages." Never admit any charge against an elder except on the evidence of two or three witnesses. As for those who persist in sin, rebuke them in the presence of all, so that the rest may stand in fear.

No longer drink only water, but use a little wine for the sake of your stomach and your frequent ailments.

The sins of some men are conspicuous, pointing to judgment, but the sins of others appear later. So also good deeds are conspicuous; and even when they are not, they cannot remain hidden. Let all who are under the yoke of slavery regard their masters as worthy of all honor, so that the name of God and the teaching may not be defamed. Those who have believing masters must not be disrespectful on the ground that they are brethren; rather they must serve all the better, since those who benefit by their service are believers and beloved.

Teach and urge these duties. If any one does not agree with the sound words of our Lord Jesus Christ, he is puffed up with conceit; he has a morbid craving for controversy and for disputes about words, which produce envy, dissension, slander, base suspicions, and wrangling among men who are depraved in mind and bereft of the truth, imagining that godliness is a means of gain. There is great gain in godliness with contentment; for we brought nothing into the world, and we cannot take anything out of the world; but if we have food and clothing, with these we shall be content. Those who desire to be rich fall into many senseless desires that plunge men into ruin. For the love of money is the root of all evils; it is through this craving that some have wandered from the faith and pierced their hearts with many pangs.

As for you, man of God, shun all this. Fight the good fight of the faith; take hold of the eternal life to which you were called.

In the presence of God who gives life to all things, and of Christ Jesus who in his testimony before Pontius Pilate made the good confession, I charge you to keep the commandment unstained and free from reproach until the appearing of our Lord Jesus Christ. This will be made manifest at the proper time by the blessed and only Sovereign, the King of kings and Lord of lords, who alone has immortality and dwells in unapproachable light, whom no man has ever seen or can see. To him be honor and eternal dominion. Amen.

As for the rich, charge them not to be haughty, nor to set their hopes on uncertain riches but on God, who richly furnishes us with everything. They are to be rich in good deeds, thus laying up for themselves a good foundation for the future, so that they may take hold of the life which is life indeed.

O Timothy, guard what has been entrusted to you. Avoid the godless chatter and contradictions of what is falsely called knowledge, for by professing it some have missed the mark as regards the faith. Grace be with you.

2 TIMOTHY

In 2 Timothy, a much more personal letter than 1 Timothy, the author urges endurance as an essential quality for a preacher of the gospel. The emphasis is on courage and fidelity in standing fast against false teaching, and in becoming a vessel fit for the Master's use. The author warns Timothy of sufferings that are bound to come, and he closes with a moving reference to his own impending martyrdom. For modern opinion concerning date and authorship, see the Introduction to 1 Timothy.

PAUL, AN APOSTLE of Christ Jesus by the will of God according to the promise of the life which is in Christ Jesus, to Timothy, my beloved child: Grace, mercy, and peace from God the Father and Christ Jesus our Lord.

I thank God, whom I serve with a clear conscience, when I remember you in my prayers. As I remember your tears, I long to see you, that I may be filled with joy. I am reminded of your sincere faith, a faith that dwelt first in your grandmother Lois and your mother Eunice and now dwells in you. Rekindle the gift of God that is within you through the laying on of my hands; God did not give us a spirit of timidity but a spirit of power and love and self-control.

Do not be ashamed then of testifying to our Lord, nor of me his prisoner. Share in suffering for the gospel in the power of God, who called us with a holy calling in virtue of his own purpose and the grace which he gave us in Christ Jesus ages ago, and now through the appearing of our Savior Christ Jesus, who abolished death and brought life and immortality. For this gospel I was appointed a preacher and apostle and teacher, and therefore I suffer as I do. But I am not ashamed, for I know whom I have believed. Follow the pattern of the sound words which you have heard from me, in the faith and love which are in Christ Jesus; guard the truth that has been entrusted to you by the Holy Spirit who dwells within us.

My son, be strong in the grace that is in Christ Jesus, and what you have heard from me, entrust to faithful men who will be able to teach others also. Share in suffering as a good soldier of Christ Jesus. No soldier on service gets entangled in civilian pursuits, since his aim is to satisfy the one who enlisted him. An athlete is not crowned unless he competes according to the rules.

Remember Jesus Christ, risen from the dead, descended from David, as preached in my gospel, the gospel for which I am suffering and wearing fetters like a criminal. But the word of God is not fettered. Therefore I endure everything for the sake of the elect, that they also may obtain salvation in Christ Jesus with its eternal glory. The saying is sure: If we have died with him, we shall also live with him; if we endure, we shall also reign with him; if we deny him, he also will deny us; if we are faithless, he remains faithful—for he cannot deny himself.

Remind them of this, and charge them before the Lord to avoid disputing about words, which does no good, but only ruins the hearers. Do your best to present yourself to God as one approved, a workman who has no need to be ashamed, rightly handling the word of truth. Avoid godless chatter, for it will lead people into more and more ungodliness, and their talk will eat its way like gangrene. Among them are Hymenaeus and Philetus, who have swerved from the truth by holding that the resurrection is past already. They are upsetting the faith of some. But God's firm foundation stands, bearing this seal: "The Lord knows those who are his," and, "Let every one who names the name of the Lord depart from iniquity."

In a great house there are not only vessels of gold and silver but also of wood and earthenware, and some for noble use, some for ignoble. If any one purifies himself from what is ignoble, then he will be a vessel for noble use, consecrated and useful to the master of the house, ready for any good work. So shun youthful passions and aim at righteousness, faith, love, and peace, along with those who call upon the Lord from a pure heart. Have nothing to do with stupid, senseless controversies; you know that they breed quarrels. And the Lord's servant must not be quarrelsome but kindly to every one, an apt teacher, forbearing, correcting his opponents with gentleness.

But understand this, that in the last days there will come times of stress. For men will be lovers of self, lovers of money, proud, arrogant, abusive, disobedient to their parents, ungrateful, unholy, inhuman, implacable, slanderers, profligates, fierce, haters of good, treacherous, reckless, swollen with conceit, lovers of pleasure rather than lovers of God, holding the form of religion but denying the power of it. Avoid such people. As Jannes and Jambres opposed Moses, so these men also oppose the truth, men of corrupt mind and counterfeit faith; but they will not get very far, for their folly will be plain to all, as was that of those two men.

Now you have observed my teaching, my conduct, my aim in life, my faith, my patience, my love, my steadfastness, my persecutions, my sufferings, what befell me at Antioch, at Iconium, and at Lystra, what persecutions I endured; yet from them all the Lord rescued me. Indeed all who desire to live a godly life in Christ Jesus will be persecuted, while evil men and impostors will go on from bad to worse, deceivers and deceived. But as for you, continue in what you have learned and have firmly believed, knowing from whom you learned it and how from childhood you have been acquainted with the sacred writings which are able to instruct you for salvation through faith in Christ Jesus. All scripture is inspired by God and profitable for teaching, for reproof, for correction, and for training in righteousness, that the man of God may be complete, equipped for every good work.

I charge you in the presence of God and of Christ Jesus who is to judge the living and the dead, preach the word, be urgent in season and out of season, convince, rebuke, and exhort, be unfailing in patience and in teaching. For the time is coming when people will not endure sound teaching, but having itching ears they will accumulate for themselves teachers to suit their own likings, and will turn away from listening to the truth and wander into myths.

I am already on the point of being sacrificed; the time of my departure has come. I have fought the good fight, I have finished the race, I have kept the faith. Henceforth there is laid up for me the crown of righteousness, which the Lord, the righteous judge, will award to me on that Day, and not only to me but also to all who have loved his appearing.

Do your best to come to me soon. For Demas, in love with this present world, has deserted me and gone to Thessalonica; Crescens has gone to Galatia, Titus to Dalmatia. Luke alone is with me. Get Mark and bring him with you; for he is very useful in serving me. Bring the cloak that I left with Carpus at Troas, also the books, and above all the parchments. Alexander the coppersmith did me great harm; the Lord will requite him for his deeds. At my first defense no one took my part; all deserted me. May it not be charged against them! But the Lord stood by me and gave me strength to proclaim the message fully, that all the Gentiles might hear it. So I was rescued from the lion's mouth. The Lord will rescue me from every evil and save me for his heavenly kingdom. To him be the glory for ever and ever. Amen.

Do your best to come before winter. Eubulus sends greetings to you, as do Pudens and Linus and Claudia and all the brethren. The Lord be with your spirit. Grace be with you.

LETTER OF PAUL
TITUS

Titus, a Greek, was probably one of the first Gentile Christians. For a time he served as a missionary companion of the apostle Paul. This brief letter to him, classed with 1 and 2 Timothy as Paul's Pastoral Letters, deals with those qualities that are required of leaders in the church. It treats the duties of various classes in society, sums up the Christian virtues, and closes with a warning against becoming entangled in theoretical arguments that only distract the attention and divert energy from the Christian cause. For modern opinion concerning date and authorship, see the Introduction to 1 Timothy.

———

PAUL, A SERVANT of God and an apostle of Jesus Christ, to further the faith of God's elect and their knowledge of the truth which accords with godliness, in hope of eternal life which God, who never lies, promised ages ago and at the proper time manifested in his word through the preaching with which I have been entrusted by command of God our Savior; to Titus, my true child in a common faith: Grace and peace from God the Father and Christ Jesus our Savior.

This is why I left you in Crete, that you might amend what was defective, and appoint elders in every town, if any man is blameless, the husband of one wife, and his children are believers and not profligate or insubordinate. A bishop must not be arrogant or quick-tempered or a drunkard or violent or greedy, but hospitable, a lover of goodness, master of himself, and holy. He must hold firm to the sure word as taught, that he may be able to give instruction in sound doctrine and confute those who contradict it.

For there are many insubordinate men, deceivers, especially the circumcision party; they must be silenced, since they are upsetting whole families by teaching for base gain what they have no right to teach. One of themselves, a prophet, said, "Cretans are always liars, evil beasts, lazy gluttons." This testimony is true. Therefore rebuke them sharply, that they may be sound in the faith, instead of giving heed to Jewish myths or to men who reject the truth. To the pure all things are pure, but to the corrupt and unbelieving nothing is pure; their very minds and consciences are corrupted. They profess to know God, but they deny him by their deeds; they are detestable, disobedient, unfit for any good deed.

As for you, teach what befits sound doctrine. Bid the older men be temperate, serious, sound in faith, in love, and in steadfastness. Bid the older women be reverent in behavior, not slanderers or slaves to drink; they are to train the young women to love their husbands and children, to be sensible, chaste, domestic, kind, and submissive to their husbands. Urge the younger men to control themselves. Show yourself a model of good deeds, and in your teaching show integrity, gravity, and speech that cannot be censured, so that an opponent may have nothing evil to say of us. Bid slaves be submissive to their masters, not to pilfer, but to show entire fidelity.

For the grace of God has appeared for the salvation of all, training us to renounce irreligion and worldly passions, and to live sober, godly lives, awaiting our blessed hope, the appearing of the glory of our God and Savior Jesus Christ, who gave himself for us to redeem us from all iniquity and to purify for himself a people of his own who are zealous for good deeds.

Declare these things; exhort and reprove with all authority. Let no one disregard you.

Remind our people to be submissive to rulers and authorities, to be ready for any honest work, to speak evil of no one, to avoid quarreling, to be gentle, and to show perfect courtesy toward all. For we ourselves were once foolish, led astray, slaves to passions and pleasures, passing our days in malice and envy, hated by men and hating one another. But when the goodness and loving kindness of God our Savior appeared, he saved us, not because of deeds done by us in righteousness, but in virtue of his own mercy, by the washing of regeneration and renewal in the Holy Spirit, which he poured out upon us richly through Jesus Christ our Savior, that we might be justified by his grace and become heirs in hope of eternal life.

I desire you to insist on these things, so that those who have believed in God may be careful to apply themselves to good deeds. But avoid stupid controversies, dissensions, and quarrels over the law, for they are futile. As for a man who is factious, after admonishing him once or twice, have nothing more to do with him, knowing that such a person is perverted and sinful; he is self-condemned.

When I send Artemas or Tychicus to you, do your best to come to me at Nicopolis, for I have decided to spend the winter there. Speed Zenas the lawyer and Apollos on their way; see that they lack nothing. And let our people learn to help cases of urgent need, and not to be unfruitful.

All who are with me send greetings to you. Greet those who love us in the faith. Grace be with you all.

LETTER OF PAUL
PHILEMON

Philemon was a Christian of Colossae in Phrygia, whose slave Onesimus had run away. Somehow the fugitive had come to meet Paul, who sent him back to his master with this brief personal note, the shortest of the Pauline Letters. Paul asks Philemon, for the sake of friendship, to forgive Onesimus, who is now a fellow Christian. As a runaway slave, Onesimus could be severely punished, and Paul's plea shows how Christian ways were changing the old harsh customs, though it was many generations before slavery was ended.

———

PAUL, A PRISONER for Christ Jesus, and Timothy our brother, to Philemon our beloved fellow worker and Apphia our sister and Archippus our fellow soldier, and the church in your house: Grace to you and peace from God our Father and the Lord Jesus Christ.

I thank my God always when I remember you in my prayers, because I hear of your love and of the faith which you have toward the Lord Jesus and all the saints, and I pray that the sharing of your faith may promote the knowledge of all the good that is ours in Christ. For I have derived much joy and comfort from your love, my brother, because the hearts of the saints have been refreshed through you.

Accordingly, though I am bold enough in Christ to command you to do what is required, yet for love's sake I prefer to appeal to you—I, Paul, an ambassador and now a prisoner also for Christ Jesus—I appeal to you for my child, Onesimus, whose father I have become in my imprisonment. (Formerly he was useless to you, but now he is indeed useful to you and to me.) I am sending him back to you, sending my very heart. I would have been glad to keep him with me, in order that he might serve me on your behalf during my imprisonment for the gospel; but I preferred to do nothing without your consent in order that your goodness might not be by compulsion but of your own free will.

Perhaps this is why he was parted from you for a while, that you might have him back for ever, no longer as a slave but more than a slave, as a beloved brother, especially to me but how much more to you, both in the flesh and in the Lord. So if you consider me your partner, receive him as you would receive me. If he has wronged you at all, or owes you anything, charge that to my account. I, Paul, write this with my own hand, I will repay it—to say nothing of your owing me even your own self. Yes, brother, I want some benefit from you in the Lord. Refresh my heart in Christ.

Confident of your obedience, I write to you, knowing that you will do even more than I say. At the same time, prepare a guest room for me, for I am hoping through your prayers to be granted to you.

Epaphras, my fellow prisoner in Christ

Jesus, sends greetings to you, and so do Mark, Aristarchus, Demas, and Luke, my fellow workers.

The grace of the Lord Jesus Christ be with your spirit.

LETTER TO THE
HEBREWS

This anonymous treatise, the longest sustained argument of any book in the Bible, was written to Jewish Christians who were on the point of returning to Judaism, perhaps because of persecution. In order to win them back to the Christian faith, the author emphasizes three points: the superiority of Jesus Christ over Old Testament figures (the prophets, the angels, and Moses himself); the superiority of Christ's priesthood over the priesthood of Aaron; and the superiority of Christ's sacrifice of himself over the Levitical sacrifices. Into his argument the author weaves sections of earnest exhortation, urging his readers to be steadfast, to persevere, and to have greater faith. Though the letter is traditionally ascribed to the apostle Paul, features of style and vocabulary show that it was written by some other leader in the early church. It is probably to be dated before the fall of Jerusalem in A.D. 70.

IN MANY AND various ways God spoke of old to our fathers by the prophets; but in these last days he has spoken to us by a Son, whom he appointed the heir of all things, through whom also he created the world. He reflects the glory of God and bears the very stamp of his nature, upholding the universe by his word of power. When he had made purification for sins, he sat down at the right hand of the Majesty on high, having become as much superior to angels as the name he has obtained is more excellent than theirs. For to what angel did God ever say, "Thou art my Son, today I have begotten thee"? To what angel has he ever said, "Sit at my right hand, till I make thy enemies a stool for thy feet"?

Therefore we must pay the closer attention to what we have heard, lest we drift away from it. For how shall we escape if we neglect such a great salvation? It was declared at first by the Lord, and it was attested to us by those who heard him, while God also bore witness by signs and wonders and various miracles and by gifts of the Holy Spirit.

For it was not to angels that God subjected the world to come, of which we are speaking. It has been testified somewhere, "What is man that thou art mindful of him, or the son of man, that thou carest for him? Thou didst make him for a little while lower than the angels, thou hast crowned him with glory and honor, putting everything in subjection under his feet." Now in putting everything in subjection to him, he left nothing outside his control. As it is, we do not yet see everything in subjection to him. But we see Jesus, who for a little while was made lower than the angels, crowned with glory and honor because of the suffering of death, so that by the grace of God he might taste death for every one.

It was fitting that he, for whom and by whom all things exist, should make the pioneer of their salvation perfect through suffering. For he who sanctifies and those who are sanctified have all one origin. That is why he is not ashamed to call them brethren, saying, "I will proclaim thy name to my brethren." And again, "Here am I, and the children God has given me." Since therefore the children share in flesh and blood, he himself likewise partook of the same nature, that through death he might destroy him who has the power of death, that is, the devil, and deliver all those who through fear of death were subject to lifelong bondage. He had to be made like his brethren in every respect, so that he might become a merciful and faithful high priest in the service of God, to make expiation for the sins of the people. Because he himself has suffered and been tempted, he is able to help those who are tempted.

Therefore, holy brethren, consider Jesus, the apostle and high priest of our confession. He was faithful to him who appointed him, just as Moses also was faithful in God's house as a servant, to testify to the things that were to be spoken later. But Christ was faithful over God's house as a son. And we are his house if we hold fast our confidence and pride in our hope.

Take care, brethren, lest there be in any of you an evil, unbelieving heart, leading you to fall away from the living God. But exhort one another every day, that none of you may be hardened by the deceitfulness of sin. For we share in Christ, if only we hold our first confidence firm to the end. The word of God is living and active, sharper than any two-edged sword, piercing to the division of soul and spirit, of joints and marrow, and discerning the thoughts and intentions of the heart. And before him no creature is hidden, but all are open and laid bare to the eyes of him with whom we have to do.

Since, then, we have a great high priest who has passed through the heavens, Jesus, the Son of God, let us hold fast our confession. For we have not a high priest who is unable to sympathize with our weaknesses, but one who in every respect has been tempted as we are, yet without sin. Let us, then, with confidence draw near to the throne of grace, that we may receive mercy and find grace to help in time of need.

For every high priest chosen from among men is appointed to act on behalf of men in relation to God, to offer gifts and sacrifices for sins. He can deal gently with the ignorant and wayward, since he himself is beset with weakness. Because of this he is bound to offer sacrifice for his own sins as well as for those of the people. And one does not take the honor upon himself, but he is called by God, just as Aaron was. So also Christ did not exalt himself to be made a high priest, but was appointed by him who said to him, "Thou art my Son, today I have begotten thee."

In the days of his flesh, Jesus offered up prayers and supplications, with loud cries and tears, to him who was able to save him from death, and he was heard for his godly fear. Although he was a Son, he learned obedience through what he suffered; and being made perfect he became the source of eternal salvation to all who obey him, being designated by God a high priest after the order of Melchizedek.

When God made a promise to Abraham, since he had no one greater by whom to swear, he swore by himself, saying,

"Surely I will bless you and multiply you."
And thus Abraham, having patiently endured, obtained the promise. Men indeed
swear by a greater than themselves, and in
all their disputes an oath is final for confirmation. So when God desired to show
more convincingly to the heirs of the
promise the unchangeable character of his
purpose, he interposed with an oath, so
that through two unchangeable things, in
which it is impossible that God should
prove false, we who have fled for refuge
might have strong encouragement to seize
the hope set before us. We have this as a
sure and steadfast anchor of the soul, a
hope that enters into the inner shrine behind the curtain, where Jesus has gone as a
forerunner on our behalf, having become a
high priest for ever, after the order of
Melchizedek.

For this Melchizedek, king of Salem,
priest of the Most High God, met Abraham returning from the slaughter of the
kings and blessed him; and to him Abraham apportioned a tenth part of everything. He is first, by translation of his
name, king of righteousness, and then he is

also king of Salem, that is, king of peace. He is without father or mother or genealogy, and has neither beginning of days nor end of life, but resembling the Son of God he continues a priest for ever.

See how great he is! Abraham the patriarch gave him a tithe of the spoils. And those descendants of Levi who receive the priestly office have a commandment in the law to take tithes from the people, that is, from their brethren, though these also are descended from Abraham. But this man who has not their genealogy received tithes from Abraham and blessed him who had the promises. It is beyond dispute that the inferior is blessed by the superior. Here tithes are received by mortal men; there, by one of whom it is testified that he lives. One might even say that Levi himself, who receives tithes, paid tithes through Abraham, for he was still in the loins of his ancestor when Melchizedek met him.

Now if perfection had been attainable through the Levitical priesthood (for under it the people received the law), what further need would there have been for another priest to arise after the order of

Melchizedek, rather than one named after the order of Aaron? For when there is a change in the priesthood, there is necessarily a change in the law as well. The one of whom these things are spoken belonged to another tribe, from which no one has ever served at the altar. For it is evident that our Lord was descended from Judah, and in connection with that tribe Moses said nothing about priests.

This becomes even more evident when another priest arises in the likeness of Melchizedek, who has become a priest, not according to a legal requirement concerning bodily descent but by the power of an indestructible life. For it is witnessed of him, "Thou art a priest for ever, after the order of Melchizedek."

On the one hand, a former commandment is set aside because of its weakness and uselessness (for the law made nothing perfect); on the other hand, a better hope is introduced, through which we draw near to God.

And it was not without an oath. Those who formerly became priests took their office without an oath, but this one was addressed with an oath, "The Lord has sworn and will not change his mind, 'Thou art a priest for ever.'" This makes Jesus the surety of a better covenant.

The former priests were many in number, because they were prevented by death from continuing in office; but he holds his priesthood permanently, because he continues for ever. Consequently he is able for all time to save those who draw near to God through him, since he always lives to make intercession for them.

It was fitting that we should have such a high priest, holy, blameless, unstained, separated from sinners, exalted above the heavens. He has no need to offer sacrifices daily, first for his own sins and then for those of the people; he did this once for all when he offered up himself. Indeed, the law appoints men in their weakness as high priests, but the word of the oath, which came later than the law, appoints a Son who has been made perfect for ever.

Now the point in what we are saying is this: we have such a high priest, one who is seated at the right hand of the throne of the Majesty in heaven, a minister in the sanctuary and the true tent which is set up not by man but by the Lord. If he were on earth, he would not be a priest at all, since there are priests who offer gifts according to the law. They serve a copy and shadow of the heavenly sanctuary. But as it is, Christ has obtained a ministry which is as much more excellent than the old as the covenant he mediates is better, since it is enacted on better promises. For if that first covenant had been faultless, there would have been no occasion for a second.

Now even the first covenant had regulations for worship and an earthly sanctuary. For a tent was prepared, the outer one, in which were the lampstand and the table and the bread of the Presence; it is called the Holy Place. Behind the second curtain stood a tent called the Holy of Holies, having the golden altar of incense and the ark of the covenant covered on all sides with gold, which contained a golden urn holding the manna, and Aaron's rod that budded, and the tables of the covenant; above it were the cherubim of glory overshadowing the mercy seat.

These preparations having been made,

the priests go continually into the outer tent, performing their ritual duties; but into the second only the high priest goes, and he but once a year, and not without taking blood, which he offers for himself and for the errors of the people. By this the Holy Spirit indicates that the way into the sanctuary is not yet opened as long as the outer tent is still standing (which is symbolic for the present age). According to this arrangement, gifts and sacrifices are offered which cannot perfect the conscience of the worshiper, but deal only with food and drink and various ablutions, regulations for the body imposed until the time of reformation.

But when Christ appeared as a high priest, then through the greater and more perfect tent (not made with hands, that is, not of this creation) he entered once for all into the Holy Place, taking not the blood of goats and calves but his own blood, thus securing an eternal redemption. For if the sprinkling of defiled persons with the blood of goats and bulls and with the ashes of a heifer sanctifies for the purification of the flesh, how much more shall the blood of Christ, who through the eternal Spirit offered himself without blemish to God, purify your conscience from dead works to serve the living God.

Therefore he is the mediator of a new covenant, so that those who are called may receive the promised eternal inheritance, since a death has occurred which redeems them from the transgressions under the first covenant. He has appeared once for all at the end of the age to put away sin by the sacrifice of himself. And just as it is appointed for men to die once, and after that comes judgment, so Christ, having been offered once to bear the sins of many, will appear a second time, not to deal with sin but to save those who are eagerly waiting for him. We have been sanctified through the offering of the body of Jesus Christ once for all.

Therefore, brethren, since we have confidence to enter the sanctuary by the blood of Jesus, by the new and living way which he opened for us through the curtain, that is, through his flesh, let us draw near in full assurance of faith, with our hearts sprinkled clean from an evil conscience and our bodies washed with pure water. Let us hold fast the confession of our hope without wavering, for he who promised is faithful; and let us consider how to stir up one another to love and good works, not neglecting to meet together, as is the habit of some, but encouraging one another, and all the more as you see the Day drawing near.

For if we sin deliberately after receiving the knowledge of the truth, there no longer remains a sacrifice for sins, but a fearful prospect of judgment, and a fury of fire which will consume the adversaries. A man who has violated the law of Moses dies without mercy at the testimony of two or three witnesses. How much worse punishment do you think will be deserved by the man who has spurned the Son of God, and profaned the blood of the covenant by which he was sanctified, and outraged the Spirit of grace? For we know him who said, "Vengeance is mine, I will repay." And again, "The Lord will judge his people." It is a fearful thing to fall into the hands of the living God.

But recall the former days when, after

you were enlightened, you endured a hard struggle with sufferings, sometimes being publicly exposed to abuse and affliction, and sometimes being partners with those so treated. For you had compassion on the prisoners, and you joyfully accepted the plundering of your property, since you knew that you yourselves had a better possession and an abiding one. Therefore do not throw away your confidence, which has a great reward. For you have need of endurance, so that you may do the will of God and receive what is promised.

Now faith is the assurance of things hoped for, the conviction of things not seen. For by it the men of old received divine approval. By faith we understand that the world was created by the word of God, so that what is seen was made out of things which do not appear.

By faith Abel offered to God a more acceptable sacrifice than Cain; he died, but through his faith he is still speaking. By faith Enoch was taken up so that he should not see death; now before he was taken he was attested as having pleased God. And without faith it is impossible to please him. For whoever would draw near to God must believe that he exists and that he rewards those who seek him.

By faith Noah, being warned by God concerning events as yet unseen, took heed and constructed an ark for the saving of his household. By faith Abraham obeyed when he was called to go out to a place which he was to receive as an inheritance; and he went out, not knowing where he was to go. By faith Sarah herself received power to conceive, even when she was past the age. Therefore from one man, and him as good as dead, were born descendants as many as the stars of heaven and as the innumerable grains of sand by the seashore.

These all died in faith, not having received what was promised, but having seen it and greeted it from afar, and having acknowledged that they were strangers and exiles on the earth. They desire a better country, that is, a heavenly one. Therefore God is not ashamed to be called their God, for he has prepared for them a city.

By faith Moses left Egypt, not being afraid of the anger of the king; for he endured as seeing him who is invisible. By faith he kept the Passover and sprinkled the blood, so that the Destroyer of the first-born might not touch them. By faith the people crossed the Red Sea as if on dry land; but the Egyptians, when they attempted to do the same, were drowned. By faith the walls of Jericho fell down after they had been encircled for seven days. By faith Rahab the harlot did not perish with those who were disobedient, because she had given friendly welcome to the spies.

And what more shall I say? For time would fail me to tell of Gideon, Barak, Samson, Jephthah, of David and Samuel and the prophets—who through faith conquered kingdoms, enforced justice, received promises, stopped the mouths of lions, quenched raging fire, escaped the edge of the sword, won strength out of weakness, became mighty in war, put foreign armies to flight. Women received their dead by resurrection. Some were tortured, refusing to accept release, that they might rise again to a better life. Others suffered mocking and scourging, and even chains and imprisonment. They were stoned, they were sawn in two, they were killed with the sword; they went about in skins of sheep and goats, destitute, afflicted, ill-treated, wandering over deserts and mountains, and in dens and caves of the earth.

And all these, though well attested by their faith, did not receive what was promised, since God had foreseen something better for us, that apart from us they should not be made perfect.

Therefore, since we are surrounded by so great a cloud of witnesses, let us also lay aside every weight, and sin which clings so closely, and let us run with perseverance the race that is set before us, looking to Jesus the pioneer and perfecter of our faith, who for the joy that was set before him endured the cross, despising the shame, and is seated at the right hand of the throne of God.

Consider him who endured from sinners such hostility against himself, so that you may not grow weary or fainthearted. In your struggle against sin you have not yet resisted to the point of shedding your blood. And have you forgotten the exhortation which addresses you as sons?—"My son, do not regard lightly the discipline of the Lord, nor lose courage when you are punished by him. For the Lord disciplines him whom he loves, and chastises every son whom he receives."

God is treating you as sons; for what son is there whom his father does not discipline? If you are left without discipline, in which all have participated, then you are illegitimate children and not sons. Besides this, we have had earthly fathers to discipline us and we respected them. Shall we not much more be subject to the Father of spirits and live? For they disciplined us for a short time at their pleasure, but he disciplines us for our good, that we may share his holiness. For the moment all discipline seems painful rather than pleasant; later it yields the peaceful fruit of righteousness to those who have been trained by it.

Therefore lift your drooping hands and strengthen your weak knees, and make straight paths for your feet, so that what is lame may not be put out of joint but rather be healed. Strive for peace with all men, and for the holiness without which no one will see the Lord. See to it that no one fail to obtain the grace of God; that no "root of bitterness" spring up and cause trouble, and by it the many become defiled; that no one be immoral or irreligious like Esau, who sold his birthright for a single meal. You know that afterward, when he desired to inherit the blessing, he was rejected, for he found no chance to repent, though he sought it with tears.

You have not come to what may be touched, a blazing fire, and darkness, and gloom, and a tempest, and the sound of a trumpet, and a voice whose words made the hearers entreat that no further messages be spoken to them. You have come to Mount Zion and to the city of the living God, the heavenly Jerusalem, and to innumerable angels in festal gathering, and to the assembly of the first-born who are enrolled in heaven, and to a judge who is God of all, and to the spirits of just men made perfect, and to Jesus, the mediator of a new covenant, and to the sprinkled blood that speaks more graciously than the blood of Abel.

See that you do not refuse him who is

speaking. For if they did not escape when they refused him who warned them on earth, much less shall we escape if we reject him who warns from heaven. His voice then shook the earth; but now he has promised, "Yet once more I will shake not only the earth but also the heaven." This phrase, "Yet once more," indicates the removal of what is shaken, as of what has been made, in order that what cannot be shaken may remain. Therefore let us be grateful for receiving a kingdom that cannot be shaken, and thus let us offer to God acceptable worship, with reverence and awe; for our God is a consuming fire.

Let brotherly love continue. Do not neglect to show hospitality to strangers, for thereby some have entertained angels unawares. Remember those who are in prison, as though in prison with them; and those who are ill-treated, since you also are in the body. Let marriage be held in honor among all, and let the marriage bed be undefiled; for God will judge the immoral and adulterous. Keep your life free from love of money, and be content with what you have; for he has said, "I will never fail you nor forsake you."

Remember your leaders, those who spoke to you the word of God; consider the outcome of their life, and imitate their faith. Jesus Christ is the same yesterday and today and for ever. Do not be led away by diverse and strange teachings; for it is well that the heart be strengthened by grace. Here we have no lasting city, but we seek the city which is to come. Through him, then, let us continually offer up a sacrifice of praise to God, that is, the fruit of lips that acknowledge his name. Do not neglect to do good and to share what you have, for such sacrifices are pleasing to God.

Now may the God of peace who brought again from the dead our Lord Jesus, the great shepherd of the sheep, by the blood of the eternal covenant, equip you with everything good, that you may do his will, working in you that which is pleasing in his sight, through Jesus Christ; to whom be glory for ever and ever. Amen.

LETTER OF
JAMES

Forceful in style, the Letter of James is more like a sermon than a letter. Its content, which is concerned with Christian conduct, is not very orderly, supplying many diverse admonitions, some more than once. Except for the opening greeting *"to the twelve tribes in the Dispersion"*—meaning all God's faithful scattered abroad—none of the usual parts of an ancient letter is present. Tradition ascribes the letter to James, the Lord's brother, writing about A.D. 45, but modern opinion is uncertain, and differs widely on both origin and date.

———

JAMES, A SERVANT of God and of the Lord Jesus Christ, to the twelve tribes in the Dispersion: Greeting.

Count it all joy, my brethren, when you meet various trials, for you know that the testing of your faith produces steadfastness. And let steadfastness have its full effect, that you may be perfect and complete, lacking in nothing.

If any of you lacks wisdom, let him ask God, and it will be given him. But let him ask in faith, with no doubting, for he who doubts is like a wave of the sea that is driven and tossed by the wind. Do not suppose that a double-minded man will receive anything from the Lord.

Blessed is the man who endures trial, for he will receive the crown of life which God has promised to those who love him. Let no one say when he is tempted, "I am tempted by God"; for God cannot be tempted with evil and he himself tempts no one; but each person is tempted when he is enticed by his own desire. Then desire when it has conceived gives birth to sin; and sin when it is full-grown brings forth death.

Do not be deceived, my beloved brethren. Every good endowment and every perfect gift is from above, coming down from the Father of lights, with whom there is no variation or shadow due to change. Of his own will he brought us forth by the word of truth, that we should be a kind of first fruits of his creatures.

Know this, my beloved brethren. Let every man be quick to hear, slow to speak, slow to anger, for the anger of man does not work the righteousness of God. But be doers of the word, and not hearers only, deceiving yourselves. For if any one is a hearer of the word and not a doer, he is like a man who observes his natural face in a mirror, and goes away and at once forgets what he was like. But he who looks into the perfect law, and perseveres, being a doer that acts, he shall be blessed.

If any one thinks he is religious, and does not bridle his tongue but deceives his heart, this man's religion is vain. Religion that is pure and undefiled before God and the Father is this: to visit orphans and widows in their affliction, and to keep oneself unstained from the world.

My brethren, show no partiality. If a man with gold rings and in fine clothing comes into your assembly, and a poor man in shabby clothing also comes in, and to the one who wears the fine clothing you say, "Have a seat here, please," while you say to the poor man, "Stand there," or, "Sit at my feet," have you not made distinctions among yourselves, and become judges with evil thoughts? Has not God chosen those who are poor in the world to be rich in faith and heirs of the kingdom which he has promised to those who love him?

If you really fulfil the royal law, "You shall love your neighbor as yourself," you do well. But if you show partiality, you commit sin, and are convicted by the law as transgressors. For whoever keeps the whole law but fails in one point has become guilty of all of it. Speak and act as those who are to be judged under the law of liberty. For judgment is without mercy to one who has shown no mercy; yet mercy triumphs over judgment.

What does it profit, my brethren, if a man says he has faith but has not works? Can his faith save him? If a brother or sister is ill-clad and in lack of daily food, and one of you says to them, "Go in peace, be warmed and filled," without giving them the things needed for the body, what does it profit? So faith by itself, if it has no works, is dead.

But some one will say, "You have faith and I have works." Show me your faith apart from your works, and I by my works will show you my faith. Do you want to be shown, you shallow man, that faith apart from works is barren? Was not Abraham our father justified by works, when he offered his son Isaac upon the altar? You see that faith was active along with his works, and faith was completed by works. You see that a man is justified by works and not by faith alone. As the body apart from the spirit is dead, so faith apart from works is dead.

Look at the ships; though they are so great and are driven by strong winds, they are guided by a very small rudder. So the tongue is a little member and boasts of great things. How great a forest is set ablaze by a small fire! And the tongue is a fire. The tongue is an unrighteous world among our members, setting on fire the cycle of nature, and set on fire by hell. For every kind of beast can be tamed and has been tamed by humankind, but no human being can tame the tongue—a restless evil, full of deadly poison. With it we bless the Lord and Father, and with it we curse men, who are made in the likeness of God. From the same mouth come blessing and cursing. My brethren, this ought not to be so.

Who is wise and understanding among you? By his good life let him show his works in the meekness of wisdom. But if you have bitter jealousy and selfish ambition in your hearts, do not boast and be false to the truth. This wisdom is not such as comes down from above, but is earthly, unspiritual, devilish. For where jealousy and selfish ambition exist, there will be disorder and every vile practice. But the wisdom from above is first pure, then peaceable, gentle, open to reason, full of mercy and good fruits, without uncertainty or insincerity.

What causes wars, and what causes fightings among you? Is it not your passions that are at war in your members? You desire and do not have; so you kill.

And you covet and cannot obtain; so you fight and wage war. You do not have, because you do not ask. You ask and do not receive, because you ask wrongly, to spend it on your passions. Unfaithful creatures! Do you not know that friendship with the world is enmity with God? Therefore whoever wishes to be a friend of the world makes himself an enemy of God. Resist the devil and he will flee from you. Draw near to God and he will draw near to you. Humble yourselves before the Lord and he will exalt you.

Do not speak evil against one another, brethren. He that speaks evil against a brother or judges his brother, speaks evil against the law and judges the law. There is one lawgiver and judge, he who is able to save and to destroy. But who are you that you judge your neighbor?

Come now, you who say, "Tomorrow we will go into town and trade and get gain"; whereas you do not know about tomorrow. You are a mist that appears for a little time and then vanishes. Instead you ought to say, "If the Lord wills, we shall live and we shall do this or that." As it is, you boast in your arrogance. All such boasting is evil. Whoever knows what is right to do and fails to do it, for him it is sin.

Come now, you rich, weep and howl for the miseries that are coming upon you. Your riches have rotted and your garments are moth-eaten. Your gold and silver have rusted, and their rust will be evidence against you and will eat your flesh like fire. Behold, the wages of the laborers who mowed your fields, which you kept back by fraud, cry out; and the cries of the harvesters have reached the ears of the Lord of hosts.

Be patient, therefore, brethren, until the coming of the Lord. Behold, the farmer waits for the precious fruit of the earth, being patient over it until it receives the early and the late rain. You also be patient. Establish your hearts, for the coming of the Lord is at hand. Do not grumble, brethren, against one another, that you may not be judged; behold, the Judge is standing at the doors. But above all, my brethren, do not swear, either by heaven or by earth or with any other oath, but let your yes be yes and your no be no, that you may not fall under condemnation.

Is any one among you suffering? Let him pray. Is any cheerful? Let him sing praise. Is any among you sick? Let him call for the elders of the church, and let them pray over him, anointing him with oil in the name of the Lord; and the prayer of faith will save the sick man, and the Lord will raise him up; and if he has committed sins, he will be forgiven. Therefore confess your sins to one another, and pray for one another, that you may be healed. The prayer of a righteous man has great power in its effects.

My brethren, if any one among you wanders from the truth and some one brings him back, let him know that whoever brings back a sinner from the error of his way will save his soul from death and will cover a multitude of sins.

FIRST LETTER OF
PETER

Written to the Christians of five Roman provinces in Asia Minor (modern Turkey), this letter offers encouragement in difficult times. Some of the Christians in these provinces, threatened with renewed serious persecution, had already suffered in various ways for their faith. The author begins by reminding them of the central place occupied by Christ's redeeming death and resurrection in the Christian plan of salvation. He then passes to Christian duties: unity with each other and with God, and the obligations to be observed by various classes of believers, with repeated reference to the example of Christ. According to tradition, the apostle Peter wrote the letter from Rome, perhaps after the outbreak of persecution by the emperor Nero in A.D. 64. But this is questioned by some modern scholars, who prefer to date the letter nearer A.D. 100, with authorship unknown. In any case, it was accepted as canonical in the earliest times.

———

PETER, AN APOSTLE of Jesus Christ, to the exiles of the Dispersion in Pontus, Galatia, Cappadocia, Asia, and Bithynia, chosen and destined by God the Father and sanctified by the Spirit for obedience to Jesus Christ and for sprinkling with his blood: May grace and peace be multiplied to you.

Blessed be the God and Father of our Lord Jesus Christ! By his great mercy we have been born anew to a living hope through the resurrection of Jesus Christ from the dead, and to an inheritance which is imperishable, undefiled, and unfading, kept in heaven for you, who by God's power are guarded through faith for a salvation ready to be revealed in the last time. In this you rejoice, though now for a little while you may have to suffer various trials, so that the genuineness of your faith, more precious than gold which though perishable is tested by fire, may redound to praise and glory and honor at the revelation of Jesus Christ. Without having seen him, you love him; though you do not now see him, you believe in him and rejoice with unutterable and exalted joy.

The prophets who prophesied of the grace that was to be yours searched and inquired about this salvation; they inquired what person or time was indicated by the Spirit of Christ within them when predicting the sufferings of Christ and the subsequent glory. It was revealed to them that they were serving not themselves but you, in the things which have now been announced to you, things into which angels long to look.

Gird up your minds, be sober, set your hope fully upon the grace that is coming to you at the revelation of Jesus Christ. As he who called you is holy, be holy yourselves, since it is written, "You shall be holy, for I am holy." And if you invoke as Father him who judges each one impartially according to his deeds, conduct yourselves with fear throughout the time of your exile. You know that you were ransomed from the

futile ways inherited from your fathers, not
with perishable things such as silver or
gold, but with the precious blood of
Christ, like that of a lamb without blemish
or spot. He was destined before the foundation of the world but was made manifest
at the end of the times for your sake.

Having purified your souls, love one another earnestly from the heart. You have
been born anew, not of perishable seed but
of imperishable, through the living and
abiding word of God; for "All flesh is like
grass and all its glory like the flower of
grass. The grass withers, and the flower
falls, but the word of the Lord abides for
ever." That word is the good news which
was preached to you. So put away all malice and all guile and insincerity and envy
and all slander. Like newborn babes, long
for the pure spiritual milk, that by it you
may grow up to salvation; for you have
tasted the kindness of the Lord.

You are a chosen race, a royal priesthood, a holy nation, God's own people,
that you may declare the wonderful deeds
of him who called you out of darkness into
his marvelous light. Once you were no

people but now you are God's people; once you had not received mercy but now you have received mercy.

Beloved, I beseech you as aliens and exiles to abstain from the passions of the flesh that wage war against your soul. Maintain good conduct among the Gentiles, so that in case they speak against you as wrongdoers, they may see your good deeds and glorify God on the day of visitation.

Be subject for the Lord's sake to every human institution, whether it be to the emperor as supreme, or to governors as sent by him to punish those who do wrong and to praise those who do right. For it is God's will that by doing right you should put to silence the ignorance of foolish men. Live as free men, yet without using your freedom as a pretext for evil; but live as servants of God. Honor all men. Love the brotherhood. Fear God. Honor the emperor.

Servants, be submissive to your masters with all respect, not only to the kind and gentle but also to the overbearing. For one is approved if, mindful of God, he endures pain while suffering unjustly. For what credit is it, if when you do wrong and are beaten for it you take it patiently? But if when you do right and suffer for it you take it patiently, you have God's approval. For to this you have been called, because Christ also suffered for you, leaving you an example, that you should follow in his steps. He committed no sin; no guile was found on his lips. When he was reviled, he did not revile in return; when he suffered, he did not threaten; but he trusted to him who judges justly. He himself bore our sins in his body on the tree, that we might die to sin and live to righteousness. By his wounds you have been healed. For you were straying like sheep, but have now returned to the Shepherd and Guardian of your souls.

Likewise you wives, be submissive to your husbands, so that some, though they do not obey the word, may be won without a word by the behavior of their wives, when they see your reverent and chaste behavior. Let not yours be the outward adorning with braiding of hair, decoration of gold, and wearing of fine clothing, but let it be the hidden person of the heart with the imperishable jewel of a gentle and quiet spirit, which in God's sight is very precious.

Likewise you husbands, live considerately with your wives, bestowing honor on the woman as the weaker sex, since you are joint heirs of the grace of life, in order that your prayers may not be hindered.

Finally, all of you, have unity of spirit, sympathy, love of the brethren, a tender heart, and a humble mind. Do not return evil for evil or reviling for reviling; but on the contrary bless, that you may obtain a blessing.

Now who is there to harm you if you are zealous for what is right? But even if you do suffer for righteousness' sake, you will be blessed. Have no fear of them, nor be troubled, but in your hearts reverence Christ as Lord. Always be prepared to make a defense to any one who calls you to account for the hope that is in you, yet do it with gentleness and reverence; and keep your conscience clear, so that when you are abused, those who revile your good behavior in Christ may be put to shame. For it is better to suffer for doing right, if that should be God's will, than for doing wrong.

Since therefore Christ suffered in the flesh, arm yourselves with the same thought, for whoever has suffered in the flesh has ceased from sin, so as to live for the rest of the time in the flesh no longer by human passions but by the will of God. Let the time that is past suffice for doing what the Gentiles like to do, living in licentiousness, passions, drunkenness, revels, carousing, and lawless idolatry. They are surprised that you do not now join them in the same wild profligacy, and they abuse you; but they will give account to him who is ready to judge the living and the dead. For this is why the gospel was preached even to the dead, that though judged in the flesh like men, they might live in the spirit like God.

The end of all things is at hand; therefore keep sane and sober for your prayers. Above all, hold unfailing your love for one another, since love covers a multitude of sins. Practice hospitality ungrudgingly to one another. As each has received a gift, employ it for one another, as good stewards of God's varied grace: whoever speaks, as one who utters oracles of God; whoever renders service, as one who renders it by the strength which God supplies; in order that in everything God may be glorified through Jesus Christ. To him belong glory and dominion for ever and ever. Amen.

Beloved, do not be surprised at the fiery ordeal which comes upon you to prove you, as though something strange were happening to you. But rejoice in so far as you share Christ's sufferings, that you may also rejoice and be glad when his glory is revealed. If you are reproached for the name of Christ, you are blessed, because the spirit of glory and of God rests upon you. But let none of you suffer as a murderer, or a thief, or a wrongdoer, or a mischief-maker; yet if one suffers as a Christian, let him not be ashamed, but under that name let him glorify God. For the time has come for judgment to begin with the household of God; and if it begins with us, what will be the end of those who do not obey the gospel of God?

So I exhort the elders among you, as a fellow elder and a witness of the sufferings of Christ as well as a partaker in the glory that is to be revealed. Tend the flock of God that is your charge, not by constraint but willingly, not for shameful gain but eagerly, not as domineering over those in your charge but being examples to the flock. And when the chief Shepherd is manifested you will obtain the unfading crown of glory. Likewise you that are younger be subject to the elders. Clothe yourselves, all of you, with humility toward one another, for "God opposes the proud, but gives grace to the humble."

Humble yourselves therefore under the mighty hand of God, that in due time he may exalt you. Cast all your anxieties on him, for he cares about you. Be sober, be watchful. Your adversary the devil prowls around like a roaring lion, seeking some one to devour. Resist him, firm in your faith, knowing that the same experience of suffering is required of your brotherhood throughout the world. And after you have suffered a little while, the God of all grace, who has called you to his eternal glory in

Christ, will himself restore, establish, and strengthen you. To him be the dominion for ever and ever. Amen.

By Silvanus, a faithful brother as I regard him, I have written briefly to you, exhorting and declaring that this is the true grace of God; stand fast in it. She who is at Babylon, who is likewise chosen, sends you greetings; and so does my son Mark. Greet one another with the kiss of love. Peace to all of you that are in Christ.

SECOND LETTER OF
PETER

Markedly different in content and manner from 1 Peter, this brief letter is addressed to all Christians. It begins with an exhortation to maintain holiness of character, followed by a warning (based on the Letter of Jude) against heresy, which leads to immorality. It concludes with a reminder of the Second Coming of Christ, a hope that some individuals in that time had begun to ridicule. Because the author refers to the letters of Paul as "scripture," a term apparently not applied to them until long after Paul's death, most modern scholars think that this letter was drawn up in Peter's name sometime between A.D. 100 and 150.

———

Simeon Peter, a servant and apostle of
Jesus Christ, to those who have obtained a
faith of equal standing with ours in the
righteousness of our God and Savior Jesus
Christ: May grace and peace be multiplied
to you in the knowledge of God and of
Jesus our Lord.

His divine power has granted to us all
things that pertain to life and godliness,
through the knowledge of him who called
us to his own glory and excellence, by
which he has granted to us his precious
and very great promises, that through
these you may escape from the corruption
that is in the world because of passion,
and become partakers of the divine nature.
For this very reason make every effort to
supplement your faith with virtue, and virtue with knowledge, and knowledge with
self-control, and self-control with steadfastness, and steadfastness with godliness,
and godliness with brotherly affection, and
brotherly affection with love. For if these
things are yours and abound, they keep
you from being ineffective or unfruitful in
the knowledge of our Lord Jesus Christ.

I think it right, as long as I am in this

body, to arouse you by way of reminder, since I know that the putting off of my body will be soon, as our Lord Jesus Christ showed me. And I will see to it that after my departure you may be able at any time to recall these things.

For we did not follow cleverly devised myths when we made known to you the power and coming of our Lord Jesus Christ, but we were eyewitnesses of his majesty. For when he received honor and glory from God the Father and the voice was borne to him by the Majestic Glory, "This is my beloved Son, with whom I am well pleased," we heard this voice borne from heaven, for we were with him on the holy mountain. And we have the prophetic word made more sure. You will do well to pay attention to this as to a lamp shining in a dark place, until the day dawns and the morning star rises in your hearts. First of all you must understand this, that no prophecy of scripture is a matter of one's own interpretation, because no prophecy ever came by the impulse of man, but men moved by the Holy Spirit spoke from God.

But false prophets also arose among the

people, just as there will be false teachers among you, who will secretly bring in destructive heresies, even denying the Master who bought them, bringing upon themselves swift destruction. For if God did not spare the angels when they sinned, but cast them into hell and committed them to pits of nether gloom until the judgment; if he did not spare the ancient world, but preserved Noah, a herald of righteousness, with seven others; if by turning the cities of Sodom and Gomorrah to ashes he condemned them to extinction; and if he rescued righteous Lot, then the Lord knows how to rescue the godly from trial, and to keep the unrighteous under punishment until the day of judgment, and especially those who indulge in the lust of defiling passion and despise authority.

Bold and wilful, they are not afraid to revile the glorious ones, whereas angels, though greater in might and power, do not pronounce a reviling judgment upon them before the Lord. But these, like irrational animals, creatures of instinct, born to be caught and killed, reviling in matters of which they are ignorant, will be destroyed in the same destruction with them, suffering wrong for their wrongdoing. They count it pleasure to revel in the daytime. They are blots and blemishes, reveling in their dissipation, carousing with you. They have eyes full of adultery, insatiable for sin. They entice unsteady souls. They have hearts trained in greed. Accursed children! They have followed the way of Balaam, who loved gain from wrongdoing, but was rebuked; a dumb ass spoke with human voice and restrained the prophet's madness.

These are waterless springs and mists driven by a storm; for them the nether gloom of darkness has been reserved. For they entice men who have barely escaped from those who live in error. They promise freedom, but they themselves are slaves of corruption; for whatever overcomes a man, to that he is enslaved. If, after men have escaped the defilements of the world through Jesus Christ, they are again entangled, the last state has become worse than the first. It has happened to them according to the true proverb: The dog turns back to his own vomit, and the sow is washed only to wallow in the mire.

This is now the second letter that I have written to you, beloved, and in both of them I have aroused your sincere mind by way of reminder; that you should remember the predictions of the holy prophets and the commandment of the Lord and Savior through your apostles. First of all you must understand this, that scoffers will come in the last days, following their own passions and saying, "Where is the promise of his coming? For ever since the fathers fell asleep, all things have continued as they were from the beginning of creation." They deliberately ignore this fact, that by the word of God heavens existed long ago, and an earth formed out of water and by means of water, through which the world that then existed was deluged with water and perished. But by the same word the heavens and earth that now exist have been stored up for fire, being kept until the day of judgment and destruction of ungodly men.

But do not ignore this one fact, beloved, that with the Lord one day is as a thousand years, and a thousand years as one day. The Lord is not slow about his promise as some count slowness, but is forbearing toward you, not wishing that any should perish, but that all should reach repentance. But the day of the Lord will come like a thief, and then the heavens will pass away with a loud noise, and the elements will be dissolved with fire, and the earth and the works that are upon it will be burned up.

Since all these things are thus to be dissolved, what sort of persons ought you to be in lives of holiness and godliness, waiting for and hastening the coming of the day of God, because of which the heavens will be kindled and dissolved, and the elements will melt with fire! But according to his promise we wait for new heavens and a new earth in which righteousness dwells.

Therefore, beloved, since you wait for these, be zealous to be found by him without spot or blemish, and at peace. And count the forbearance of our Lord as salvation. So also our beloved brother Paul wrote to you according to the wisdom given him, speaking of this as he does in all his letters. There are some things in them hard to understand, which the ignorant and unstable twist to their own destruction, as they do the other scriptures. You therefore, beloved, knowing this beforehand, beware lest you be carried away with the error of lawless men and lose your own stability. But grow in the grace and knowledge of our Lord and Savior Jesus Christ. To him be the glory both now and to the day of eternity. Amen.

FIRST LETTER OF
JOHN

The three letters of John give us a fascinating glimpse into the life of the Christian church in Asia Minor toward the close of the first century. Tradition ascribes all three to John the Apostle, author of the fourth Gospel. The writer, however, identifies himself only as "the Elder" (letters 2 and 3), though in the first letter he stresses that he knew Jesus in the flesh. Whoever he was, he obviously held a position of spiritual authority in the early church. Woven into the first letter are theology and ethics, doctrine and behavior, making it resemble a sermon or theological treatise. It was written to deepen the spiritual life of its readers and to correct false doctrines on the Person of Christ. The conception of God as light and life, prominent in the fourth Gospel, recurs here. Special emphasis is laid on the love of God, manifested in his Son, who was sent into the world as the remedy for sin and to give eternal life to all believers. The mark of Christians is love for God and for one another, and victory over sin.

THAT WHICH WAS from the beginning, which we have heard, which we have seen with our eyes and touched with our hands, concerning the word of life made manifest—this we proclaim to you so that you may have fellowship with us. Our fellowship is with the Father and with his Son Jesus Christ, and we are writing this that our joy may be complete.

This is the message we have heard from him, that God is light and in him is no darkness at all. If we say we have fellowship with him while we walk in darkness, we lie. But if we walk in the light, we have fellowship with one another, and the blood of Jesus his Son cleanses us from all sin. If we say we have no sin, we deceive ourselves. If we confess our sins, he will cleanse us from all unrighteousness.

My little children, I am writing this to you so that you may not sin; but if any one does sin, we have an advocate with the Father, Jesus Christ the righteous. He is the expiation for our sins, and for the sins of the whole world. We may be sure that we know him if we keep his commandments. He who says "I know him" but disobeys his commandments is a liar, but whoever keeps his word, in him love for God is perfected. He who says he abides in him ought to walk in the same way in which he walked.

Beloved, I am writing you no new commandment, but an old commandment which you had from the beginning, the word which you have heard. Yet I am writing you a new commandment, which is true in him and in you, because the darkness is passing away and the true light is already shining. He who says he is in the light and hates his brother is in the darkness still. He who loves his brother abides in the light, and there is no cause for stumbling.

I am writing to you, little children, because your sins are forgiven for Jesus' sake. I am writing to you, fathers, because you know him who is from the beginning. I write to you, young men, because you are strong, and the word of God abides in you, and you have overcome the evil one.

Do not love the world or the things in the world. If any one loves the world, love for the Father is not in him. For all that is in the world, the lust of the flesh and the lust of the eyes and the pride of life, is not of the Father but is of the world. And the world passes away, and the lust of it; but he who does the will of God abides for ever.

Children, it is the last hour; and as you have heard that antichrist is coming, so now many antichrists have come; therefore we know that it is the last hour. They went out from us, but they were not of us; they went out that it might be plain that they all are not of us. But you have been anointed by the Holy One, and you all know. I write to you, not because you do not know the truth, but because you know it, and know that no lie is of the truth. Who is the liar but he who denies that Jesus is the Christ?

This is the antichrist, he who denies the Father and the Son. No one who denies the Son has the Father. He who confesses the Son has the Father also. If what you heard from the beginning abides in you, then you will abide in the Son and in the Father. And this is what he has promised us, eternal life.

I write this to you about those who would deceive you; but the anointing which you received from him abides in you, and you have no need that any one should teach you. As his anointing teaches you about everything, and is true, abide in him, so that when he appears we may not shrink from him in shame. You may be sure that every one who does right is born of him.

See what love the Father has given us, that we should be called children of God; and so we are. The reason why the world does not know us is that it did not know him. Beloved, we are God's children now; it does not yet appear what we shall be, but we know that when he appears we shall be like him, for we shall see him as he is. And every one who thus hopes in him purifies himself as he is pure.

Every one who commits sin is guilty of lawlessness. You know that he appeared to take away sins, and in him there is no sin. No one who abides in him sins; no one who sins has either seen him or known him. He who commits sin is of the devil; for the devil has sinned from the beginning. The reason the Son of God appeared was to destroy the works of the devil. No one born of God commits sin; by this it may be seen who are the children of God, and who are the children of the devil.

This is the message you have heard from the beginning, that we should love one another, and not be like Cain, who was of the evil one and murdered his brother. And why did he murder him? Because his own deeds were evil and his brother's righteous. Do not wonder, brethren, that the world hates you. We know that we have passed out of death into life, because we love the brethren. He who does not love abides in death. Any one who hates his brother is a murderer, and you know that no murderer has eternal life abiding in him. By this we know love, that he laid down his life for us; and we ought to lay down our lives for the brethren. But if any one has the world's goods and sees his brother in need, yet closes his heart against him, how does God's love abide in him? Little children, let us not love in word or speech but in deed and in truth.

By this we shall know that we are of the truth, and reassure our hearts before him whenever our hearts condemn us; for God is greater than our hearts, and he knows everything. Beloved, if our hearts do not condemn us, we have confidence before God; and we receive from him whatever we ask, because we keep his commandments. And this is his commandment, that we should believe in the name of his Son Jesus Christ and love one another. We know that he abides in us, by the Spirit which he has given us.

Beloved, do not believe every spirit, but test the spirits to see whether they are of God; for many false prophets have gone out into the world. Every spirit which confesses that Jesus Christ has come in the flesh is of God, and every spirit which does not confess Jesus is not of God. This is the spirit of antichrist, of which you heard that it was coming, and now it is in the world already. Little children, we are of God. Whoever knows God listens to us, and he who is not of God does not listen to us. By this we know the spirit of truth and the spirit of error.

Beloved, let us love one another; for love is of God, and he who loves is born of God. He who does not love does not know God; for God is love. In this the love of God was made manifest among us, that God sent his only Son into the world, so that we might live through him. In this is love, not that we loved God, but that he loved us and sent his Son to be the expiation for our sins. Beloved, if God so loved us, we also ought to love one another. No man has ever seen God; if we love one another, God abides in us and his love is perfected in us.

By this we know that we abide in him and he in us, because he has given us of his own Spirit. And we have seen and testify that the Father has sent his Son as the Savior of the world. Whoever confesses that Jesus is the Son of God, God abides in him, and he in God. God is love, and he who abides in love abides in God, and God abides in him. We may have confidence for the day of judgment, because as he is, so are we in this world. There is no fear in love, but perfect love casts out fear. For fear has to do with punishment, and he who fears is not perfected in love. We love, because he first loved us. If any one says, "I love God," and hates his brother, he is a liar; for he who does not love his brother whom he has seen, cannot love God whom he has not seen.

Every one who believes that Jesus is the Christ is a child of God, and every one who loves the parent loves the child. By this we know that we love the children of God, when we obey God's commandments. For this is the love of God, that we keep his commandments. Whatever is born of God overcomes the world; and this is the victory that overcomes the world, our faith.

This is he who came by water and blood, Jesus Christ, not with the water only but with the water and the blood. And the Spirit is the witness, because the

Spirit is the truth. There are three witnesses, the Spirit, the water, and the
blood; and these three agree. If we receive
the testimony of men, the testimony of
God is greater; for this is the testimony of
God, that he has borne witness to his Son.
He who believes in the Son of God has the
testimony in himself. He who does not believe God has made him a liar, because he
has not believed in the testimony that God
has borne to his Son. And this is the testimony, that God gave us eternal life, and
this life is in his Son. He who has the Son
has life; he who has not the Son of God
has not life.

I write this to you who believe in the
name of the Son of God, that you may
know that you have eternal life. And this is
the confidence which we have in him, that
if we ask anything according to his will he
hears us. If we know that he hears us, we
know that we have obtained the requests
made of him. If any one sees his brother
committing what is not a mortal sin, he
will ask, and God will give him life for
those whose sin is not mortal. There is sin
which is mortal; I do not say that one is to

pray for that. All wrongdoing is sin, but there is sin which is not mortal.

We know that we are of God, and the whole world is in the power of the evil one. And we know that the Son of God has come and has given us understanding to know him who is true; and we are in him who is true, in his Son Jesus Christ. This is the true God and eternal life. Little children, keep yourselves from idols.

SECOND LETTER OF
JOHN

The author, who calls himself "the Elder," repeats in briefer form the main
teaching of 1 John, and adds a warning
against showing hospitality to itinerant
teachers of false doctrines. The address-
ees (*"the elect lady and her children"*) are
usually understood to be a local church
and its members. At the close of the letter the writer extends the greetings of the
members of the "sister" church where he
is now resident.

———

THE ELDER TO the elect lady and her children, whom I love in the truth, and not
only I but also all who know the truth,
because of the truth which abides in us
and will be with us for ever: Grace, mercy,

and peace will be with us, from God the Father and from Jesus Christ the Father's Son, in truth and love.

I rejoiced greatly to find some of your children following the truth, just as we have been commanded by the Father. And now I beg you, lady, not as though I were writing you a new commandment, but the one we have had from the beginning, that we love one another. And this is love, that we follow his commandments; this is the commandment, as you have heard from the beginning, that you follow love. For many deceivers have gone out into the world, men who will not acknowledge the coming of Jesus Christ in the flesh; such a one is the deceiver and the antichrist. Look to yourselves, that you may not lose what you have worked for, but may win a full reward. Any one who goes ahead and does not abide in the doctrine of Christ does not have God; he who abides in the doctrine has both the Father and the Son. If any one comes to you and does not bring this doctrine, do not receive him into the house or give him any greeting; for he who greets him shares his wicked work.

Though I have much to write to you, I would rather not use paper and ink, but I hope to come to see you and talk with you face to face, so that our joy may be complete.

The children of your elect sister greet you.

THIRD LETTER OF
JOHN

In this personal letter the Elder expresses thanks to Gaius, an influential member of an unidentified church, for showing kindness and hospitality to Christian travelers. Mention is also made of a certain Diotrephes, who had opposed the Elder, and of someone named Demetrius, who is commended. The word "friends," at the letter's conventional close, refers to those members of the church who are loyal to the Elder and who oppose Diotrephes.

———

THE ELDER TO the beloved Gaius, whom I love in the truth.

Beloved, I pray that all may go well with you and that you may be in health; I know that it is well with your soul. For I greatly rejoiced when some of the brethren arrived and testified to the truth of your life, as indeed you do follow the truth. No greater joy can I have than this, to hear that my children follow the truth.

Beloved, it is a loyal thing you do when you render any service to the brethren, especially to strangers, who have testified to your love before the church. You will do well to send them on their journey as befits God's service. For they have set out for his sake and have accepted nothing from the heathen. So we ought to support such men, that we may be fellow workers in the truth.

I have written something to the church; but Diotrephes, who likes to put himself first, does not acknowledge my authority. So if I come, I will bring up what he is doing, prating against me with evil words. And not content with that, he refuses himself to welcome the brethren, and also stops those who want to welcome them and puts them out of the church.

Beloved, do not imitate evil but imitate good. He who does good is of God; he who does evil has not seen God. Demetrius has testimony from every one, and from the truth itself; I testify to him too, and you know my testimony is true.

I had much to write to you, but I would rather not write with pen and ink; I hope to see you soon, and we will talk together face to face.

Peace be to you. The friends greet you. Greet the friends, every one of them.

LETTER OF
JUDE

The purpose of this forceful letter was to combat doctrines that were being spread by heretical teachers. Using examples drawn from the Old Testament, the writer graphically illustrates the dangers of such doctrines. The letter's date and destination cannot be determined with any precision; its author has usually been identified as one of the "brethren" of Jesus. Containing references to two Jewish apocryphal books (Enoch and the Assumption of Moses), the letter closes with a beautiful and moving benediction.

———

JUDE, A SERVANT of Jesus Christ and brother of James, to those who are called, beloved in God the Father and kept for Jesus

Christ: May mercy, peace, and love be multiplied to you.

Beloved, being very eager to write to you of our common salvation, I found it necessary to write appealing to you to contend for the faith which was once for all delivered to the saints. For admission has been secretly gained by some who long ago were designated for this condemnation, ungodly persons who pervert the grace of our God into licentiousness and deny our only Master and Lord, Jesus Christ.

Now I desire to remind you, though you were once for all fully informed, that he who saved a people out of the land of Egypt, afterward destroyed those who did not believe. And the angels that did not keep their own position but left their proper dwelling have been kept by him in eternal chains in the nether gloom until the judgment of the great day; just as Sodom and Gomorrah and the surrounding cities, which likewise acted immorally and indulged in unnatural lust, serve as an example by undergoing a punishment of eternal fire.

Yet in like manner these men in their dreamings defile the flesh, reject authority, and revile the glorious ones. But when the archangel Michael, contending with the devil, disputed about the body of Moses, he did not presume to pronounce a reviling judgment upon him, but said, "The Lord rebuke you." But these men revile whatever they do not understand, and by those things that they know by instinct as irrational animals do, they are destroyed. Woe to them! For they walk in the way of Cain, and abandon themselves for the sake of gain to Balaam's error, and perish in Korah's rebellion. These are blemishes on your love feasts, as they boldly carouse together, looking after themselves; waterless clouds, carried along by winds; fruitless trees in late autumn, twice dead, uprooted; wild waves of the sea, casting up the foam of their own shame; wandering stars for whom the nether gloom of darkness has been reserved for ever.

It was of these also that Enoch in the seventh generation from Adam prophesied, saying, "Behold, the Lord came with his holy myriads, to execute judgment on all, and to convict all the ungodly of all their deeds of ungodliness which they have committed in such an ungodly way, and of all the harsh things which ungodly sinners have spoken against him." These are grumblers, malcontents, following their own passions, loudmouthed boasters, flattering people to gain advantage.

But you must remember, beloved, the predictions of the apostles of our Lord Jesus Christ; they said to you, "In the last time there will be scoffers, following their own ungodly passions." It is these who set up divisions, worldly people, devoid of the Spirit. But you, beloved, build yourselves up on your most holy faith; pray in the Holy Spirit; keep yourselves in the love of God; wait for the mercy of our Lord Jesus Christ unto eternal life. And convince some who doubt; save some, by snatching them out of the fire; on some have mercy with fear, hating even the garment spotted by the flesh.

Now to him who is able to keep you from falling and to present you without blemish before the presence of his glory with rejoicing, to the only God, our Savior through Jesus Christ our Lord, be glory, majesty, dominion, and authority, before all time and now and for ever. Amen.

THE
REVELATION
TO JOHN

Fifty miles offshore from Miletus in Asia Minor lies the rocky island of Patmos. Here a Christian prophet named John, who had been exiled for refusing to worship the image of the emperor Domitian (A.D. 81–96), experienced a series of remarkable visions. Some were beautiful, some horrible, but all of them proved to him the reality of his Christian faith, strengthening his belief that Christ and his church would ultimately triumph. When his harsh exile was over and he could obtain writing materials, John wrote the substance of his visions in a book in order to inspire hope, courage, and endurance among persecuted Christians. His book is arranged in elaborate patterns of sevens, and contains prophetic symbolism derived from Daniel and Zechariah. John's final visions of a new heaven and a new earth, predicted by Isaiah, describe the renewal of all creation, freed from imperfection and transformed by the glory of God.

―――――

THE REVELATION OF Jesus Christ, which God gave him to show to his servants what must soon take place; and he made it known by sending his angel to his servant John, who bore witness to the word of God and to the testimony of Jesus Christ, even to all that he saw. Blessed is he who reads aloud the words of the prophecy, and blessed are those who hear, and who keep what is written therein; for the time is near.

JOHN TO THE seven churches that are in Asia:

Grace to you and peace from him who is and who was and who is to come, and from the seven spirits before his throne, and from Jesus Christ the faithful witness, the first-born of the dead, and the ruler of kings on earth.

To him who loves us, and has freed us from our sins by his blood, and made us a kingdom, priests to his God and Father, to him be glory and dominion for ever. Behold, he is coming with the clouds, and every eye will see him, every one who pierced him; and all tribes of the earth will wail on account of him.

"I am the Alpha and the Omega," says the Lord God, who is and who was and who is to come, the Almighty.

I John, your brother, who share with you in Jesus the tribulation, was on the island called Patmos on account of the word of God and the testimony of Jesus. I was in the Spirit on the Lord's day, and I heard behind me a loud voice like a trumpet saying, "Write what you see in a book and send it to the seven churches."

Then I turned, and I saw seven golden lampstands, and in the midst one like a son of man, clothed with a long robe and with a golden girdle round his breast; his head and his hair were white as white wool; his eyes like a flame of fire, his feet like burnished bronze, and his voice like the sound of many waters; in his right hand he held seven stars, from his mouth issued a sharp two-edged sword, and his face was like the sun shining in full strength.

I fell at his feet as though dead, but he laid his right hand upon me, saying, "Fear not, I am the first and the last; I died, and behold, I am alive for evermore, and I have the keys of Death and Hades. Now write what you see, what is and what is to take place hereafter. As for the mystery of the seven stars, they are the angels of the seven churches, and the lampstands are the seven churches.

"To the angel of the church in Ephesus write: 'The words of him who holds the seven stars in his right hand, who walks among the seven golden lampstands.

" 'I know your works, and how you cannot bear evil men, but have tested those who call themselves apostles but are not, and found them to be false; I know you are enduring patiently for my name's sake. But I have this against you, that you have abandoned the love you had at first. Remember from what you have fallen, repent and do the works you did at first. If not, I will remove your lampstand from its place. To him who conquers I will grant to eat of the tree of life, in the paradise of God.'

"And to the angel of the church in Smyrna write: 'The words of the first and the last, who died and came to life.

" 'I know your tribulation and your poverty (but you are rich) and the slander of those who say that they are Jews and are not, but are a synagogue of Satan. Behold, the devil is about to throw some of you into prison, that you may be tested, and for ten days you will have tribulation. Be faithful unto death, and I will give you the crown of life. He who conquers shall not be hurt by the second death.'

"And to the angel of the church in Pergamum write: 'The words of him who has the sharp two-edged sword.

" 'I know you dwell where Satan's throne is; you did not deny my faith even in the days of Antipas my witness, who was killed among you. But I have a few things against you: you have some there who hold the teaching of Balaam, who taught Balak to put a stumbling block before the sons of Israel, that they might eat food sacrificed to idols and practice immorality. Repent then. If not, I will soon war against them with the sword of my mouth. To him who conquers I will give some of the hidden manna, and I will give him a white stone, with a new name written on the stone which no one knows except him who receives it.'

"And to the angel of the church in Thyatira write: 'The words of the Son of God, who has eyes like a flame of fire, and feet like burnished bronze.

" 'I know your works, your faith and patient endurance, and that your latter works exceed the first. But the woman Jezebel, who calls herself a prophetess, is beguiling my servants to practice immorality and to eat food sacrificed to idols. I gave her time to repent, but she refuses. Behold, I will throw her and those with her into great tribulation, unless they repent; and I will strike her children dead. And all the churches shall know that I am he who searches mind and heart, and I will give to each of you as your works deserve. To the rest of you, who have not learned what some call the deep things of Satan, I say, hold fast what you have, until I come. He who keeps my works until the end, I will give power over the nations, even as I myself have received power from my Father; and I will give him the morning star.'

"And to the angel of the church in Sardis write: 'The words of him who has the seven spirits of God and the seven stars.

" 'I know your works; you have the name of being alive, and you are dead. Awake, and strengthen what remains. Remember what you received, and repent. If you will not awake, I will come like a thief, and you will not know at what hour. Yet you have still a few in Sardis who have not soiled their garments; and they shall walk with me in white, for they are worthy. He who conquers shall be clad thus, and I will not blot his name out of the book of life; I will confess his name before my Father and before his angels.'

"And to the angel of the church in Philadelphia write: 'The words of the holy one, the true one, who has the key of David, who opens and no one shall shut, who shuts and no one opens.

" 'I know your works. Behold, I have set before you an open door, which no one is able to shut; I know that you have but little power, and yet you have kept my word and have not denied my name. Those who say that they are Jews and are not, but lie—behold, I will make them come and bow down before your feet, and learn that I have loved you. Because you have kept my word, I will keep you from the hour of trial which is coming on the whole world. I am coming soon; hold fast what you have. He who conquers, I will make him a pillar in the temple of my God; I will write on him the name of my God, and of the city of my God, the new Jerusalem which comes down from my God out of heaven, and my own new name.'

"And to the angel of the church in La-odicea write: 'The words of the Amen, the faithful and true witness, the beginning of God's creation.

" 'I know your works: you are neither cold nor hot. Because you are lukewarm, I will spew you out of my mouth. For you say, I am rich, I need nothing; not knowing that you are wretched, pitiable, poor, blind, and naked. Therefore I counsel you to buy from me gold refined by fire, that you may be rich, and white garments to keep the shame of your nakedness from being seen, and salve to anoint your eyes, that you may see. Those whom I love, I reprove and chasten; so be zealous and repent. Behold, I stand at the door and knock; if any one hears my voice and opens the door, I will come in to him and eat with him, and he with me. He who conquers, I will grant him to sit with me on my throne, as I myself conquered and sat down with my Father on his throne.' "

AFTER THIS I looked, and lo, in heaven an open door! And the first voice, like a trumpet, said, "Come up hither, and I will show you what must take place after this." At once I was in the Spirit, and lo, a throne stood in heaven, with one seated on it who appeared like jasper and carnelian, and round the throne was a rainbow that looked like an emerald. Round the throne were twenty-four thrones, and seated on them twenty-four elders, clad in white garments, with golden crowns. From the throne issue flashes of lightning, and voices and peals of thunder, and before the throne burn seven torches of fire, which are the seven spirits of God; and before the throne there is as it were a sea of glass, like crystal. On each side of the throne are four living creatures, full of eyes in front and behind: the first living creature like a lion, the second like an ox, the third with the face of a man, and the fourth like a flying eagle. And the creatures, each with six wings, never cease to sing, "Holy, holy, holy, is the Lord God Almighty, who was and is and is to come!" And whenever the living creatures give glory and honor and thanks to him who is seated on the throne, who lives for ever and ever, the twenty-four elders fall down before him and worship, singing, "Worthy art thou, our Lord and God, to receive glory and honor and power, for thou didst create all things, and by thy will they existed and were created."

And I saw in the right hand of him seated on the throne a scroll sealed with seven seals; and I saw a strong angel proclaiming with a loud voice, "Who is worthy to open the scroll and break its seals?" No one in heaven or on earth or under the earth was able to open the scroll, and I wept much that no one was found. Then one of the elders said to me, "Weep not; lo, the Lion of the tribe of Judah, the Root of David, has conquered, so that he can open the scroll and its seven seals."

And I saw a Lamb standing, as though it had been slain, with seven horns and seven eyes, which are the seven spirits of God sent out into all the earth; and he took the scroll. Then the four living creatures and the twenty-four elders fell down before the Lamb, each holding a harp, and with golden bowls full of incense, which are the prayers of the saints; and they sang a new song, saying, "Worthy art thou to take the scroll and to open its seals, for thou wast slain and by thy blood didst ransom men for God from every tribe and tongue and people and nation, and hast made them a kingdom and priests to our God, and they shall reign on earth."

Then I heard around the throne the voice of many angels, numbering myriads of myriads and thousands of thousands, saying with a loud voice, "Worthy is the Lamb who was slain, to receive power and wealth and wisdom and might and honor and glory and blessing!" And I heard every creature in heaven, earth and sea saying, "To him who sits upon the throne and to the Lamb be blessing and honor and glory and might for ever and ever!" And the four living creatures said, "Amen!" and the elders fell down and worshiped.

When the Lamb opened one of the seven seals, I heard one of the four living creatures say, as with a voice of thunder, "Come!" And I saw a white horse, and its rider had a bow; and a crown was given to him, and he went out conquering and to conquer.

When he opened the second seal, I heard the second living creature say, "Come!" And out came another horse, bright red; its rider was permitted to take peace from the earth, so that men should slay one another; and he was given a great sword.

When he opened the third seal, I heard the third living creature say, "Come!" And behold, a black horse, and its rider had a balance in his hand; and I heard a voice in the midst of the four living creatures saying, "A quart of wheat for a denarius, and three quarts of barley for a denarius; but do not harm oil and wine!"

When he opened the fourth seal, I heard the voice of the fourth living creature say, "Come!" And I saw a pale horse, and its rider's name was Death, and Hades followed him; and they were given power over a fourth of the earth, to kill with sword and famine and pestilence and by wild beasts.

When he opened the fifth seal, I saw under the altar the souls of those who had been slain for the word of God and for the witness they had borne; they cried out, "O Sovereign Lord, holy and true, how long before thou wilt judge and avenge our blood on those who dwell upon the earth?" Then they were each given a white robe and told to rest a little longer, until the number of their fellow servants and their brethren should be complete, who were to be killed as they themselves had been.

When he opened the sixth seal, behold,

there was a great earthquake; the sun became black as sackcloth, the full moon
became like blood, and the stars of the sky
fell to the earth as the fig tree sheds its
winter fruit when shaken by a gale; the sky
vanished like a scroll that is rolled up, and
every mountain and island was removed
from its place. Then the kings of the earth
and the great men and the generals and
the rich and the strong, and every one,
slave and free, hid in the caves and among
the rocks of the mountains, calling to
the mountains and rocks, "Fall on us and
hide us from the face of him seated on
the throne, and from the wrath of the
Lamb; for the great day of their wrath has
come, and who can stand before it?"

After this I saw four angels standing at
the four corners of the earth, holding back
the four winds of the earth. Then I saw
another angel ascend from the rising of the
sun, with the seal of the living God, and he
called to the four angels, saying, "Do not
harm the earth or the sea or the trees, till
we have sealed the servants of our God
upon their foreheads." And I heard the
number of the sealed, a hundred and forty-

four thousand, out of every tribe of the sons of Israel, twelve thousand out of each.

After this, behold, a multitude which no man could number, from every nation, standing before the throne and before the Lamb, clothed in white robes, with palm branches in their hands, and crying out, "Salvation belongs to our God, who sits upon the throne, and to the Lamb!" And all the angels round the throne fell on their faces and worshiped God, saying, "Amen! Blessing and glory and wisdom and thanksgiving and honor and power and might be to our God for ever and ever! Amen."

Then one of the elders addressed me, saying, "Who are these, clothed in white robes, and whence have they come?" I said to him, "Sir, you know." And he said to me, "These are they who have come out of the great tribulation; they have washed their robes and made them white in the blood of the Lamb. Therefore are they before the throne of God, and serve him day and night within his temple; and he who sits upon the throne will shelter them with his presence. They shall hunger no more, neither thirst any more; the sun shall not strike them, nor any scorching heat. For the Lamb in the midst of the throne will be their shepherd, and he will guide them to springs of living water; and God will wipe away every tear from their eyes."

When the Lamb opened the seventh seal, there was silence in heaven for about half an hour. Then I saw the seven angels who stand before God, and seven trumpets were given to them. And another angel came and stood at the altar with a golden censer; and the smoke of the incense rose with the prayers of the saints. Then the angel took the censer and filled it with fire from the altar and threw it on the earth; and there were peals of thunder, voices, flashes of lightning, and an earthquake.

Now the seven angels made ready to blow the trumpets.

The first angel blew, and there followed hail and fire, mixed with blood, which fell on the earth; and a third of the earth was burned up, and a third of the trees, and all green grass.

The second angel blew, and something

like a great mountain, burning with fire, was thrown into the sea; and a third of the sea became blood, a third of the living creatures in the sea died, and a third of the ships were destroyed.

The third angel blew, and a great star fell from heaven, blazing like a torch, and it fell on a third of the rivers and on the fountains of water. The name of the star is Wormwood. A third of the waters became wormwood, and many men died of the water, because it was made bitter.

The fourth angel blew, and a third of the sun was struck, and a third of the moon, and a third of the stars, so that a third of their light was darkened.

Then I heard an eagle crying as it flew in midheaven, "Woe, woe, woe to those who dwell on the earth, at the blasts of the other trumpets which the three angels are about to blow!"

And the fifth angel blew his trumpet, and I saw a star fallen from heaven to earth, and he was given the key of the shaft of the bottomless pit. He opened the shaft, and from it rose smoke like the smoke of a great furnace, and the sun and the air were darkened. Then from the smoke came locusts on the earth, and they were given power like the power of scorpions of the earth; they were told not to harm the grass of the earth or any green growth or any tree, but only those of mankind who have not the seal of God upon their foreheads; they were allowed to torture them for five months, but not to kill them, and their torture was like the torture of a scorpion, when it stings a man. And in those days men will long to die, and death will fly from them. In appearance the locusts were like horses arrayed for battle; on their heads were what looked like crowns of gold; their faces were like human faces, their hair like women's hair, and their teeth like lions' teeth; they had scales like iron breastplates, and the noise of their wings was like the noise of many chariots with horses rushing into battle. They have tails like scorpions, and stings. They have as king over them the angel of the bottomless pit; his name in Hebrew is Abaddon, and in Greek Apollyon.

The first woe has passed; behold, two woes are still to come.

Then the sixth angel blew his trumpet, and I heard a voice from the golden altar before God, saying to the sixth angel, "Release the four angels who are bound at the great river Euphrates." So the four angels were released, who had been held ready for the hour, the day, the month, and the year, to kill a third of mankind. The number of the troops of cavalry was twice ten thousand times ten thousand; I heard their number. And in my vision the riders wore breastplates the color of fire and of sapphire and of sulphur, and the heads of the horses were like lions' heads, and fire and smoke and sulphur issued from their mouths. A third of mankind was killed by the fire and smoke and sulphur. The horses' tails are like serpents, with heads, and by means of them they wound. The rest of mankind, who were not killed, did not repent of the works of their hands nor give up worshiping demons and idols; nor did they repent of their murders or their sorceries or their immorality or their thefts.

THEN I SAW another mighty angel coming down from heaven, wrapped in a cloud, with a rainbow over his head, his face like the sun, and his legs like pillars of fire. He had a little scroll open in his hand. And he set his right foot on the sea, and his left foot on the land, and called out like a lion roaring; when he called out, the seven thunders sounded. I was about to write, but I heard a voice from heaven saying, "Seal up what the seven thunders have said, and do not write it down." And the angel lifted up his right hand to heaven and swore by him who lives for ever and ever, who created heaven and earth and sea, that there should be no more delay, but that in the days of the trumpet call to be sounded by the seventh angel, the mystery of God, as he announced to his servants the prophets, should be fulfilled.

Then the voice which I had heard from heaven spoke to me again, saying, "Go, take the scroll." So I went to the angel and told him to give me the little scroll; and he said to me, "Take it and eat; it will be bitter to your stomach, but sweet as honey in your mouth." And I took the little scroll from the hand of the angel and ate it; it was sweet as honey in my mouth, but when I had eaten it my stomach was made bitter. And I was told, "You must again prophesy about many peoples and nations and tongues and kings."

Then I was given a measuring rod like a staff, and I was told: "Rise and measure the temple of God and the altar and those who worship there, but do not measure the court outside the temple; that is given over to the nations, and they will trample over the holy city for forty-two months. And I will grant my two witnesses power to prophesy for one thousand two hundred and sixty days." These are the two olive trees and the two lampstands which stand before the Lord of the earth. And if any one would harm them, fire pours from their mouth and consumes their foes. They have power to shut the sky, that no rain may fall during the days of their prophesying, and they have power over the waters to turn them into blood, and to smite the earth with every plague.

And when they have finished their testimony, the beast that ascends from the bottomless pit will conquer and kill them, and their dead bodies will lie in the street of

the great city where their Lord was crucified. For three days and a half men from
the peoples and nations gaze at their dead
bodies and refuse to let them be placed in
a tomb, and those who dwell on the earth
will make merry, because these two prophets had been a torment to them. But after
the three and a half days a breath of life
from God entered them, and they stood
up, and great fear fell on those who saw
them. A loud voice from heaven said to
them, "Come up hither!" And in the sight
of their foes they went up to heaven in a
cloud. At that hour there was a great
earthquake, and a tenth of the city fell;
seven thousand people were killed, and the
rest were terrified and gave glory to the
God of heaven.

The second woe has passed; behold, the
third woe is soon to come.

Then the seventh angel blew his trumpet, and there were loud voices in heaven,
saying, "The kingdom of the world has
become the kingdom of our Lord and of
his Christ, and he shall reign for ever and
ever." And the twenty-four elders fell on
their faces and worshiped God, saying,

"We give thanks to thee, Lord God Almighty, who art and who wast, that thou hast taken thy great power and begun to reign. The nations raged, but thy wrath came, and the time for the dead to be judged, for rewarding thy servants, the prophets and saints, and those who fear thy name, both small and great, and for destroying the destroyers of the earth."

Then God's temple in heaven was opened, and the ark of his covenant was seen within; and there were flashes of lightning, voices, peals of thunder, an earthquake, and heavy hail.

A GREAT PORTENT appeared in heaven, a woman clothed with the sun, with the moon under her feet, and on her head a crown of twelve stars; she was with child and she cried out in her pangs of birth. And another portent appeared in heaven, a great red dragon, with seven heads and ten horns, and seven diadems upon his heads. His tail swept down a third of the stars of heaven, and cast them to the earth. And the dragon stood before the woman, that he might devour her child when she brought it forth. Then she brought forth a male child, one who is to rule all the nations with a rod of iron, but her child was caught up to God and to his throne, and the woman fled into the wilderness, where she has a place prepared by God, in which to be nourished for one thousand two hundred and sixty days.

Now war arose in heaven, Michael and his angels fighting against the dragon; and the dragon and his angels fought, but they were defeated and there was no longer any place for them in heaven. The great dragon, that ancient serpent, who is called the Devil and Satan, the deceiver of the whole world—he was thrown down to the earth, and his angels with him. I heard a loud voice in heaven, saying, "Now the salvation and the power and the kingdom of our God and the authority of his Christ have come, for the accuser of our brethren has been thrown down, who accuses them day and night before our God. They have conquered him by the blood of the Lamb and by the word of their testimony, for they loved not their lives even unto death. Rejoice then, O heaven and you that dwell therein! But woe to you, O earth and sea, for the devil has come down to you in great wrath, because he knows that his time is short!"

When the dragon saw that he had been thrown down to the earth, he pursued the woman who had borne the male child. But the woman was given the two wings of the great eagle, that she might fly into the wilderness, where she is to be nourished for a time, and times, and half a time. The serpent poured water like a river out of his mouth after the woman, to sweep her away with the flood. But the earth came to the help of the woman, and swallowed the river. Then the dragon was angry with the woman, and went off to make war on the rest of her offspring, on those who keep the commandments of God and bear testimony to Jesus.

And I saw a beast rising out of the sea, with ten horns and seven heads, with ten diadems upon its horns and a blasphemous name upon its heads. And the beast was like a leopard, its feet were like a bear's, and its mouth was like a lion's. To it the dragon gave his power and his throne and great authority. One of its heads seemed to have a mortal wound, but its mortal wound was healed, and the whole earth followed the beast with wonder. Men worshiped the dragon, for he had given his authority to the beast, and they worshiped the beast, saying, "Who is like the beast, and who can fight against it?"

And the beast was given a mouth uttering blasphemous words, and it was allowed to exercise authority for forty-two months, blaspheming God's name and his dwelling, that is, those who dwell in heaven. Also it was allowed to make war on the saints and to conquer them. And authority was given it over every tribe and nation, and all who dwell on earth will worship it, every one whose name has not been written before the foundation of the world in the book of life of the Lamb that was slain.

Then I saw another beast which rose out of the earth; it had two horns like a lamb and it spoke like a dragon. It exercises all the authority of the first beast in its presence, and makes the earth and its inhabitants worship the first beast, whose mortal wound was healed. It works great signs, even making fire come down from heaven to earth in the sight of men; and by the signs it deceives those who dwell on earth, bidding them make an image for the first beast; and it was allowed to give breath to the image, so that it should speak, and to cause those who would not worship the image to be slain. Also it causes all, both small and great, both rich and poor, both free and slave, to be marked on the right hand or the forehead, so that no one can buy or sell unless he has the mark, that is, the name of the beast or the number of its name. This calls for wisdom: let him who has understanding reckon the number of the beast, for it is a human number, its number is six hundred and sixty-six.

Then lo, on Mount Zion stood the Lamb, and with him a hundred and forty-four thousand who had his name and his Father's name written on their foreheads. And I heard a voice from heaven like the sound of many waters and like loud thunder; the voice I heard was like the sound of harpers, and they sing a new song before the throne. No one could learn that song except the hundred and forty-four thousand. It is these who are chaste; it is these who follow the Lamb wherever he goes; these have been redeemed from mankind as first fruits for God and the Lamb, and in their mouth no lie was found, for they are spotless.

Then I saw another angel flying in mid-heaven, with an eternal gospel to proclaim on earth to every nation; and he said with a loud voice, "Fear God and give him glory, for the hour of his judgment has come; and worship him who made heaven and earth, the sea and the fountains of water."

A second angel followed, saying, "Fallen, fallen is Babylon the great, she who made all nations drink the wine of her impure passion."

And a third followed, saying with a loud voice, "If any one worships the beast and its image, and receives a mark on his forehead or hand, he also shall drink the wine of God's wrath, and shall be tormented with fire and sulphur in the presence of the holy angels and of the Lamb. And the smoke of their torment goes up for ever and ever; and they have no rest, day or night."

I heard a voice from heaven saying, "Write this: Blessed are the dead who die in the Lord henceforth." "Blessed indeed," says the Spirit, "that they may rest from their labors, for their deeds follow them!"

Then lo, a white cloud, and seated on the cloud one like a son of man, with a golden crown on his head, and a sharp sickle in his hand. And another angel came out of the temple, calling to him upon the cloud, "Put in your sickle, and reap, for the hour to reap has come, for the harvest of the earth is fully ripe." So he swung his sickle on the earth, and the earth was reaped.

And another angel came out, and he too had a sharp sickle. Then another angel came out from the altar, the angel who has power over fire, and he called to him who had the sharp sickle, "Put in your sickle and gather the clusters of the vine of the earth, for its grapes are ripe." So the angel swung his sickle and gathered the vintage of the earth, and threw it into the great wine press of the wrath of God; and the wine press was trodden outside the city, and blood flowed from it, as high as a horse's bridle, for one thousand six hundred stadia.

T<small>HEN</small> I <small>SAW</small> another portent in heaven, great and wonderful, seven angels with seven plagues, which are the last, for with them the wrath of God is ended.

And I saw what appeared to be a sea of glass mingled with fire, and those who had conquered the beast, standing beside the sea with harps of God in their hands. And they sing the song of Moses and the song of the Lamb, saying, "Great and wonderful are thy deeds, O Lord God the Almighty! Just and true are thy ways, O King of the ages! Who shall not fear and glorify thy name, O Lord? For thou alone art holy. All nations shall come and worship thee, for thy judgments have been revealed."

After this I looked, and the temple of the tent of witness in heaven was opened, and out came the seven angels with the seven plagues, robed in pure bright linen, and their breasts girded with golden girdles. And one of the four living creatures gave the angels seven golden bowls full of the wrath of God; and the temple was filled with smoke from the glory and power of God, and no one could enter the temple until the seven plagues were ended.

Then I heard a loud voice from the temple telling the seven angels, "Go and pour out on the earth the seven bowls of the wrath of God."

So the first angel poured his bowl on the earth, and foul sores came upon the men who bore the mark of the beast and worshiped its image.

The second angel poured his bowl into the sea, and it became like the blood of a dead man, and every living thing died that was in the sea.

The third angel poured his bowl into the rivers and the fountains of water, and they became blood. And I heard the angel of water say, "Just art thou in these thy judgments, O Holy One. For men have shed the blood of saints and prophets, and thou hast given them blood to drink. It is their due!"

The fourth angel poured his bowl on the sun, and it was allowed to scorch men with fire and fierce heat, and they cursed the name of God who had power over these plagues, and they did not repent.

The fifth angel poured his bowl on the throne of the beast, and its kingdom was in darkness; men gnawed their tongues in anguish and cursed the God of heaven for their pain and sores, and did not repent of their deeds.

The sixth angel poured his bowl on the great river Euphrates, and its water was dried up, to prepare the way for the kings from the east. And I saw, issuing from the mouths of the dragon and the beast and the false prophet, three foul spirits like frogs; for they are demonic spirits, performing signs, who go abroad to the kings of the whole world, to assemble them for battle on the great day of God the Almighty. And they assembled them at the place which is called in Hebrew Armageddon.

The seventh angel poured his bowl into the air, and a loud voice came out of the temple, from the throne, saying, "It is done!" And there were flashes of lightning, voices, peals of thunder, and a great earthquake such as had never been since men were on the earth. The great city was split into three parts, and the cities of the nations fell, and God remembered great Babylon, to make her drain the cup of the fury of his wrath.

THEN ONE OF the angels said to me, "Come, I will show you the judgment of the great harlot who is seated upon many waters, with whom the kings of the earth have committed fornication." And he carried me away in the Spirit into a wilderness, and I saw a woman sitting on a scarlet beast which had seven heads and ten horns. The woman was arrayed in purple and scarlet, and bedecked with jewels, holding in her hand a golden cup full of abominations and the impurities of her fornication; and on her forehead was written a name of mystery: "Babylon the great, mother of harlots and of earth's abominations." And I saw the woman, drunk with the blood of the saints.

"I will tell you the mystery of the woman," the angel said, "and of the beast. The beast that you saw was, and is not, and is to ascend from the bottomless pit and go to perdition. The seven heads are seven mountains on which the woman is seated; they are also seven kings, five of whom have fallen. The ten horns are ten kings who have not yet received power, but they are to receive authority for one hour, together with the beast. They will make war on the Lamb, and the Lamb will conquer them, for he is Lord of lords and King of kings."

And he said to me, "The waters where the harlot is seated are peoples and nations. The ten horns and the beast will hate the harlot; they will make her desolate and naked. And the woman is the great city which has dominion over the kings of the earth."

After this I saw another angel coming down from heaven, and the earth was made bright with his splendor. And he called out with a mighty voice, "Fallen, fallen is Babylon the great! It has become a dwelling place of demons, a haunt of every foul spirit, and the merchants of the earth have grown rich with the wealth of her wantonness."

Then I heard another voice from heaven saying, "Come out of her, my people, lest you take part in her sins, for God has remembered her iniquities. Render to her as she herself has rendered, and repay her double for her deeds. So shall her plagues come in a single day, pestilence and mourning and famine, and she shall be burned with fire; for mighty is the Lord God who judges her."

And the kings of the earth will weep over her when they see the smoke of her burning, and they will say, "Alas! thou mighty city, Babylon! In one hour has thy judgment come."

And the merchants of the earth mourn for her, since no one buys their cargo any more. And all shipmasters and seafaring men stood far off and cried out, "What city was like the great city, where all who had ships at sea grew rich by her wealth? In one hour she has been laid waste. Rejoice over her, O heaven, O saints and apostles and prophets, for God has given judgment for you against her!"

After this I heard what seemed to be the loud voice of a great multitude in heaven, crying, "Hallelujah! Salvation and glory and power belong to our God, for his judgments are true and just; he has judged the great harlot, and he has avenged on her the blood of his servants. The smoke from her goes up for ever and ever." And the twenty-four elders and the four living creatures fell down and worshiped God, who is seated on the throne, saying, "Amen. Hallelujah!" Again I heard what seemed to be the voice of a great multitude, like the sound of many waters and of mighty thunderpeals, crying, "Hallelujah! For the Lord our God the Almighty reigns. Let us rejoice, for the marriage of the Lamb has come, and his Bride has made herself ready; it was granted her to be clothed with fine linen, bright and pure"— for the fine linen is the righteous deeds of the saints. And the angel said to me, "Write this: Blessed are those who are invited to the marriage supper of the Lamb."

Then I saw heaven opened, and behold, a white horse! He who sat upon it is called Faithful and True, and in righteousness he judges and makes war. His eyes are like a flame, and on his head are many diadems;

and he has a name inscribed which no one knows but himself. He is clad in a robe dipped in blood, and the name by which he is called is The Word of God. And the armies of heaven, arrayed in fine linen, white and pure, followed him on white horses. From his mouth issues a sharp sword with which to smite the nations, and he will rule them with a rod of iron; he will tread the wine press of the wrath of God the Almighty. On his robe and on his thigh he has a name inscribed, King of kings and Lord of lords.

Then I saw an angel standing in the sun, and with a loud voice he called to all the birds that fly in midheaven, "Come, gather for the great supper of God, to eat the flesh of kings, of captains, of mighty men, the flesh of horses and their riders." And I saw the beast and the kings of the earth with their armies gathered to make war against him who sits upon the horse and against his army. And the beast was captured, and with it the false prophet who by signs had deceived those who had received the mark of the beast and worshiped its image. These two were thrown alive into the lake of fire that burns with sulphur. And the rest were slain by the sword of him who sits upon the horse, and all the birds were gorged with their flesh.

Then I saw an angel coming down from heaven, holding the key of the bottomless pit and a great chain. And he seized the dragon, that ancient serpent, the Devil and Satan, and bound him for a thousand years, and threw him into the pit, and shut it and sealed it over him, that he should deceive the nations no more, till the thousand years were ended. After that he must be loosed for a little while.

Then I saw thrones, and seated on them were those to whom judgment was committed. Also I saw the souls of those who had been beheaded for their testimony to Jesus and for the word of God. They came to life, and reigned with Christ a thousand years. The rest of the dead did not come to life until the thousand years were ended. This is the first resurrection. Blessed and holy is he who shares in the first resurrection! Over such the second death has no power, but they shall be priests of God and of Christ, and they shall reign with him a thousand years.

And when the thousand years are ended, Satan will be loosed from his prison and will come out to deceive the nations which are at the four corners of the earth, that is, Gog and Magog, to gather them for battle; their number is like the sand of the sea. And they marched up over the broad earth and surrounded the camp of the saints and the beloved city; but fire came down from heaven and consumed them, and the devil was thrown into the lake of fire and sulphur where the beast and the false prophet were, and they will be tormented day and night for ever.

Then I saw a great white throne and him who sat upon it; from his presence earth and sky fled away. And I saw the dead, great and small, standing before the throne, and books were opened. Also another book was opened, which is the book of life. And the dead were judged by what was written in the books, by what they had done. And the sea gave up the dead in it, Death and Hades gave up the dead in them, and all were judged by what they had done. Then Death and Hades were thrown into the lake of fire. This is the second death, the lake of fire; and if any one's name was not found written in the book of life, he was thrown into the lake of fire.

THEN I SAW a new heaven and a new earth; for the first heaven and the first earth had passed away, and the sea was no more. And I saw the holy city, new Jerusalem, coming down out of heaven from God, prepared as a bride adorned for her husband; and I heard a loud voice from the throne saying, "Behold, the dwelling of God is with men. They shall be his people; God will wipe away every tear from their eyes, and death shall be no more, neither shall there be mourning nor crying nor pain any more, for the former things have passed away."

And he who sat upon the throne said, "Behold, I make all things new. I am the Alpha and the Omega, the beginning and the end. To the thirsty I will give from the fountain of the water of life without payment. He who conquers shall have this heritage, and I will be his God and he shall be my son. But as for the cowardly, the faithless, the polluted, as for murderers, fornicators, sorcerers, idolaters, and all liars, their lot shall be in the lake that burns with fire and sulphur, which is the second death."

Then one of the seven angels who had the bowls full of the seven last plagues spoke to me, saying, "Come, I will show you the Bride, the wife of the Lamb." And in the Spirit he carried me away to a high mountain, and showed me the holy city Jerusalem coming down out of heaven from God, having the glory of God, its radiance like a most rare jewel. It had a great, high wall, with twelve gates, and at the gates twelve angels, and on the gates the names of the twelve tribes of Israel were inscribed. And the wall had twelve foundations, and on them the names of the twelve apostles of the Lamb. The city lies foursquare, twelve thousand stadia; its length and breadth and height are equal.

The wall was built of jasper, while the city was pure gold, clear as glass. The foundations of the wall were adorned with every jewel: jasper, sapphire, agate, emerald, onyx, carnelian, chrysolite, beryl, topaz, chrysoprase, jacinth, amethyst. The twelve gates were each made of a single pearl, and the street of the city was pure gold, transparent as glass. And I saw no temple in the city, for its temple is the Lord God the Almighty and the Lamb. And the city has no need of sun or moon to shine upon it, for the glory of God is its light, and its lamp is the Lamb. By its light shall the nations walk; and the kings of the earth shall bring their glory into it, and its gates shall never be shut by day—and there shall be no night there. But nothing unclean shall enter it, nor any one who practices abomination or falsehood, but only those who are written in the Lamb's book of life.

Then he showed me the river of the water of life, bright as crystal, flowing from the throne of God and of the Lamb through the middle of the street of the city; also, on either side of the river, the tree of life with its twelve kinds of fruit, yielding its fruit each month; and the leaves of the tree were for the healing of the nations. There shall no more be anything accursed, but the throne of God and of the Lamb shall be in it, and his servants shall worship him; they shall see his face, and his name shall be on their foreheads. And they shall reign for ever and ever.

AND HE SAID to me, "The Lord, the God of the spirits of the prophets, has sent his angel to show his servants what must soon take place. And behold, I am coming soon."

Blessed is he who keeps the words of the prophecy of this book.

I John am he who heard and saw these things. And when I heard and saw them, I fell down to worship at the feet of the angel who showed them to me; but he said to me, "You must not do that! I am a fellow servant with you and your brethren the prophets, and with those who keep the words of this book. Worship God." And he said to me, "Do not seal up the words of the prophecy of this book, for the time is near. Let the evildoer still do evil, and the filthy still be filthy, and the righteous still do right, and the holy still be holy."

Blessed are those who wash their robes,

that they may have the right to the tree of life and that they may enter the city by the gates. Outside are the dogs and sorcerers and fornicators and murderers and idolaters, and every one who loves and practices falsehood.

"I Jesus have sent my angel to you with this testimony for the churches. I am the root and the offspring of David, the bright morning star."

The Spirit and the Bride say, "Come." And let him who hears say, "Come." And let him who is thirsty come, let him who desires take the water of life without price.

He who testifies to these things says, "Surely I am coming soon." Amen. Come, Lord Jesus!

The grace of the Lord Jesus be with all the saints. Amen.